THE ROLE OF PERFORMANCE PAY SYSTEMS IN COMPREHENSIVE SCHOOL REFORM

Considerations for Policy Making and Planning

Warren A. Hodge

University Press of America,® Inc.
Lanham · New York · Oxford

Copyright © 2003 by
University Press of America,® Inc.
4501 Forbes Boulevard
Suite 200
Lanham, Maryland 20706
UPA Acquisitions Department (301) 459-3366

PO Box 317
Oxford
OX2 9RU, UK

All rights reserved
Printed in the United States of America
British Library Cataloging in Publication Information Available

ISBN 0-7618-2554-1 (paperback : alk. ppr.)

∞™ The paper used in this publication meets the minimum
requirements of American National Standard for Information
Sciences—Permanence of Paper for Printed Library Materials,
ANSI Z39.48—1984

This book is dedicated to all educators who—while they may not know it, at times forget it, and are inadequately compensated and rewarded for it—contribute nobly to the development of the world's most precious resources.

CONTENTS

LIST OF FIGURES AND TABLES ix

FOREWORD xi

PREFACE AND INTRODUCTION xiii

ACKNOWLEDGMENTS xvii

CHAPTER 1: Historical and Theoretical Overview 1
    The Move to Comprehensive
        School Reform and Performance Pay Programs 5
    Theoretical Framework and School Reform Programs 7

CHAPTER 2: Critical Variables in Performance Pay Systems 11
    Systemic/Comprehensive Reform Focus 12
    Teacher Motivation 15
    Performance Assessment 22
        a. Assessing Student Performance 23
        b. Assessing Teacher Performance 25
    Comprehensive Program Evaluation 28
    Participation and Collaboration 34
    Funding Performance Pay Programs 37
    Chapter Summary 45

CHAPTER 3: Professional Development and Performance Pay 47
    Theories/Models of Adult
        Development and Learning 50
    Time 54

Linkage with Student Achievement 55
Funding 57
Professional Development Models and Approaches 58
Exemplars of Comprehensive Professional Development 60
    a. Model One 61
    b. Model Two 62
    c. Model Three 63
Chapter Summary 66

CHAPTER 4: Prevalent Performance Pay Programs 69
Major Compensation and Incentive Approaches 72
    a. Knowledge-, Skills-Based,
       and Career Award Programs 73
    b. Group-Based/School Award Systems 81
    c. Recognition Incentive Programs 84
Other Incentive Programs 85
Chapter Summary 86

CHAPTER 5: Design and Planning
Considerations for Incentive Programs 89
Assumptions 89
Goals and Objectives of Incentive Programs 92
Standards of Adequacy Guidelines 95
Chapter Summary 97

CHAPTER 6: Research on Performance Pay Programs 99
Research on the Influence of Incentive Programs on
    Teacher Motivation, Performance,
    Attitudes and Attributions 100
    a. Motivation and Performance 100
    b. Attitudes 102
    c. Attributions 106
Research on Performance Pay
    Programs and Student Achievement 106
    a. The Arizona Program 107
    b. The Kentucky Program 109
    c. The Dallas Independent School District Program 111
    d. The North Carolina Program 111
Chapter Summary 114

CHAPTER 7: Conclusions and Observations 117
    Some Final Observations 126

Appendices
    A. Standards of Adequacy Checklist for
        Designing Performance Pay Programs 133
    B. Seven Examples of Design and Decision
        Making Processes for Performance Pay Programs 145
    C. Public Attitudes toward Linking Teachers'
        Salary to Students' Academic Achievement 157

NOTES 161

REFERENCES 167

AUTHOR INDEX 189

SUBJECT INDEX 197

LIST OF FIGURES AND TABLES

Figures

Figure 1 Linkages between Subject, Strands, Standards and Benchmarks

Figure 2 New American Schools Evaluation Process

Figure 3 Cincinnati, Ohio, Knowledge- and Skills-Based Salary Schedule

Figure 4 Factors Influenced by Reward Programs

Tables

Table 1 Motivation Theories and Their Relevance to Teacher Incentive Programs

Table 2 Key Findings on Teacher Motivation and Incentives

Table 3 2000-2002 Reward Programs in Selected SREB States

Table 4 Costs and Funding of Performance Pay Programs

Table 5 Districts with Knowledge- and Skills-Based Pay

Table 6 Examples of a District's Conceptual Model of a Knowledge- and Skill-Based Pay Program

Table 7   SASS Data on Public School Favorability Ratings of Pay Incentives

Table 8   Rewards and Sanctions Associated with the Kentucky Accountability Program

FOREWORD

Warren Hodge tells me that I am in part responsible for the existence of *The Role of Performance Pay Systems in Comprehensive School Reform: Considerations for Policy Making and Planning.* If that is so, I am proud of whatever small role I may have played. Several years ago I became convinced that those of us in educational leadership programs needed to be much better informed about performance pay systems. As we looked at the literature, the names of Allan Odden and Carolyn Kelley were prominent. Because of some available endowment money through the Andrew A. Robinson Chair for Educational Policy and Economic Development at the University of North Florida, I was able to make it possible for Warren along with union and administrative representatives from Duval County Public Schools to attend one of the workshops on performance pay led by Odden and Kelley at the University of Wisconsin-Madison. I asked Warren to submit a report on what he learned.

While I would like to take credit for the rest, Warren really took that assignment and ran with it. Warren's expertise in research, school law, school finance, and human resource management has served him well as he gathered together the literature on performance pay and organized it into a coherent overview of an emerging field. That review of the literature eventually became this book.

What he has delivered in this book is the framework that policymakers will need as they consider the benefits and hazards of performance-based compensation systems. Warren correctly grounds our understandings of pay systems in theories of motivation, theories of adult development and learning, and systems theory. His point of view is neither that of an advocate nor a critic. Instead, he provides a well-balanced perspective on the issues.

Warren also avoids over-simplification. He never misleads us into believing that crafting a well-designed pay for performance system is easily done. Instead, the standards of adequacy checklist he includes in the book will challenge anyone contemplating the adoption of a system to consider carefully all of the relevant issues.

This book should be required reading for legislative staff in every state, for school board members and union officials. Teachers' salaries are not competitive with those of others in occupations requiring similar education and training. Legislators and business leaders seem reluctant to raise salaries without some assurance that additional quality will be obtained. Pay for performance systems seem a likely way to break the stalemate. We should, however, move cautiously, taking care to avoid unintended effects. If Warren's book helps others to understand the possibilities offered by pay for performance systems or prevents the hasty implementation of one ill-conceived incentive system, the field will have been well served.

Katherine Kasten, Ph.D.
Dean, College of Education and Human Services
University of North Florida
May 2002

PREFACE AND INTRODUCTION

Shortly after the National Commission on Excellence in Education (NCEE) published *A Nation at Risk* (1983), several states provided what they deemed credible evidence that they were already reforming their schools and implementing a number of recommendations cited in the report. In one account, *Meeting the Challenge: Present Efforts to Improve Education Across the Nation* (NCEE, 1983), the states responded to the NCEE's report by presenting several reform initiatives that they had implemented or were considering implementing. In their responses, the states cited renewed emphasis on parental responsibility and reported trends toward performance-based salary schedules. They also cited major initiatives such as curriculum reform, increased graduation requirements, enhancement of student evaluation and testing, longer school days, increased requirements for teacher certification and preparation, and more professional development for teachers. Educators called these attempts to improve education "first wave" reform initiatives because they were among initial endeavors to improve the quality of education after the NCEE published its report.

These first initiatives, however, not only failed to arrest the decline in student achievement, but at a more substantive level, they also failed to address the missing "theoretical linkage between structural changes (e.g., site-based management) and the bridging variables (e.g., teacher attitudes and performance) and connect them to measurable outcomes (e.g., enhanced student learning)" (Murphy, 1991, p. 75). Malen, Ogawa, and Kranz (1989) went on to explain that the linkages

> are neither direct nor dependable, simple or linear. A host of factors combine to offset the impact of normal structural changes. Some of those

factors relate to the characteristics of participants (e.g., their attitudes, orientations, predispositions, skill and will in deploying resources to acquire influence) while others relate more to systemic forces (e.g., deeply engrained norms, the discretion afforded by the formal structural arrangements, the availability and stability of critical resources). Unfortunately, little is known about the manner in which these and other factors combine and interact to shape responses to the formal alteration of governance structure. (cited in Murphy, 1991, p. 75-76)

Now that almost two decades have elapsed since *A Nation at Risk* was published, the education policy planning and research community is showing signs of embracing the promises of structural changes necessary for improving student achievement. The new school accountability movement has spawned substantive changes in the way educators regard schooling. The new view of accountability acknowledges the importance of standards-based, systemic reform and places importance on the alignment of curriculum development and effective instruction. It defines district and school success in terms of student performance on standardized tests that measure knowledge and skill acquisition, requires public reporting of the success and failure of individual schools, advocates consequences to limit excuses for failure, and restructures the way teachers are compensated and rewarded (Fuhrman, 1999).

The emphasis on standards-based, high-stakes accountability reform is partly reflected in the Obey-Potter legislation, which resulted in the Comprehensive School Reform Demonstration Program (CSRDP) managed by the United States Department of Education (U.S. DOE, 1998). The CSRDP encourages states and districts to implement sweeping "comprehensive and revitalized" reform of entire schools as opposed to piecemeal changes reflected in typical responses to *A Nation at Risk*. Among the numerous comprehensive reform initiatives are performance-based incentive or reward programs, which some school districts have adopted and some policymakers are beginning to embrace. These programs are the focus of this book.

Organization of the Book

This book addresses several dimensions of the accountability movement in education. Specifically, it addresses performance pay for teachers as one approach to achieving success with enhancing student achievement within the framework of comprehensive school reform (CSR). The discussion evolves through seven chapters. Chapter 1 presents a brief historical background of CSR initiatives with special attention given to performance pay systems. Chapter 2 details some critical variables that are essential for an effective performance pay system. Professional development and the role it plays in pay systems are discussed in Chapter 3. Chapter 4 discusses three prevalent teacher incentive or performance pay approaches—(a) knowledge and skill-based systems, (b) school-based or group-based award systems, and (c) nonmonetary or recognition performance systems—and presents the major advantages and disadvantages of each. Chapter 5 explores assumptions and objectives necessary for planning performance pay systems (PPS) and addresses decision and design processes used to develop, implement, and evaluate them. This chapter also explains the contents of Appendix A, a Standards of Adequacy Checklist for designing performance pay programs. Chapter 6 presents emerging empirical evidence on various aspects of incentive programs, and, finally, Chapter 7 offers eight conclusions and some observations regarding performance pay systems.

ACKNOWLEDGMENTS

One never can take total credit for any book. The process always involves the help of others during the research and writing processes. The author may toil with the drudgery and loneliness of putting words on paper, but he or she in the end must give credence to the reality that the effort was not singular. It is the same with this book, a venture for me that turned out to be deeply rewarding. The people to whom I owe a great debt of gratitude contributed to its completion and deserve the thanks I now extend.

To Kathe Kasten, I will not prevaricate, but rightly admit that the book was largely your idea. Thank you for getting the ball rolling by turning my attention to what is certainly now a significant emerging initiative in education reform. Thank you also for making funds available during the research and writing stages, your meticulous editing, and your suggestions for improvement. They all contributed much to improving the depth and scope of the book.

To Larry Daniel, I owe a great depth of gratitude for the initial editing. Know that I was consoled by the fact that editors of your caliber are accustomed to the rough, tumbled world of first expressions and are well schooled in mind reading and divining authors' true intentions. Thank you for all that and for your substantive suggestions.

To Charles Galloway, thank you for your fine editing and for your encouraging words. Your honesty and forthrightness gave me much to ponder and led to numerous substantive changes and improvements in the first draft. Please know that your reputation for "telling it like it is" and your penchant for fine scholarship are the reasons I sought you out. You did not disappoint me.

To John Venn, Deborah Inman, and Tammi Horn, thank you for taking time from family and all the demands of your position to read the manuscript.

To Shannon McLeish, our assiduous, conscientious, and proficient secretary, thank you for reading, editing, and making many substantive suggestions. Please know that you possess two of the keenest editorial eyes I have encountered. I will not forget that you took time from your extremely busy schedule to help polish a manuscript whose subject may not be of interest to everyone. You did it in grand style.

To Claribel Torres, my doctoral student, for reading the manuscript and for setting me straight on several omissions and incoherent scribblings. Your contributions helped clarify several misunderstandings about the actual distribution of rewards and bonuses in several Florida school districts.

To all the librarians at the University of North Florida and the University of Florida who assisted with numerous requests for interlibrary loans and difficult-to-find sources—thank you.

I would also like to thank several individuals and organizations for granting permission to adapt material from their published work: To Allen Odden for the use of information from his compensation design seminars at the University of Wisconsin and from the Consortium for Policy Research in Education; to Tony Melanowski at the University of Wisconsin for use of his data on knowledge- and skills-based pay designs; to Claudine McCrary, Lynn Cornett, Gale Gaines, and the Southern Regional Education Board for use of their data on incentive pay programs in SREB states; to Erling Boe, Professor of Education at the University of Pennsylvania, for use of his data from the 1987-1988 School and Staffing Survey; to Joyce Pollard at the Southwest Educational Development Laboratory for use of information from their publication on performance-based incentive plans; to Adam Hirschberg at Prentice-Hall for permission to use information from published work; to Grenda Hudson at The Urban Institute for permission to use information from published work; to Terri Hampton at Phi Delta Kappa for use of information from two issues of the *Kappan*; to SAGE Publication, Inc. and Corwin Press, Inc. for permission to use information from Carolyn Kelley's published work; to John Wiley & Sons for permission to reprint information from published work; and to all the folks at the U.S. Department of Education for information on the 1999 School Survey and Staffing study. I thank you all for the contributions you have made to this project.

Finally, I extend special thanks to my wife, Emilia, who has been a constant source of support and inspiration from the first day of research and writing to the last. Thank you for helpful comments that influenced and contributed to shaping the manuscript into something of value. Your educational journey provided a rewarding opportunity for me to straddle two education environments that truly stimulate and encourage scholarship.

1

HISTORICAL AND THEORETICAL OVERVIEW

> History will view the 1980s not as the decade of education reform, but as the decade of education debate.... However, our immobility is now coming to an end, and we stand on the verge of a wave of reform that could transform the landscape of education. Futrell, (1989)

Much of the research driving comprehensive school reform (CSR) is being conducted by education and policy research agencies, foundations, think tanks, and consortia such as the Center for the Study of Teaching and Policy, the National Center on Education and the Economy, The Urban Institute, Teacher Union Reform Network, and, most notably, the Consortium for Policy Research in Education. Two observations emerged from studies conducted by these entities: (a) there is a concerted and resolute determination by both the public and private sectors to hold educators, especially teachers, accountable for student achievement, and (b) there is an equally resolute determination by education policymakers to use standards focused on quality instruction and valid measures of student progress as major components in new pay systems for compensating and rewarding teachers (Tucker & Codding, 1998).

Considering the trend towards building a global economy, the reform movement in education is not restricted to the United States. Policymakers and professional educators in Canada, Taiwan, Australia, South Africa, Great Britain and other countries have also embraced CSR as a path to better schools (Ingvarson, Chadbourne, & Culton, 1995; Mungazi & Kay, 1997; Levin & Young, 1998; Reynolds & Cruz, 1998).

As some countries adopt CSR and others search for alternative approaches to improving the quality of education, the debate about the causes of poorly performing schools remains polarized. In this country, conservatives and liberals blame and criticize each other. In much of Europe, the Christians and social democrats do the same. In both settings, multiple causes for poor performance include poverty, disinterested parents, insufficient resources, inadequately trained and underpaid teachers, and moral decay of these societies. Likewise, both camps propose numerous solutions, or, as they are called, "reform initiatives," which, are often implemented and then prematurely abandoned. Researchers (Carpenter, 2000; Tyack & Cuban, 1995; Wong & Meyer, 1998) have identified several of the "good ideas" that have not resulted in convincing improvement in student achievement. Indeed, results from international comparisons of student performance such as the Third International and Science Survey and national studies such as the National Assessment of Education Progress (NAEP), seem to confirm that achievement has remained relatively stable over the past fifteen years (Bracey, 1998; Mak, 2000; Martin & Kelly, 1996; Quinn, 2000; Viadero, 1998).

At both the national and international levels, the accountability movement is clearly defined by core reform values and characteristics that have evolved and sharpened since the watershed *A Nation at Risk* report galvanized attention to severe problems in education. In a policy brief for CPRE, Fuhrman (1999) identified core educational reform characteristics as (a) focus on student performance, (b) schools as the unit of performance, (c) continuous improvement strategies, (d) evaluative inspections, (e) more accountability categories, (f) public reporting of results, and (g) consequences attached to performance levels. Proponents of standards, accountability, and efficiency in education say all these factors must be aligned and addressed in a comprehensive way if schools are to be successful in preparing students to function successfully in a global economy. In other words, education reform must have an all-inclusive and systemic focus that embraces every aspect of schooling and not be narrowly confined to piecemeal and incremental revisions. According to some observers

(Carlson, 1996; Darling-Hammond, 1997; Ravitch, 1995, 2000; Tucker & Codding, 1998; Zemelman, et al., 1998), school reform initiatives should not be determined solely by state policy mandates and private-sector expectations but should be proactively determined by schools themselves.

The emerging reform initiative now refocusing much of the debate about "reengineering" schooling has been broadly referred to as teacher incentive pay, school-based performance pay, group-based pay, or pay for performance. The focus on adequately compensating teachers is significant for two reasons: (a) research has consistently shown that teacher effect accounts for 55% to 80% of the variance associated with student achievement (Jordan, Mendro, & Weerasinghe, 1997; Sanders & Rivers, 1996), and (b) the policy planning and research community has acknowledged that teachers are inadequately compensated. Some, such as Matthews (1999), have argued that teachers are underpaid because there is "little competition at the K-12 level ... and as a result public school teachers' pay is less than it could be" (p. A-24). Furthermore, he suggested that "a teacher should be paid a professional salary, the market should determine that level, and we should be able to offer that salary to a teacher. If the teacher is not performing at that salary level, the contract should not be renewed" (p. A-24). Others have articulated similar views by suggesting that teachers should not be paid simply for getting older, but rather for learning from experience, for professional development, and for performing better (Tomlinson, 1996).

Teacher compensation has evolved from the 1880s practice of compensating teachers by boarding them in students' homes ("boarding round"), to grade-based compensation, and finally to the single salary schedule. The single salary schedule became prevalent during the first half of the 1900s because teachers liked its objective focus on preparation and experience. The structure of this form of pay is simple: teachers are paid for academic preparation and for their years of experience. Most teachers are accustomed to this system; they readily embrace it because it provides "objective" criteria on which pay is determined. They are generally reluctant to entertain ideas about other compensation systems.

Nevertheless, as supported by many policy analysts and researchers (Berends, 1999; Firestone, 1994; Hassel, 2002; Levin, 1983; Wise, 1984), while teacher salaries make up the largest portion of a district's budget, individual salaries generally do not reflect a consistent relationship between teacher skills and teacher compensation. It has been noted that "salary steps are not tied to student performance, which result in little incentive for teachers to increase their efforts or improve their skills" (Firestone, 1994). It is also difficult to find any convincing relationship between resources expended on education—particularly teacher pay—and student achievement. In fact, Childs and Shakeshaft's (1986) meta-analytic study of the relationship between educational expenditures and student achievement led them to conclude that the relationship "is minimal with those expenditures which relate directly to instruction, such as teacher salary and instructional supplies, having the most positive relationship to student achievement" (p. 259). Other researchers such as Hanushek (1989), Ludwig and Bassi (1999), and Whitehead (2000) have corroborated these findings. Ludwig and Bassi further contended that "whether additional school spending translates into overall improved student learning remains unclear" (p. 385). Other researchers, however, have found a positive relationship between spending and student achievement (Lockwood & McLean, 1993; Wainer, 1993; Wenglinsky, 1998). Wenglinsky, for example, found that while teachers' level of education and spending on administration at the building level made little difference, "spending on administration at the district level, however, paid off" (cited in Bracey, 2002, p. 32). In addition, a major RAND study found convincing evidence that while additional resources had little effect on majority or more-advantaged students, "additional resources have been effective for minority and disadvantaged students" (Grissmer, Flanagan, Kawata, & Williamson, 2000, p. xxviii).

During the 1980s and early 1990s, districts attempted to reform teacher pay structures with merit pay and career ladder systems (Johnson, 1985). Their efforts were partially motivated by President Reagan's call for rewarding deserving teachers with extra pay. As discussed in detail later on, these early attempts at reforming teacher pay were only appendages to the single salary schedule, which for the most part remained unchanged. Most merit pay and some career ladder systems were proven unsuccessful and were unpopular within the education community (Boe, 1990; Elam & Gallup, 1989; Smylie & Smart, 1990).[1]

For the most part, teacher opposition to merit pay and career ladders was primarily due to what they perceived as an unworkable evaluation process fraught with bias, politics, favoritism, and "subjective evaluation of teachers by administrators"(Lenord & Tanaka, 1996, p. 34).[2] In Florida, for example, the Master Teacher Program used the school principal and a certified observer to evaluate teachers' knowledge of their content area and their instructional skills. Evaluation results were then used to determine who received merit pay. This system was severely criticized by educators who believed the process was too subjective (Arthur & Milton, 1991). The unpopularity of the program was documented in a survey that indicated only 39% of school district personnel supported merit pay, with most support coming from personnel administrators and school board members (Wiegman & Binnie, 1985). Obviously, this was not what designers of the program envisioned. Their original intent had been the implementation of a rigorous system in which all performance observers were trained and certified in a measurement system that would meet stringent criteria mandated by Florida State Board of Education (Wilson, 1985).

Merit pay programs of the 1980s failed for many reasons. In a review of the literature, Johnson (1986) found the key reasons were (a) lack of an adequate and appropriate theoretical framework, (b) incomplete implementation, (c) unintended organizational consequences, (d) failure to advance teacher development and student learning, and (e) the reality that teachers are "primarily motivated by intrinsic rather than extrinsic rewards" (p. 64). Fundamentally, contributions of the pre-1990s career ladders and merit pay systems to the accountability movement were blunted by failure on the part of policymakers and professional educators to link compensation and reward to teacher performance, and, most importantly, to student achievement.

The Move to Comprehensive School Reform and Performance Pay Programs

The failure of merit pay and career ladder incentive programs to improve instruction and student performance shifted attention to other initiatives. The new initiatives fell under the rubrics of "standards-based" and "comprehensive" reform, terms popularized by several policymakers and education stakeholders[3] (National Center on Education and the Economy, 1996; New American Schools Corporation, 1991; Ravitch, 1995; Stringfield, et al., 1996). Tucker and Codding (1998) defined standards-based education as "a way of operating schools and education systems so that standards for student performance are at the center, and the sole objective for everyone in the system is ensuring that students meet the standards" (p. 320). They further argued that the format for standards should have three essential parts: performance descriptors, samples of student work, and commentaries on student work.[4] These three components helped form the foundation of a new wave of comprehensive programs that may truly improve student achievement. By several accounts (Stringfield, Ross, & Smith, 1996; Traub, 2000), there are numerous models of "comprehensive," "school wide," "systemic programs," and more than 9000 schools across the country have adopted one or more of them. These systemic models emphasize "change that incorporates a coherent and self-consistent vision of pedagogy, curriculum and structure—a replicable, purpose-built school" (Traub, 2000, p. 56). Within the context of personnel and program evaluation, standards are considered to be

> widely shared principles for assessing the value or quality of a profession's services. They are integral to professionalism. Standards provide clients as well as evaluators with a carefully developed, periodically updated, widely shared, professionally accredited view of what constitutes current best practices and what are unacceptable. They also provide guidelines for meeting the requirements of the standards and caution against common error to anticipate and avoid. Setting and applying professional standards is a force against corrupt, careless, and incompetent evaluations. (Stufflebeam 1998, p. 290)

When applied to performance pay systems, however, standards-based education takes on a different meaning. According to Odden and Kelley (1997), the term suggests new elements for compensation, primarily "(a) competency-based pay to develop the wide array of skills needed for teaching a high-quality curriculum well and for engaging in effective school-based measurement, and (b) group performance awards for meeting specified improvement in school results" (pp. 22-23). Odden (2000a) addressed four reasons why changing from traditional ways of compensating teachers to standards- and performance-based approaches may be possible: (a) the creation of the National Board for Professional Teaching Standards (NBPTS); (b) the emergence in the private sector of new compensation structures, such as 'knowledge- and skill-based pay,' competency pay, group-based performance awards, and gainsharing, (c) the report of the National Commission on Teaching and America's Future (NCTAF); and (d) a publication by CPRE titled *Paying Teachers for What They Know and Do* (1997, 2002). While the influence of the CPRE publication is debatable, especially considering that the ideas undergirding performance pay were addressed extensively elsewhere long before 1997 (Duttweiler & Ramos-Cancel, 1986; Lawler, 1971, 1992), one would encounter great difficulty finding evidence that contradicts the impact the other three factors have had on comprehensive reform in general and performance pay in particular.

Theoretical Frameworks and School Reform Programs

Carlson (1996) articulated several theories that conceptualize and define standards-driven accountability and comprehensive school reform. They include the *common sense theory*, the *decentralization theory*, the *open systems theory*, and the *quality of work life theory*. The salient features of these theories are the following:

- Common Sense—supports inferences about the connections between organizational structures and student outcome. According to Newman (1993) 'New organization structures will presumably either increase the commitment (motivation) of adults to teach and students to learn or they will increase the competence (technical capacity) of adults to offer a better learning environment' (p. 5).

- Decentralization—builds on the proposition that the closer the governance process is to the people affected, the more responsive it is to their demands and interest. Murphy observes: 'Interwoven in this grassroots notion of responsiveness are issues of democracy, constituent influence and control over organizational decisions, ownership of public institutions, trust, and organizational accountability.'

- Open System—recognizes that schools are complex social organizations made up of numerous internal and external processes and relationships. Under this theory, schools are seen as having multiple internal subsystems and being embedded within multiple external subsystems.

- Quality of Work Life—emphasizes respect for adults; participation in decision making; frequent and stimulating professional interaction; frequent, accurate feedback, leading to a higher sense of efficacy; use of skills and knowledge; resources to carry out the job; and goal congruence. (p. 242-246)

Together these theories provide a framework within which the new era of school reform is progressing. Each theory addresses a particular dimension of comprehensive school reform. The quality of work life theory, however, comes closest to addressing the issues inherent in teacher incentive programs. It emphasizes key factors necessary for viable performance pay programs and articulates a linkage between improving the quality of education through professionalizing teaching and paying teachers for what they know and do.

More recently, Fuhrman and Odden (2001) articulated a "theory of action" that explains several dimensions of CSR. Four postulates or assumptions underpin this theory:

> First, there must be clear and ambitious goals, together with such indicators of results as coherent educational standards and sound measures of achievement. Second, when ambitious goals seek to increase performance by significant amounts, the core technology of education—instructional practice—must change dramatically. Third, achieving dramatically improved instruction in all schools requires extensive investment in continuing professional development, in strong curricula, and in leadership at the system and school levels. Finally, such systemic change requires incentives to provide positive reinforcements where improvement is occurring and to signal schools and districts that more and better change is required. (pp. 59-60)

While the quality of work life and other theories frame issues of CSR, however, specific reform models and approaches provide proscriptive blueprints and practical means by which educators can plan and implement restructuring efforts. Models and approaches that attempt to reform schooling can be classified as either "incremental" or "discontinuous." According to Conley (1993), who relied on the work of Lindblom (1959) and Tyack (1990), "Incremental change results in gradual adaptation to the existing system" and "implies a process of slowly instituting programs and projects designed to avoid the conflicts and upheaval that invariably accompany" major change. Discontinuous change on the other hand "implies activities that reinvent the way the organization functions" (p.102). It transforms the culture and structure of the organization and "reengineers" the philosophy, vision, mission, and the way things get done. Until the 1990s, most reform programs were largely incremental. Several incremental programs are detailed in *Educational Programs that Work* (U.S. DOE, 1995) and *School Improvement Programs* (Block, Everson, &

Guskey, 1995). They include programs that focused on learning (Cooperative Learning, Interactive Learning, Mastery Learning), teaching (Direct Instruction, Peer Coaching, and Writing Across the Curriculum), and schooling (Outcome-Based Education and Effective Schools).

Discontinuous programs are whole-school reform initiatives that restructure the entire school and in some cases the entire district. They address all the dimensions of restructuring evident in recent reform models. Many of these are documented in the CSRDP (1999) and explained in *Bold Plans for School Restructuring: The New American School Designs* (Stringfield, Ross, & Smith, 1996). They include Comer's School Development Program, Success for All, Co-NECT, the Child Development Project (Lewis & Barnett, 1999), and the Manitoba School Improvement Program (cited in Fullan, 1999, p. 33).

What is encouraging about discontinuous reform initiatives is their holistic and systemic focus as opposed to the fragmented, piecemeal focus of incremental approaches to reforming education. At the core of discontinuous approaches is an emphasis on standards, parent involvement, and whole-school reform. These three dimensions are among the most prevalent initiatives that define and drive the current era of reform. The particulars of discontinuous models of reform, also referred to as "high standards/high involvement," are ubiquitous throughout the literature and have been explained by several members of the research community, including Odden and Kelley (1997, 2002):

> The high standards/high involvement model is a school with ambitious goals ... and different management structures designed to better achieve those goals. High standards means that schools are to produce a high level of student achievement, with a strong focus on high outcomes for all students, extending concern of the effective schools model but with much higher performance expectations for students. Student outcomes are to include a high capacity for problem solving, the ability to adapt to a changing work environment, and the ability to access and maintain a high level of understanding of difficult subject matter. High involvement alludes to the importance of teachers centrally involved in not only school improvement but also school management for achieving the ambitious new school goals. The high involvement model means that schools are led by teacher teams that are responsible for instructional leadership and school management. (pp. 41-42)

As evident in this definition, the high standards/high involvement model recognizes neither the single-salary schedule nor merit pay as ways to compensate and reward teachers. These approaches create disincentives that are inconsistent with and anathema to the philosophy, ideals, and goals of the standards-driven movement. Equally important, advocates of the high standards/high involvement model have only recently begun to recognize the need to link standards and whole-school reform to performance pay. Many school districts (see Tables 3 and 4 in Chapter 2) have reengineered salary schedules and many others are in the process of revising their pay structure to enhance equity and efficiency, which, "requires reallocation of existing resources, incentives for improved performance, and a more market-based budgeting environment...." (Picus, 1998). Teacher incentive or performance pay programs are becoming integral parts of standards-based reform programs and are being used to ensure educational accountability for world-class instruction and learning. They may be, in Futrell's words, "among the wave of reforms that can transform the landscape of education" (1989, p. 9). They are different in some respects but share common elements.

Before states and districts adopt performance pay programs, however, they should grapple with a host of issues essential to developing a functional and effective performance program. They should also address critical variables and factors that play important roles during the development and implementation stages of a performance pay system. These factors include a systemic and comprehensive school reform focus, teacher motivation and performance, professional development, performance assessment, comprehensive program evaluation, adequate funding, and designing and developing the program within a framework of collaboration and shared decision making. The next chapter explores all these variables and their relationship to successful performance pay programs.

2

CRITICAL VARIABLES IN
PERFORMANCE PAY SYSTEMS

When and if performance pay systems are judged successful, it will be because they adhere to criteria and standards that reflect differences between success and failure, including (a) a focus on student achievement, (b) a focus on systemic, comprehensive reform, (c) knowledge of what motivates teachers, (d) an emphasis on professional development, (e) a commitment to effective performance assessment, (f) a commitment to comprehensive program evaluation, (g) the promotion and engagement in collaborative relationships, and (h) a commitment to providing adequate and sustained funding (Darling-Hammond, 1997; Eisner, 2001; Fuhrman 1993; Lieberman, 1995; Ravitch, 1995, 2000; Tucker & Codding, 1998; Zemelman, 1998). Each component contributes to the gestalt of an outcome-based school, a standards-driven high performance school, or simply an effective school. Further, these factors contribute to the milieu of what some call the "ecology of learning," or the intricate linkage of home, community, and school that collectively influences student achievement. These factors also help make the high standards/high performance model of accountability and reform functional and effective. They could be regarded as essential precursors to effective teacher incentive pay systems. A description of these factors and the role they play in performance pay systems is presented in this chapter. Note that while the first variable (focus on student achievement) is not discussed in a separate section in this chapter, its importance is acknowledged throughout the discussion and a more extensive treatment is presented in Chapter 7. Also, because professional development plays such a pivotal role in the development and implementation of performance pay systems, it is mentioned briefly in this chapter but addressed extensively in Chapter 3.

Systemic/Comprehensive Reform Focus

Current efforts to reform pay structures focus not on piecemeal, disjointed approaches, but rather on changing the way the entire system functions. System theorists were right when they contended that comprehensive change is preferable to disjointed, fragmented change. This they emphasized, is preferable; otherwise, "good solutions may be applied to the wrong problem" (Cleland, 1969; Parsons, 1951; Seiler, 1967; Von Bertalanffy, 1968). When applied to performance pay for educators, compensating and rewarding teachers are only pieces of the puzzle in CSR. They are, however, important pieces that focus attention on teacher effectiveness and student achievement. In explaining the role teacher pay plays in the broader accountability and restructuring movement, Firestone noted that "our best interest is not in reforming the salary system as an end in itself but in bringing an analysis of salaries into the broader discussion of how to reform the American educational system" (1994, p. 551).

The necessity of a broader discussion was brought to the fore when the United States Department of Education (1998) created the CSRDP. Under this initiative, states and districts may apply for funds to reform education but only if they adhere to nine criteria, one of which is using a comprehensive design that aligns curriculum, technology, professional development, and instruction with student performance. So far, the U.S. Department of Education has allocated more than $220,000,000 to help states in their effort to plan and implement comprehensive models of reform, which *may* include performance-based incentive systems.

Florida, for example, followed several CSRDP guidelines to develop its A+ System of School Improvement and Accountability. It identified eight education goals, of which Goal 3 (student performance) became the focus and pivotal point for reforming education. Goal 3 also became the foundation on which the state developed the curriculum framework, which identifies the major subjects and content domains. These are linked to nine reform domains (called chapters in the state's curriculum guide), which include Goal 3 Standards, the Sunshine State Standards, assessment, and professional development. The Sunshine Standards (expected levels of achievement students are to attain) include:

- a curriculum *strand* (a label for a category of knowledge such as mathematics),
- a *standard* (a general statement of expected learner achievement)
- *grade levels* (PreK-2, 3-5, 6-8, and 9-12),
- *benchmarks* (learner expectations or what a student should know and be able to do), and
- performance *descriptions* of students' work or examples of things a student could do to demonstrate achievement of the benchmark.

Figure 1 below shows an example of how these elements are interrelated for grade levels 3-5 mathematics.

Figure 1: Linkages between subject, strand, standard, benchmark, and sample performance description management, effective communication, creative and critical thinking.

A. Subject: Mathematics—Number Sense, Concepts, and Operations			
Level 3	**Benchmark**	**Performance Description**	**Goal**
Standards			
Grades 3-5	MA.A.2.2.1 Uses place-value concepts of grouping of ten (thousandths, hundredths, tenths, tens, hundreds, thousands) within the decimal number system.	MA.A.2.2.1.a Chooses the best estimate below of breaths per day, knowing that, on average, human beings breathe 984 times each hour. a) 28,000; b) 20,000; c) 21,600; d) 24,000	3
Grades 3-5		MA.A.2.2.1.b Writes the number represented by 7000 + 3 + 20 + 600, without adding	3

Adapted, by permission, from State of Florida, *Florida Curriculum Framework: Mathematics, PreK-12 Sunshine State Standards and Instructional Practices*, p. 53. © 1996 by State of Florida, Department of State.

The Sunshine Standards are aligned with Goal 3 Standards, which include information management, effective communication, creative and critical thinking, numeric problem solving, and system management. The state developed the *Florida Comprehensive Assessment Test (*FCAT) and uses it to assess students' performance on numeric problem solving, information management, effective communication, and creative/critical thinking. While mathematics and reading competencies are assessed in grades 3-10 using FCAT, writing skills are assessed in grades 4, 8, and 10 using *FCAT Writing!*, another standardized test.

Florida also uses results from the FCAT to calculate "annual learning gains" and assigns school performance grades of F to A based on their annual gains. According to State Board of Education Rule 6A-1.09981, which governs implementation of Florida's A+ System of School Improvement and Accountability,

- Schools designated School Performance Grade A and schools improving at least one (1) performance grade shall be eligible for school recognition and awards.

- Schools designated School Performance Grade A and schools improving at least two (2) performance grades shall be eligible for deregulated status and increased budget authority.

- Intensive assistance and intervention including on-site assistance preference for awarding grants, and priority for other discretionary funds as specified in subsections (9), (10), and (11) of this rule shall be provided to schools designated School Performance Grade F and School Performance Grade D. Renegotiation of bargained contracts as specified in subsection (9) of this rule may be provided to schools designated School Performance Grade F.

Financial rewards ($100 per student) distributed to designated A schools and schools improving at least one (1) performance grade must be used "as determined by the school's staff and school advisory council for nonrecurring bonuses to the faculty and staff or for nonrecurring expenditures for educational equipment or materials or temporary personnel for the school to assist in maintaining and improving student performance" (F.S. 231.2905). On the other hand, students attending schools that receive two F grades in a four-year period become eligible for vouchers, which may be used to attend nonpublic schools. Additionally, teacher professional development and student achievement are linked. Educators in all state public schools must analyze student achievement data and design professional development activities that match and address student needs. So for example, if student mathematics scores on the FCAT are low, teacher professional development activities must reflect that reality.

Many school districts in other states have developed comprehensive accountability systems similar to Florida's (McGinn, 1999; U.S. DOE, 1998). In doing so, these states have made the transition required by the CSRDP while others are still in the planning stages (Swanson & Stevenson, 2002). Importantly, while some districts have adopted the new performance pay systems and integrated them with their school improvement and accountability systems, many have not (Odden & Kelley, 2002).

Teacher Motivation

The adult development and psychology literature is replete with human motivational theories. There are motivational theories that focus on outcome behavior of individuals and their perception of past events, theories that focus on changing behavior through modification and reinforcement techniques, and theories that focus on how motivation occurs. Motivational theories may be characterized and distinguished as either *content* or *process* theories. According to Lunenburg and Ornstein (2000), content theories focus on the question of "what energizes human behavior" while process theories are concerned with "how motivation occurs" (p. 90). Table 1 presents information on ten prevalent motivational theories, several of which are used by performance pay developers. The table depicts the name of the theory, the individual(s) most responsible for its development, the key idea undergirding the theory, and the idea that connects the theory with teacher incentive programs.[5] The table also identifies whether the theory is content- or process-oriented.

Each of the motivational theories shown in Table 1 addresses, to some degree, the key motivational concepts of *extrinsic* rewards (e.g., income, prestige, power over others), *intrinsic* rewards (e.g., psychic, internal and intangible rewards, such as pride and satisfaction when students learn), and *ancillary* rewards (e.g., work schedule, good working conditions, availability of teaching materials, professional growth opportunities, security of retirement benefits).[6] All three concepts have been related to teachers and the instructional process in studies by Lortie (1975), Johnson (1986),

Kottkamp, Provenzo, & Cohn (1986), and Ozcan (1996). These researchers found, among other things, that teachers emphasize the importance of intrinsic rewards, have a tendency to de-emphasize or overlook the importance of extrinsic rewards, and use the lack of or insufficiency of both extrinsic and ancillary rewards to decide whether to continue or leave teaching.[7]

While intrinsic and extrinsic rewards play significant roles in teacher motivation and productivity, ancillary rewards play an equally important role. Ancillary awards are components of the job environment that Johnson (1986), Lortie (1975), and Lieberman (1995) identified as "learning facilitators." Among these are facilities that are conducive to teaching and learning, class size, amount of instructional time, active parent involvement, and an adequate supply of teaching materials.

Motivational theories depicted in Table 1 as well as extrinsic, intrinsic, and ancillary rewards, to varying degrees, rely on the same assumptions Ozcan identified:

- Teachers as human beings are naturally motivated to survive, utilize their potential, and realize themselves.
- Teachers engage in their occupation to earn their survival and self-realization resources.
- As humans, teachers are cultural beings and live as the members of various social groups. (1996, p. 6)

These assumptions suggest that, in terms of rewards, teachers are no different from other workers (Lawler, 1971, 1998). What motivates teachers, the rewards and incentives that excite their spirit and fire their imagination, work virtually the same way with all workers. Teachers have the same needs (Alderfer, 1972; Maslow, 1970), are satisfied or dissatisfied with the same "hygiene" or "motivator" factors (Herzberg, 1966), desire the same optimal experiences (Csikszentmihalyi, 1990), anticipate the same level of quality in their working environments and want working conditions that are facilitative and conducive for professional growth and development (Lortie, 1975), and, like other workers, expect their efforts and energy to result in equitable and meaningful rewards (Adams, 1964; Vroom, 1964; Weick, 1966). Key findings about teacher motivation and its linkage to performance pay programs are summarized in Table 2. Note especially Item #1, that professional efficacy ranks as *the* key motivator for teachers. It explains a major reason why many teachers, despite deplorable working conditions, despite being underpaid and largely unappreciated, choose to continue teaching.

Teachers receive personal satisfaction and a deep sense of professional efficacy when they are able to teach a student to read, understand math concepts, play an instrument, draw a picture, speak a second language, or solve a personal problem. These accomplishments mean more to them than salary increases or bonuses. Collectively, the accomplishments are examples of what Fullan (1993, 1999) calls the "moral purpose" of education because they make noticeable and verifiable differences in students' lives, helping them to acquire knowledge and skills with which to navigate their way through life.

Table 1: Motivation Theories and their Relevance to Teacher Incentive Programs

Theory	Theorist(s)	Key Idea	Linkage to Teacher Incentives
Expectancy Theory (Process)	Vroom, 1964	Individuals strive in their work if there is an anticipated reward that they value.	Teachers must anticipate the connection between their actions and subsequent monetary rewards and bonuses.
Goal Setting Theory (Process)	Locke & Latham, 1995	Goals motivate, inspire, and lead to higher task performance if they are specific, challenging, attainable, and if individuals are committed to them.	Teachers are more likely to achieve higher levels of performance if they are adequately compensated and rewarded for attaining specific curriculum and instructional goals.
Equity Theory (Process)	Adams, 1964; Weick, 1966	Individuals are dissatisfied if they are unjustly compensated for their efforts.	As a professional group, teachers feel they are inadequately compensated.

...continued

Table 1 continued

Theory	Author	Description	Implication
Job Enrichment Theory (Process)	Argyris, 1957	Individuals are more motivated when their work is varied and challenging.	Performance pay programs should challenge teachers and offer multiple opportunities for advancement.
Flow Theory and Rewards (Content)	Csikszentmihalyi, 1990	Individuals are more productive when they have optimal experience or the ability to derive moment-by-moment enjoyment from their work.	Teachers are more likely to be motivated by a comprehensive pay program that creates optimal work experiences by considering standards, opportunities for growth and development, performance assessment, and equitable compensation.
Contingency Theory (Content)	Lawler III, 1990	Individuals are more likely to be motivated when compensation and reward programs are consistent with organizational goals and practices.	Districts' goals and practices should create an atmosphere within which teachers see compensation and rewards as integral parts of a results-oriented philosophy.
Means/Rewards (Process)	Ozcan, 1996	Teachers' motivation increases when they are given opportunities to earn economic, honorific, political, intrinsic, and means rewards.	Address teacher motivation through a smorgasbord of rewards (e.g., economic, honorific, political, intrinsic, ancillary, and means).
Hierarchy of Needs (Content)	Maslow, 1970	All human beings have five kinds of needs—physical, safety, social, self-esteem, and self-actualization.	Take time to ascertain where teachers are on the need-hierarchy and consider individualizing parts of the reward structure to fit their situation.

. . . continued

Table 1 continued

Motivation-Hygiene (Content)	Herzberg, 1966	Motivation factors are the primary causes of satisfaction, and hygiene factors the primary causes of unhappiness on the job.	Pay does not motivate, but can be a source of dissatisfaction.
ERG (Content)	Alderfer, 1972	Humans have three core needs—existence, relatedness, and growth.	The less existence needs (pay, fringe benefits, working conditions) are satisfied, the more they will be desired.

Table 2: Key Findings on Teacher Motivation and Incentives

1. Processional efficacy ranked as the key intrinsic motivator for teachers (Lortie, 1975; Johnson, 1986).
2. The linkage between performance pay and professional efficacy is weak (Lortie, 1975; Johnson, 1986).
3. When teachers are members of high performing teacher groups and effective schools, they report higher satisfaction from their work, especially when high performance was tied to higher pay (Michaels & McCulloh, 1976).
4. Perceived school effectiveness is related to satisfaction of teachers with coworkers, with supervision, and with work itself (Knopp & O'Reilly, 1978).
5. While incentives can motivate people to change their behavior, the change may not be permanent (Mitchell, Ortiz, & Mitchell, 1983).
7. Inadequate pay ranked second as a reason for leaving teaching (Johnson, 1986).
8. Extrinsic rewards such as money will improve the performance of 'unintended or otherwise unattractive' tasks but intrinsic motivators are sufficient for problem-solving tasks.

. . . continued

Table 2 continued

9. When monetary incentives are offered, teachers tend to adjust their labor market behaviors in much the same way as other workers. Further, the use of monetary incentives in education suggests teachers will work harder if they can earn more money (Johnson, 1986).
10. Teachers can be motivated by extrinsic rewards for specific achievements or contributions; the introduction of such rewards can encourage teachers to attend to the criteria that count while disregarding others (Johnson, 1986).
11. There is no research on the effects of school-wide incentives over a number of years and little research on the effects of existing programs on schools that fail to achieve their goals (Firestone, 1994).
12. In deciding how to pay for performance, it is crucial to focus on motivation, whereas a focus on capabilities should be used to determine what to pay the person, what market position to take, and how hierarchical the pay system should be (Lawler III, 1998).
13. Extra money in the paycheck is an incentive for everyone but hardly the only incentive worth pursuing. All things that are excellent are worth pursuing (Tucker & Codding, 1998).
14. A variety of factors contribute to teacher motivation that modify teaching practice. These include: communication of clear, challenging but achievable educational goals; the alignment of organizational systems to support teacher efforts to adjust teaching practice to new goals; the opportunity to grow professionally through participation in meaningful professional development activities; seeing student performance improve; and public recognition for teaching excellence (Kelley, 1998, 1999).
15. Teachers generally find bonuses desirable, along with other rewards pertaining to student achievement, goal attainment, and learning; small bonuses (less than $1000) are not likely to be motivating; teachers with the most favorable attitudes toward the bonus program are less satisfied with their current salary, think receiving a bonus is fair, and feel that the bonus program is procedurally fair (CPRE, 1999).

The misguided belief that teachers are intrinsically motivated by monetary rewards and bonuses is evident in many accountability programs. For example, the Florida A+ Accountability System awards bonuses to schools designated School Performance A and school improving at least one performance level. Florida teachers, however, downplay the importance of the awards and instead emphasize professional efficacy as the primary reason they work hard to help students learn. This tendency was illustrated in a written assignment submitted to a professor by a fourth grade teacher studying for her master's degree:

> Because our school earned an "A" based on Florida's A+ Plan, we were rewarded $100 per student. This resulted in a school bonus of over $100,000. With the guidance of our principal along with our Leadership Team, it was decided that part of the money would be used as bonuses for all school employees that were present during the year the grade was given and stayed the following year. This bonus turned out to be roughly $1,000 for teachers and slightly less for other school personnel, including custodians and cafeteria workers. It was wonderful to receive extra money; however, fourth and fifth grade teachers began to express animosity about the equity of distribution. Because the "A" grade was awarded due to the performance of students in fourth and fifth grade on the FCAT Math, Reading, and Writing test, many of the teachers of these students felt they should have received a larger percentage of the money. The next year fourth and fifth grade teachers worked hard to maintain our school's "A" status. Through extra planning, program development, and enhancement, before and after school tutoring, and the stress of co-workers saying they were looking forward to another bonus, we did indeed earn another "A" grade from the state and another well-deserved monetary bonus. Personally, I did not put forth the effort for the bonus. In addition, I am fairly certain my fellow fourth and fifth grade teachers did not either. The extra effort put forth was for our students, for our school, for our amazing principal, and to continue to be the best. The money is the icing on the cake. The cake is being the best we can be. Now, would I feel differently if I were rewarded more money. Probably. However, simply because of the nature of my job, I and all other dedicated educators will continue to give their all. Possibly, in other businesses the concern for quality is a factor that needs to be considered when applying rewards for performance. (Wells, 2000, pp. 8-10)

While professional efficacy is identified throughout the literature as the primary motivator or the great satisfier in teaching, policymakers and school officials would be mistaken to design incentive programs that emphasize only intrinsic motivation of teachers. The truth is that all three kinds of motivators—intrinsic, extrinsic, and ancillary—underlie teachers' behavior and should be reflected in a performance-based incentive system. One teacher articulated this truism when she observed that as a *teacher* she is motivated by helping students learn and making a difference in their lives, as an *individual* she is motivated by praise and recognition, and as a *mother* with children to support and bills to pay she is motivated by incentives and bonuses (V. Barrett, personal communication, September 14, 2000). Her sentiments are consistent with Ozcan's (1996) observation that "to consider teaching [merely] as an occupation producing mostly psychological [intrinsic] satisfaction and teachers as the hunters of intrinsic rewards is not readily acceptable and also has misleading implications" (1996, p. 11). [8] Clearly, the gestalt or holistic view of motivation is imperative when making assumptions about teacher behavior.

Performance Assessment

Evaluation and performance assessment play key roles in standards-based reform, and, in particular, comprehensive reform approaches such as performance pay systems. This is partly to prevent what Tucker and Codding called "a long and endless succession of fads masquerading as best guesses about what will work" (1998, p. 162). An effective performance pay system is founded on both the principles and functional particulars of performance assessment and program evaluation theory and practice.

This section of the book addresses performance assessment relative to teacher performance and student achievement, as well as program evaluation relative to comprehensive performance pay systems. Because student achievement is a measure of teacher performance, these assessments are discussed together. When applied to students, performance assessment is used interchangeably with "alternative assessment" and "authentic assessment" and refers to evaluation that "requires students to generate rather than choose a response" (Herman, 1997, p. 396). When applied to teachers' performance, assessment refers to expectations that require teachers to demonstrate how instructional practices improve their students' achievement. Importantly though, the following discussion will use the assumption that the school accountability movement is driven by the need to emphasize outcome measures (test scores, drop-out rates, absentee data, samples of student work) as opposed to process measures (administrator/teacher ratings, student/parent ratings, peer observation, ratings by outsiders using structured protocols).

Assessing Student Performance

All 50 states have developed and mandated rigorous testing schemes and have enacted or are in the process of enacting laws mandating standards and benchmarks for what students should know and be able to do upon graduation. Standards and tests have become indispensable in gauging academic progress as well as effective leadership and instruction. Some states, such as Texas and North Carolina, "compare one year's expected growth in student achievement to actual growth," while others such as Kentucky and Tennessee "measure change in student achievement over two- or three-year cycles" (Southern Regional Education Board [SREB], 1997, p. 4). One example of the standards and tests (ST) evaluation approach is the Tennessee Value-Added Assessment System developed by Sanders and his associates (Sanders & Horn, 1995). The system uses a statistically mixed model methodology to track and analyze teacher effects on student achievement over a number of years. A longitudinal evaluation design is then used to analyze student achievement data. After controlling for intra-classroom heterogeneity, student achievement level, and class size, the researchers in one study (Sanders & Rivers, 1996) found that:

- the most important factor affecting student learning is the teacher.
- there are wide variations in effectiveness among teachers.
- effective teachers appear to be effective with students of all achievement levels regardless of the level of heterogeneity in their classrooms.
- teacher effectiveness is the dominant factor affecting student academic gain.

In light of these findings, the researchers urged districts to devote efforts to tracking teacher success and to

> identify teachers [who] clearly get results over time, and comparing them to teachers over time who do not, seems a logical, worthwhile next step in addressing the issues raised here and in further developing general lines of inquiry about the important relationship between teacher effectiveness and teacher evaluation. (p. 67)

Another example of the ST approach to evaluation is reflected in Success for All (SFA), a researched-based district-wide reform approach developed by Slavin and his Johns Hopkins associates. The model is "based on the premise that all students can and must succeed in the early grades" (Slavin et al., 1996). Several components define and structure the program, including a systematic reading program that emphasizes story telling and retelling, one-on-one tutoring in reading, weekly assessment of student progress, professional development for teachers and tutors, a focus on parenting education, and facilitators who work with teachers and staff. Evaluation of the program consists of matching SFA schools with schools similar in many respects, including poverty level, historical achievement level, and student ethnicity. Students in each SFA and control school are then matched and given a reading test at the end of the school year. Their scores are then compared. According to Slavin et al. (1996), SFA schools are effective in increasing the reading level of disadvantaged students and students for whom English is a second language. The New Standards Assessment System detailed by Tucker and Codding (1998) is another example of the ST approach to testing that has yielded similar results.

What are evident in both the Tennessee Value-Added Assessment System and the Success for All approach are the focus on student achievement and the reliance on valid, reliable outcome data. According to the proponents of these approaches, student grades reflect the level and quality of district support, school leadership, and teacher performance—all of which influence student learning in discernable and measurable ways. Of course, this assertion is debatable as contrary evidence has shown that student grades more accurately reflect parental education and socioeconomic status (American Evaluation Association, 2002; Heubert & Houser, 1999; Hoover, 2000; Jones et al., 1999; Reese, Miller, Mazzeo, & Dossey, 1997; Stake, 1998; Walberg & Greenberg, 1999). Moreover, some observers have argued that high-stakes tests only measure what students learn as a result of being taught to the test (Heubert & Hauser, 1999; Jones et al. 1999; Lemann, 1999).

In condemning high-stakes tests as the "sole or primary means for making decisions with serious negative consequences for students, educators, and schools" (p. 1), The American Evaluation Association in its *Position Statement on High Stakes Testing in PreK-12 Education* has identified some of the most egregious consequences of high stakes testing. They include "increased dropout rates, teacher and administrator deprofessionalization, loss of curricular integrity, increased cultural insensitivity, and disproportionate allocation of educational resources into testing programs and not into hiring qualified teachers and providing sound educational programs" (2002, p. 1). In spite of these unintended consequences, however, there is an obvious need for student tests because without them schools would be handicapped in their ability to ascertain objectively and communicate the effects that schools, administrators, teachers, and curricula have on students' academic growth.

Assessing Teacher Performance

A large literature base supports teacher performance assessment. Some policymakers and researchers believe teacher assessment should be addressed comprehensively rather than as one piece of comprehensive school reform. For example, Darling-Hammond, Wise, and Pease (1983), Peterson (1995), The Joint Committee on Standards for Educational Evaluation (JCSEE, 1994), the Interstate New Teacher Assessment and Support Consortium (INTASC, 1995), Educational Testing Services (Dwyer, 1994; ETS, 1995), and the National Board for Professional Teaching Standards (NBPTS, 1996) have advocated that teacher assessment be aligned with curriculum development, professional development, and student performance. Performance appraisal system guidelines developed by several state agencies, such as the Florida Department of Education (2000), reflect the same emphasis on a comprehensive approach. Another group of policymakers and researchers value specific assessment strategies and approaches such as portfolio evaluation (Cushman, 1999; King, 1991; Oakley, 1998), teacher tests (Lortie, 1975; Murray, 1986; Popham, 1971, 1988), peer evaluation (Saavedra & Kwan, 1993; Shore, Shore, & Thorton, 1992), Total Quality Management (Andrews, 1997), parent reports (Peterson, 1995), effective practices (Wise, 1984), and performance-based assessment (Hibbard, 1996).

Emphasis on accountability, however, is drawing increasing attention to teacher assessment approaches that are either integrated or could be integrated with performance pay programs. Examples of these approaches include the Educational Testing Service's PRAXIS Series adapted in California, Colorado, Connecticut, Minnesota, and other states; the assessment techniques developed by INTASC; and Danielson's standards that are linked with PRAXIS III and NBPTS assessment (Danielson, 1996; Odden, 2000a). These are the performance assessment approaches now in vogue and represent "hot topics on the agenda of education reform" (Eisner, 1999, p. 658).[9] These standards-driven approaches focus on effective instruction and student achievement. They typically involve the professional judgment of trained assessors who observe actual or simulated practice supplemented by review of artifacts such as videos, lesson plans, assignments, and student work, and with explanations or reflections on teacher performance (Milanowski & Young, 1999).

Advantages of the performance-based assessment include an emphasis on knowledge and skills applied in the classroom, documentation of teacher credibility, and helping teachers learn standards of effective instructional practices. Some policymakers and researchers believe performance-based assessment "represents a set of strategies for the ... application of knowledge, skills, and work habits through the performance of tasks that are meaningful and engaging to students" (Hibbard, 1996, p. 6). Incentive pay proponents in particular see performance-based assessment as essential for making decisions about teachers' qualifications and readiness to move between pay levels. Administrators and teachers could learn more about this assessment approach as both an instructional and a performance assessment tool by consulting the work of Airasian (1991), Popham (1995), Stiggins (1994), Wiggins (1998; 1999), and the NBPTS (1996).[10]

There are numerous assessment approaches and techniques that are not comprehensive in their focus yet beneficial for distinguishing between effective and ineffective teaching. One such approach is portfolio assessment. The use of portfolios and dossiers as teacher assessment tools is a prevalent and widely accepted professional development approach. It is reflected in the Portfolio Assessment System (PAS), which is an effective and exemplary performance assessment approach because it links beginning teachers' performance to student achievement. The system was developed from research conducted by the National Association of State Directors of Teacher Education and Certification (NASDTEC), the NBPTS (1996), and the Interstate Teacher Assessment and Support Consortium. Oakley (1998) explained the expectations and requirements of PAS:

> Teachers develop portfolios consisting of the nine components, including a compilation of student goals, a report of teaching philosophy and practice, an assessment of students' progress toward goals, lesson plans, videotaped classroom instruction, a principal evaluation, a colleague evaluation, parent evaluations, and student evaluations. Licensed experienced educators are recruited and selected to evaluate the evidence provided in the portfolios in order to assign overall ratings. This team of assessors undergoes an intensive three-day training to develop common understanding of the criteria for teacher assessment and the gradients of teaching performance. (p. 326)[11]

From all indications, PAS has been successful and has provided credible data with which to judge teacher performance. It has also influenced officials and participants of the National School Reform Faculty Project to advocate and require the use of portfolios to increase teacher accountability and performance (Cushman, 1999; NBPTS, 1999).

Portfolios have become so prevalent that a large segment (44%) of the American population now advocates their use in assessing student performance and competence in addition to or in lieu of standardized tests (Rose & Gallup, 2000). Whether used for assessment or professional development purposes, school officials should be mindful of the four essential aspects of educational portfolios identified by LaBoskey (2000):

- First, the educational portfolio must allow for, promote, and reveal individual meaning-making.

- Second, the portfolio should provide the opportunity to interact about the content and meaning of those portfolios with people who matter and who support the reflective process.

- Third, the reflective processing occurs over an extended period.

- Fourth, the portfolio should be constructed and presented with a context that supports, promotes, and assesses such reflective thinking and moral deliberation elsewhere. (p. 594)

Another performance-based assessment approach includes the classroom assessment technique (CAT) that helps teachers conduct their owe assessment of teaching and learning in their classes. The developers of CAT claimed the system helps teachers use their knowledge and creativity to develop and apply assessment techniques to their unique teaching styles (Angelo & Cross, 1993).[12] In addition to CAT, assessment centers (Gay & Airasian, 2000; Hamilton, 1995; May, 1993) and action research (Arhar, Holly, & Kasten, 2001; Atweh, Kemmis & Weeks, 1988) can be used to help teachers increase their knowledge and improve instructional practice in ways that directly benefit students.

Whatever the approach used, consideration should be given to integrating the following elements in teacher assessment plans: (a) Boyatzis'(1993) three learning modes—performance, learning, development—between which adults shift continually during their professional career; (b) Ozcan's (1996) learning dimensions and propositions (see Note 7); and (d) Knowles' (1998) principles of adult learning. Moreover, reformers should also consider assessing the human resource development evaluation domains (satisfaction, learning, and performance) separately. This approach is necessary because, as Swanson and Holton (1997) observed,

> research shows that practitioners most satisfied with a program are not necessarily those who learned the most ...[and that] high or low satisfaction can be found among low, medium, and high achievers. Furthermore, because participants have gained knowledge and expertise does not mean that they will use it in the workplace. (p. 9)

This observation has a ring of truth to it because, in the past, professional development, and particularly transfer of training, have not resulted in appreciable increases in productivity in business settings and substantive improvement in instruction and student achievement in education settings (Gielen, 1995; Joyce & Showers, 1995).

Comprehensive Program Evaluation

While standards and tests can gauge student progress, and while several states are experiencing varying degrees of success with the standards and test approach,[13,14] districts also need to focus on evaluating the performance and effectiveness of entire performance pay systems. An alignment of standards, curriculum, professional development, assessment, and testing should serve as the foundation of evaluation efforts. What are ultimately needed, however, are evaluation designs and approaches that address all facets of comprehensive school reform, including performance pay programs. Such evaluation approaches must be systemic and comprehensive if the intent is to promote excellence in teaching and learning.

Several comprehensive evaluation models may provide guidance for systemic evaluation of comprehensive reform and performance pay systems. Some are rooted in the positivist/quantitative paradigm of evaluation research while others are rooted in the phenomenological/ qualitative and postmodern research paradigm. The JCSEE developed one mode that reflects the positivist paradigm. This body has a membership of 3 million who represent 18 professional organizations. Since 1975, JCSEE has developed standards that govern program and personnel evaluation. The standards are divided into four strands: *utility, feasibility, propriety,* and *accuracy*. Briefly, the *utility* standards define whether an evaluation serves the practical information needs of a given audience; the *feasibility* standards require evaluators to be realistic, prudent, diplomatic, and economical; the *propriety* standards facilitate protection of rights of individuals affected by an evaluation and promote sensitivity to and warn against unlawful, unscrupulous, unethical, and inept actions by those who conduct evaluation; and the *accuracy* standards convey technically adequate information about the features that determine worth and merit of the program being evaluated (JCSEE, 1994). When a comprehensive evaluation of a performance pay system is planned, developed, and implemented in accordance with these standards, the likelihood of valid and reliable data on which to based policy and programmatic decision increases, as demonstrated in several successful large-scale evaluation studies (Herman, 1997; Stufflebeam, 1998).

Developers of performance pay systems may want to consult JCSEE's work for ideas on how to evaluate an effective and fully functional performance pay program. Their standards on personnel appraisal can help structure and define the critical variables and components necessary for evaluating teacher performance because the standards "were developed to enable educators to answer questions about the design, implementation, and effectiveness of personnel evaluation systems" (Stufflebeam, 1998, p. 125).

A second comprehensive evaluation approach reflects principles from the qualitative and constructivist paradigms. Labeled "fourth generation evaluation" by its proponents, this approach emphasizes the importance of using stakeholders' "claims, concerns, and issues" as organizing themes when conducting evaluation and not only information evaluators believe to be relevant. Guba and Lincoln (1989) outlined 12 steps—from the initiating contract with client/sponsor to the recycling of the entire process—for conducting fourth generation evaluation and suggested the steps need not be followed sequentially. Criteria for judging the adequacy of the process are called "parallel criteria" because they "are intended to parallel the rigorous criteria that have been used within the conventional [positivist] paradigm" (p. 233). Criteria are classified under four headings: *credibility*, which parallels internal validity; *transferability*, which parallels external validity or generalizability; *dependability,* which parallels reliability; and *conformability*, which parallels objectivity. Performance pay programs can be evaluated with this approach, or the approach can be combined with the Joint Committee's positivist model. Other comprehensive evaluation models can be found in Levine, et al. (1981); Stufflebeam (2002), and Wholey, Harty, and Newcomer (1994).

Also worth noting is the evaluation process advocated by the New American Schools Corporation (Berends, 1999; Cicchinelli & Zoe, 1999; Ross, 2000; Ross et al., 1997). As depicted in Figure 2, the New American Schools' evaluation process is not new, and there is nothing unique about it. In fact, it mirrors the same steps advocated by the JCSEE, Stufflebeam, and others. What is different is its application of evaluation strategies and tools to comprehensive school reform. For example, benchmarking (disciplined search for best practices) is used to provide indicators of success for what some regard as the most important aspect of implementation. Then data are collected with several instruments such as the *School Climate Survey*, the *Comprehensive School Reform Teacher Questionnaire*, and the *School Observation Measure*. Interviews and focus groups are used to collect qualitative data. A diagnostic report is then developed wherein summary data from each instrument are reported and benchmark status is documented.

Comprehensive school reform evaluators (Sanders & Horn, 1995; Ross, 2000; Wright, Horn, & Sanders, 1997) also suggest using a hierarchy of evaluation strategies including:

- Evaluating program and control schools using standardized and performance measures
- Evaluating program and control schools using standardized measures only
- Evaluating program schools only using standardized and performance measures
- Evaluating program schools only using standardized measures

The effectiveness of performance pay systems should be evaluated in districts that make them integral parts of their reform efforts. But there is nothing in the literature that shows this is occurring. In fact, comprehensive school reform as defined by New American Schools more often than not focuses exclusively on the alignment of standards and benchmarks, curriculum design and development, professional development, and student outcome measures. Rarely, if ever, are reward systems mentioned. This is understandable, as performance systems and the role they play in school improvement have only recently begun to be noticed by whole-school reformists.

Figure 2: New American Schools Evaluation Process

Step 1: *Evaluation Plan*
Purpose and Objectives
Key consumers
Context
Evaluation questions

Step 2: *Methodology*
Participants
Instrumentation
*School Climate Survey (SCI)
*Comprehensive School Reform Teacher Questionnaire (CSRTQ)
*School Observation Measure (SOM)

Step 3: *Data Collection*
Management (data)
Time Line

Step 4: *Data Analysis*
Quantitative
Qualitative

Step 5: *Reporting and Feedback*
School staff
Parents/community
School district
Design teams

Step 6: *Continuous Improvement*
Identify needed improvement
Monitor progress

Adapted with permission from Ross (2002), *How to Evaluate Comprehensive School Reform Models. Getting by Design*, p. 15. © 1998 by New American Schools.

In one assessment evaluation study, Hall, Caffarella, and Burtlett (1997) examined how Colorado's Douglas County School District implemented a performance pay plan that reflected the credibility, dependability, and conformability dimensions of the "fourth generation" evaluation model. The researchers carefully distinguished between summative evaluation that is conducted to determine "whether or not the new way is better that the old" and formative evaluation used to "assess the current state of the implementation" and to "offer recommendations based in change theory about what can be done to further facilitate implementation" (p. 5). The researchers emphasized systemic, comprehensive evaluation aimed at uncovering how well the program functioned.

The evaluation design required a district-wide survey of all teachers, school-based, and district office administrators, as well as in-depth interviews with a representative sample of teachers. The researchers found, among other things, that the first-year implementation of the performance pay plan (PPP) had "gone unbelievably well." In essence, teachers and administrators accepted and supported the program. Because of this finding, the researchers were able to make meaningful and practical recommendations for program improvement, such as including classroom observation as part of the assessment process. The apparent disadvantage or weakness of the PPP system and the evaluation design was failure to include student achievement, as measured by standardized tests, as the key measure of effectiveness.

Overall, what was important about the study was its use in illustrating four dimensions of assessment:

- Avoiding summative success/failure judgments.
- Using recommendations to increase stakeholders' interest in the findings.
- Focusing on change as a process reduces pressure for immediate results and can increase the likelihood of having continuing support for implementation.
- Using change models to drive interventions. (Hall, Caffarella, & Burtlett, 1997, p. 12)

While the study illustrated these dimensions of program evaluation that education reformers need to consider when designing a performance pay program, it should be stressed that fourth generation evaluation approaches are insufficient for evaluating school-based accountability programs. Ideally, program evaluation should focus on student achievement data and must address the merit and worth of the entire performance-based program.

The third program evaluation example demonstrates how that was accomplished in the Dallas Independent School District (DISD), specifically as it relates to student performance and principal turnover. The program began in fall 1991 after the DISD school board mandated that all schools be held accountable for results that "stimulate continuous quality improvement over time" (Ladd, 1999, p. 2). The measure of student performance was the Texas Assessment of Academic Skills (TAAS), which is "linked to the state's curriculum and serves as the basis for statewide accountability" (p. 4). Grades 3 and 7 were the units of analysis. Ladd described the evaluation design:

> The relevant analytical question is not simply whether student performance on the TAAS improved in Dallas during the 1990s, but rather whether it improved relative to what would have been expected in the absence of the program. To address this question, I used panel data techniques to compare average student performance by school in specific grades in Dallas on the State administered TAAS with student performance by school in the other five large Texas cities (Austin, El Paso, Forth Worth, San Antonio, and Houston) for school-years 1990-91 to 1994-95. (p. 4)

The evaluation also focused on dropout, attendance rates, and principal turnover, variables influenced by the accountability program. In essence, four outcome measures guided the evaluation: student gain scores on the TAAS, dropout rates, attendance, and principal turnover. Gain scores and value-added analysis, similar to the Tennessee approach, reflected the extent to which schools were judged successful or unsuccessful. Schools that improved student reading and math performance were awarded $1000 for principals and teachers, $500 for staff such as secretaries and janitor, and $2000 for activity accounts.

The findings indicated that the program positively affected White and Hispanic seventh-grade students, did little for Black students, and was linked to a high turnover rate (from 6.3% to 24.4%) among principals. The program also influenced a decline in the dropout rate and an increase in school attendance. In summary, the evaluation illustrated the advantage of a comprehensive assessment approach. DISD officials were able to use evaluation results to revise the program. More attention was given, for example, to Black students as findings identified them as being affected least by the program.

Participation and Collaboration

The next critical variables in a performance pay program are participation and collaboration. The central notion here is to involve all interested parties from the inception to the completion of the program. This means that representatives from the school board, district office, teachers, parents, and community should compose the task force charged with planning a performance pay program. The principle and spirit of shared decision-making should guide interactions. Furthermore, Fullan's (1999) "inside-out" principle of collaboration could provide theoretical and practical guidance. The inside-out principle underscores the notion that schools can ill afford to be isolated and disconnected from the community at-large. According to Bryk, Sebring, Kerbow, Rollow, and Easton (1998), districts should emulate Chicago schools that "drew upon an extensive array of outside connections—including individual faculty at local colleges and universities, programs supported by area foundations, the business community, and other institutions—to guide and support their organizational development" (cited in Fullan, 1999, p. 46).

Some researchers have noted the importance of encouraging and facilitating participation and collaboration while planning and implementing teacher incentive programs. DeMitchell and Carroll (1999), for example, observed, "any proposed reform strategies that affect terms and working conditions of unionized employees must be bargained in those school districts that have collective bargaining" (p. 676). They also found that "the more the collective bargaining process was viewed as problem solving the less the contract was considered an obstacle to reform" (p. 678). Odden and Kelley (2002) noted the importance of building consensus and getting teachers to buy in. Furthermore, Fisher and Ury (1991) in *Getting to Yes: Negotiating Agreement Without Giving In* and Kerchner, Kippich, and Weeres (1997) in their timely and influential book *United Mind Workers*, documented this spirit of collegiality and camaraderie that should define relationships between teacher unions and district school boards. It is a relationship founded on trust and respect, which only results from honest interactions. This camaraderie is evident in successful attempts, such as in Cincinnati, Ohio, to plan and establish incentive pay programs that teachers support (Odden & Kellor, 2002).

The importance of participation and collaboration when developing performance pay programs is supported by several studies. Norton and Scott (1988), for example, conducted a 21-state study to discover whether "participation in incentive program influenced board members, district administrators, principals, and teachers about the ability of incentive pay to effect positively such factors as teacher motivation, quality of instruction, the public's respect for teachers, and the recruitment and retention of teachers" (p. 149). Districts with and districts without incentive pay programs were identified, and a random sample of 384 subjects was selected. A 28-item questionnaire was administered to gather data and test five null hypotheses:

> There is no significant difference between the attitudes of teachers, principals, central office administrators, and board members from school districts with incentive pay programs as compared to the attitudes of parallel groups from districts without incentive pay programs towards the:
>
> - collective effects of incentive pay (H1).
> - effects of incentive pay programs on motivation (H2).
> - effects of incentive pay programs on the improvement of the quality of instruction (H3).
> - toward the effects of incentive pay program on the public's perception of the status of the teaching profession (H4).
> - toward the effects of incentive pay program on the recruitment and retention of teachers (H5). (p. 149)

The researchers rejected Hypotheses H1, H2, and H3, and failed to reject H4 and H5. In other words, educators in districts that participated in PPPs had a more positive attitude towards the collective effects of incentive pay, the effects of PPPs on motivation, and the effects of PPPs on the quality of instruction, than did educators without PPPs. However, there was no difference between the attitudes of both groups of educators relative to the program's effects on the public's perception of the status of the teaching profession and the PPP's effects on the recruitment and retention of teachers. Clearly, while participation in a PPP did not influence educators' attitudes about the public's perception of the teaching profession and did not influence educators attitudes about the program's effects on recruitment and retention, the study did show that participation resulted in positive attitudes toward incentive pay and efforts to improve instruction.

These findings were corroborated in other studies. Hall, Caffarella, and Burtlett (1997), for example, found that the "process of involvement and trust building" resulted in community-wide involvement in the development of Colorado's Douglas County performance pay program that contributed to understanding and acceptance of the program.[15] In another study of nine incentive programs implemented in New York City Schools, Brandenburg (1992) found that the overall program was rated favorably by participants whose main desires were to be treated as individuals and to have the program fully explained before hand. The more participants were involved and treated as equals, the more likely they were to accept and support the program.

If district officials do not foster a climate of participatory decision-making and collaboration, their failure may result in disdain and disparagement. Furthermore, if officials fail to include representative of affected groups in the planning and development phase, they risk rejection of the plan, alienation of the people whose support is critical for the plan's success, and ultimately sabotage. Dorman and Fulford (1990) discovered some of these factors in their study of 21 incentive programs. Similar behaviors were exhibited when the Denver Classroom Teacher Association rejected a proposed performance pay program. Andrea Giunta, the DCTA's President, charged that the union was "not willing to accept ... a pay proposal that has not been tried, is not tied to teacher's classroom performance, and did not include teacher input in its creation" (Giunta, 1999, p. 25A). This attitude expressed by Giunta reflects the need for extensive teacher participation documented in other studies (Hawley, 1985) as well.

Fullan's (1999) ideas on developing collaborative cultures provide a framework for understanding how schools and districts may go about ensuring successful outcomes. His five characteristics of collaborative cultures are instructive:

1. First, contrary to myth, effective collaborative cultures are not based on like-minded consensus. They value diversity because that is how they get different perspectives and access to ideas to address complex problems.

2. Second, diversity, openendedness and relentlessly pursuing highly complex problems will provoke personal and group anxiety and conflict.

3. Third, stirring the emotions and motivating people and even encouraging people who are already motivated is not sufficient. Also needed are

quality ideas—knowledge, expertise and continuous development of best practices.

4. Fourth, collaborative cultures combine connectedness with open-endedness.

5. Fifth, the combined effect of collaborative cultures serves to mobilize three powerful change forces. Moral purpose (the spiritual) gains ascendancy. Power (politics) is used to maximize pressure and support for positive action. Ideas and best practices (the intellectual) are continually being generated, tested and selectively retained. (pp. 36-39)

Here we see the variables that provide "deep meaning" of effective collaboration: diversity, anxiety and conflict, quality ideas, connectedness and openendedness, and the combination of moral purpose, power, and best practice. When involvement and collaboration are understood and practiced in this spirit, they increase the likelihood of planning and implementing legitimate and effective performance pay systems.

Nevertheless, another key element must be present—adequate funding. Contrary to what some analysts (Ballou & Podgursky, 1997) may believe, money does make a difference in every facet of schooling—especially student achievement. This is exactly what one cross-state comparison study on student achievement conducted by the RAND Corporation found (Grissmer, Flanagan, Kawata, & Williamson, 2000). By extension, adequate funding likewise helps determine the success or failure of performance pay systems.

Funding Performance Pay Programs

From where should money come to fund performance pay programs? How do districts with such programs pay for them? This section posits some answers to these two questions by drawing on the work of Wood and Thompson (1996) and CPRE (2000).

The general sentiment shared by conservative policymakers about funding education was expressed by President George W. Bush, who believes federal money for education should be tied to schools' test scores. He warned that "federal money will no longer flow to failure" (Drinkard, 1999, p. 6A) and supports a voucher program whereby money ($1,500) will be given to parents to send their children to a successful school (charter or private schools) if assessment measures indicate failure. President Bush's position (which is now reflected in the No Child Behind Act of 2001), represents the consensus shared by many education officials and national leaders about how best to improve education. This position represents a shift away from emphasizing equity, a highly valued policy position advocating that "school districts with low property tax value would receive additional fiscal support so that taxpayers were not over-burdened in their attempt to fund educational programs" (Wood & Thompson, 1996, p. 17). It became the "preeminent theme in education finance" during the 1970s. During that time, states tried "to reduce spending differences across districts, including flat grants, minimum foundation programs, a guaranteed tax base, percentage equalizing formulas, and full state funding" (Odden, 1999b, p. 1). In a way, the equity theme articulates the philosophy of "Do more with less" espoused by William Bennett, Reagan's Secretary of Education, and others of his ilk because the federal government was not committed to increasing its share of educational support dollars to reduce funding inequities across districts (Fowler, 2000).

However, reliance on the equity approach to funding education proved unfruitful. Return on investment or declining achievement scores did not convince state leaders and policymakers that added investment in education increased student learning. Other factors likewise contributed to the abandonment of equity as a value position for funding education. Wood and Thompson (1996) explained:

> In the 1980s, the costs for providing educational programs continued to rise. Many states were confronted with decreased financial resources including a diminished level of support from the federal government and taxation limitations imposed by voters. Unstable economic conditions forced changes in the methods that states utilized to support public education. Those who engage in the process of determining what is equitable in education finance approach the problem from different perspectives. Some individuals argue the need to reduce the tax burden by altering the distribution of state funds; others call for increased state participation as a cost-effective long-term investment, while others call for a redefinition of wealth in order to shift the burden of the cost of education. (p. 17)

All these factors coalesced and created the dynamics that resulted in a new philosophy, which presently underpins education funding. This new philosophy of the 1990s and 2000s was articulated by the National

Research Council's Committee on Education, Finance Equity, Adequacy, and Productivity (Ladd & Hansen, 1999) and is defined largely by three values: *adequacy, accountability,* and *quality* (Alexander & Alexander, 2001; Ladd & Hansen, 1999; Minorini & Sugarman, 1999; Odden & Picus, 2000; Wood & Thompson, 1996). Adequacy embraces and communicates the idea that education funding should be sufficient to get the job done (i.e., increase student learning). Accountability says that public education should be funded at higher levels, but that schools, namely teachers, should be held responsible for improving student learning. In addition, the quality value says that standardized achievement scores, preferably high-stakes tests, should measure and determine excellence and distinction. This new philosophy emerged partly because equity approaches failed to adequately address fiscal disparities and a growing number of underachieving students. It became difficult to justify increasing education funding in the face of evidence that showed no linkage between educational expenditure and student performance (Ballou & Podgursky, 1997; Hanushek, 1989). As a result, school districts across the country became convinced they had to link education funding to standards-driven curricula, result-oriented leadership and instruction, and learning outcome measures—especially test scores.

Adequacy and accountability are now highly valued because they make the position espoused by Bush and Bennett tenable. De-emphasizing reliance on more spending while demanding more results from educators or linking spending to student outcomes shifts the burden of improving education away from the states to teachers and ultimately to students. Nevertheless, this is where performance pay systems can be either saviors or spoilers. They can save educators by providing them with equitable and well-earned incentives and rewards for producing the results demanded of them. Alternatively, they can spoil the accountability and adequacy arguments advance by New American Schools and other comprehensive school reform advocates by revealing and demonstrating the need to treat teachers fairly and pay them what they are truly worth. Among other things, that is what a global economy expects and demands.

One funding framework consistent with the adequacy-accountability-quality philosophy was developed and disseminated by the CPRE (Odden, 1999b). It specifies new spending roles for the state, district, and federal levels. The state role consists of four elements:

1. A base spending level considered adequate for the average child to reach high standards.
2. An additional amount of money for low income, disabled, and LEP students to reach standards.
3. A price adjustment for all dollar figures to ensure comparable spending power.
4. Annual inflation adjustments for stabilized base spending. (pp. 2-5)

The district role consists of providing school sites with greater control over their resources, reinventing teacher compensation, and providing school-based performance incentives. And, the federal role consists of providing vision and financial assistance, especially in those states unable to increase spending at the national median. Odden contended that in order for the new national goals of accountability to be realized, the adequate base spending level may have to be set at the "national or state median, whichever is higher" (p. 6). In those instances where state median spending is below national median spending, he suggests, "outside sources may well probably be necessary to bring spending up to an adequate level." (p. 6). (Recently, Odden (2001) proffered several new approaches—"economic cost function " and "cost of all models"—for determining adequate funding levels and efficient resource allocation for schools adapting standards-based reform.)

But some policy analysts have warned against relying on outside sources to fund reform initiatives such as incentive programs because "they often die out with the first economic downturn or change in elected officials" (Firestone, 1994, p. 566). This reality was evident in Dallas where the business community supported the performance reward system. The community contributed $1.2 million the first year, $900,000 in the second year, and only $500,000 in the third year (Mendro, Olivarez, Maureen, Milanowski, 1999). This trend was also evident in the Granite School District of Salt Lake City where a merit pay incentive program contributed to increased teacher participation and performance, but where funding the program was reduced and subsequently eliminated (Farnsworth, Deberham, & Smith, 1991, p. 325). Furthermore, the practice of proposing performance pay programs without adequate, sustained funding was also evident in Iowa where lawmakers voted to replace the traditional salary schedule with a knowledge- and skills-based system. As one lawmaker observed, "There is no stable, ongoing funding stream," which made it an unfunded mandate (Blair, 2001, p. 5). Policy analysts such as Firestone (1994) advocate an "up-front budget allocation," which makes sense because it not only insures the incentive program will have a permanent allocation, but will also reflect a long-term commitment to truly reforming the way teachers are rewarded for what they do.

One idea for funding performance pay programs was examined by Garris and Cohn (1996). They conducted a study of 91 South Carolina school districts from 1985-86 to 1990-91 to test a model of full-state funding based on student performance as assessed by the *Comprehensive Test of Basic Skills* and other outcome measures.[16] They examined the model "at three different levels of performance: 10, 20, and 30% of total per pupil expenditures" (p. 117). Because South Carolina has a foundation system of funding education and distributing state aid, which creates an inverse relationship between state aid allocation and district wealth, the researchers based the study on the assumption of full-state funding. While adjusting for dropouts, they predicted residual scores for performance indicators using regression analysis and used "percent of students in each school district qualifying for free and reduce-free or reduced-free lunch as a proxy of socioeconomic status" (p. 118). The researchers found:

> At both the 10 and 20 percent levels of the proposed funding model, the analysis showed a marked increase in the equity over that found for actual expenditures between 1986 and 1991.... [Furthermore], current operating expenditures that would have occurred between 1986-87 and 1990-91 based on the proposed 10 and 20 percent allocation methodology (combined with full-state funding) were far more equitable than actual expenditures, primarily because of the full-state funding component of the proposed allocation formula. Equity at the 30 percent performance level was about the same as for actual expenditures. Clearly, the 10 percent allocation in the study resulted in the most equitable distribution of resources. Moving from the actual (foundation program) to the 10 percent allocation (full state funding) would, therefore, improve both equity and efficiency. (pp. 121, 1132-133)

To date, many states have funded incentive programs and provided rewards to schools, teachers, and principals who have attained prescribed standards. Table 3 shows six SREB states that gave awards to schools and teachers who helped improve student performance during the 2001-2002 school year. As depicted in the table, total expenditures for awards across these six states ranged from a low of $2.9 million in Delaware to a high of $76.4 million in Florida. The six states include examples of awards that went to schools, teachers, and, in one case, certified staff. The average award per school ranged from a low of $18,354 in Delaware to a high of $107,368 in Georgia. The last column in the table shows that in addition to test scores, the six states used several criteria for awards, including attendance, graduation, and dropout rates.

While full-state funding and incentive awards are viable approaches to financing reform efforts, there are other practical strategies districts and schools can employ. Among them are class size reduction (Grissmer, et al., 2000; Krueger, 1998; Krueger, 2000; Wainer, 1993; Wenglinsky, 1998), employing instructional facilitators and tutors (Shanahan, 1998), and using professional development programs that focus on student achievement as the primary outcome measure (Odden, 1999a; Odden, Archibald, & Tychsen, 1999). In addition, Table 4 depicts both costs of pay and sources of funds for seven school districts with functional knowledge- and skills-based programs. Note that to fund their performance pay program, two of the seven districts (Cincinnati and Limon) use a combination of reallocation and higher local taxes; two (Coventry and Vaughn) used a combination of reallocation and increases from state funding; one (Douglas County) relied on funds raised from local tax base; one (Manitowoc) relied on new money from a tax base; and one (Robbinsdale) simply reallocated existing funds to cover additional pay costs. What is evident then is that these districts relied on reallocation, higher local taxes, and an increase in state funding to finance performance pay programs.

It is evident from the literature that money from federal, state, and local sources should fund incentive programs. However, these programs should be funded over a long period and at a sustainable level. The results should be "a win-win" situation where students achieve, schools are rewarded for verifiable performance, districts and states can convincingly justify allocations, and the public is likely to understand how tax dollars make a difference in student learning. Importantly, evidence suggests that there is substantial financial benefit to linking pay to performance, which was demonstrated convincingly in one business demonstration project (Boudreau, Sturman, Trevor, & Gerhart, 1999). Whether this holds true across school districts is yet to be demonstrated.

Table 3: 2001-2002 Reward Programs in Selected SREB States

	Total of Awards (in millions)	Awards Go to	Average Award per School	Criteria for Awards In Addition to Tests
Delaware	$2.9	Schools ($10,000 to $30,000)	$18,354	
Florida	$76.4	Schools ($100 per student)	$90,736	Graduation/ dropout; postsecondary readiness
Georgia	$10.2	Schools ($2,000 per teacher)	$107,368	Individual school goals
Kentucky	$22.4	Schools ($959 per teacher)	$31,908	Graduation/ dropout; attendance
Maryland	$2.8	Schools (per school and per student)	$45,082	Graduation/ dropout; attendance
North Carolina	$75.5	Teacher/certified staff ($750-$1,500)	$58,618	Dropout rates; course taking

Adapted with permission from L. M. Cornett & G. F.Gaines, (2002). *Quality teachers: Can incentive policies make a difference?* Atlanta, GA: Southern Regional Education Board, p.16.

Table 4: Costs and Funding of Performance Pay Programs

Site	Cost of Pay and Administration	Source of Funds for Pay and Administration
Cincinnati, Ohio	Transition costs to new pay schedule estimated at 0.2-0.4% of payroll; ultimate extra costs of administration not estimated	Reallocation of some of the dollars spent on degrees and credits in the current pay schedule, reallocation of staff time and budget resources to administer the system. Some new money raised via higher local taxes.
Coventry, Rhode Island	Estimate not available because program had just began.	Most funding appeared to have come from increases in state funding. Reallocation of existing time and funds used to cover administration, most notably conversion of an administrator position to Dir. of Professional Development
Douglas County, Colorado	District estimate of cost of additional knowledge and skill pay elements was about 0.5% of payroll. No estimate of administrative costs is available.	Additional funds raised from local tax base.
Limon, Colorado	District has mot made an estimate, but if all teachers received the professional growth bonus, the cost would be about 1.4% of payroll.	Reallocation of existing funds and additional funds raised from local tax base.
Manitowoc, Wisconsin	No estimate of additional salary costs solely due to knowledge and skill elements was available. Total package increase estimated at 1.5% to 2% of operating budget, and 3.8% of payroll. No additional administrative costs expected by district.	Local Academy was expected to be self-financing. New money available from tax base within legal limits used to finance pay costs.

. . . *continued*

Table 4 continued

Robbinsdale, Minnesota	No estimate available from district. Since the program would be applied initially to new teachers, immediate additional costs would likely be quite low.	Plan was to reallocate existing funds to cover additional pay.
Vaughn, California	Total performance plan cost about 3.5% of payroll in 1999-2000, expected to rise to 6% in 2000-2001. No estimate of administrative costs available, but some of the three new administrative positions should be considered part of the administrative cost.	Reallocation of savings from efficiencies in management and in managing funds provided by formula from the state and district; also, new money provided in the state funding formula was allocated to pay.

Adapted with permission from Milanowski, T. (2001). *The Varieties of Knowledge and Skill-Bases Pay Designs: A Comparison of Seven New Pay Systems for K-12 Teachers*. Madison, WI: Consortium for Policy Research in Education.

Chapter Summary

It is a difficult task to implement an effective performance pay system without understanding the role played by the factors addressed in this chapter. First, a comprehensive approach to performance-based incentive systems provides the proper framework for understanding critical factors that contribute to effective instruction and increased student achievement. Second, understanding that teachers are motivated by both intrinsic, extrinsic, and ancillary motivators helps planners to distinguish between incentives that are likely to work versus those that are not. Even more useful is the idea that effectiveness and success in the classroom accounts for much of the satisfaction teachers derive from what they do. Third, comprehensive assessment that reflects knowledge of both quantitative and qualitative evaluation approaches helps provide data with which to make meaningful decisions. Such assessment should address both student and teacher performance. Fourth, teacher incentive programs that are developed and implemented with contribution from all interested parties, and which use both inside-out and outside-in collaboration, stand a better chance of being successful than programs that attach little or no importance to these factors. Lastly, funding schemes consistent with adequacy and accountability values rather than with equity values are preferable to traditional funding approaches such as those detailed by Wood and Thompson (1996). While these five factors are not exhaustive, they help provide a framework for understanding performance pay and may serve as guidelines for pursuing comprehensive school reform through well-planned incentive pay programs. However, they should be coupled with capacity building opportunities or effective professional development before they can realistically inform performance pay programs that are likely to influence teacher and student performance. This is the subject of Chapter 3.

3

PROFESSIONAL DEVELOPMENT AND PERFORMANCE PAY

Professional development is a critical component in effective teacher incentive programs. Analogous terms include in-service education, continuing education, recurrent education, on-the-job staff development and training, human resource development, staff improvement, and staff renewal (Sparks & Loucks-Horsley, 1990; Webb & Norton, 1999). These terms denote different things to different people. Nevertheless, professional development and its synonyms are used here to refer to a process of activities, strategies, and approaches that in one way or another help teachers (a) increase knowledge about themselves, their students, and their instructional practices; (b) improve skills and competencies; and (c) change behaviors and habits associated with professional practices. The anticipated results from professional development are improved instruction and higher student achievement.

The extent to which professional development programs in schools accomplish these tasks is debatable. Several observers (Elmore, 1997, 2002; Joyce & Belitzky, 1997; Lieberman & McLaughlin, 1999; Webb & Norton, 1999; UNICEF, 2000) regard them as simply ineffective. The major reasons for failure include (a) lack of coordination with other programs aimed at improving instruction, (b) absence of continuity in training, (c) focus on changing behavior with no provision for collaborative learning, (d) weakness in design, and (e) a lack of an overall strategy for school improvement (Elmore, 2002; Howey & Vaughn, 1983; Seyfarth, 1996). In a study of New Jersey teachers and principals, Monahan found contemporary systems of incentives and rewards "encourage teachers to engage in more traditional, and perhaps outdated forms of professional development" (1996, p. 46). Monahan concluded that if teachers were given incentives to engage in developmental activities such as peer collaboration and peer coaching, they would use them more frequently. In Florida, Joyce and Belitzky (1997) highlighted the status of staff development in a statewide evaluation study. After analyzing data from a series of in-depth interviews and a carefully designed survey, the researcher found:

1. The scale of staff development in Florida is enormous, but an effective, coordinated system of staff development does not exist.

2. Time for effective staff development is not built into school schedules.

3. Staff development efforts reflect state and federal initiatives but do not necessarily conform to student needs.

4. Despite its importance, staff development is not generally supported by funding at the local level. State and federal dollars are nearly exclusively utilized.

5. The current system of staff development is largely a product of state activity.

In a national study using "exploratory case studies" and "in-depth case studies," Birman, Desimone, Porter, and Garet (2000) examined effective staff development using 1000 teachers (mostly science and mathematics) in the Eisenhower Professional Development Program. While controlling a number of variables (subject area, school poverty level, school level, teacher gender, certification, and years of experience), the researchers identified three *structural* features (form, duration, and participation) and three *core* features (content focus, active learning, and coherence) that they claimed "set the context for professional development" (p. 29). Among other factors, they also found

The majority of teachers (79 percent) in [their] study participate in Eisenhower-supported staff development that is traditional in form; the median number of hours of an activity is 15; and most teachers (64 percent) participate in activities that last only a week or less. Further, few teachers (20 percent) participate in activities that include collective participation. Fifty-one percent of teachers participate in Eisenhower-supported activities that emphasize content, but relatively few (between 5 and 16 percent) report opportunities for specific active-learning activities, such as being observed teaching or leading a group discussion. (p. 32)

In another national study that examined recruitment, retention, and staff development in public and private school, researchers found that "less experienced teachers receive more help and on-the-job training in the private sector" (Ballou & Podursky, 1998, p. 413). Other researchers such as Guskey (1999) have regarded traditional staff development programs as insufficient but effective and others such as Mizell (1999) have found them to be sporadic and rudimentary.

The findings from Monahan's study in New Jersey; Joyce and Belitzky's study in Florida; Ballou and Podgursky's; and Birman et al.'s national studies approximate the condition of staff development programs in other states (Birman et al., 2000; Lieberman & McLaughlin, 1999; Little, 1993). Many programs lack alignment with the curriculum, teacher assessment, and student achievement, and some programs are ineffective because they were founded on the mistaken assumption that satisfying employees through extrinsic and ancillary rewards will motivate them to achieve excellence and become more productive.

The literature, however, suggests otherwise. Employees who achieve excellence and are highly productive become, overall, satisfied employees (Swanson & Holton, 1997). They can achieve and maintain high levels of productivity and excellence, but only for so long. Eventually they too reduce their level of productivity or may experience burnout and switch jobs or retire. However, this group of workers can be motivated to continue high levels of productivity through a mix of caring leadership and a work culture that encourages, nurtures, and rewards self-development and continuous learning (Anderson, 2000; London & Smither, 1999).

On both state and district levels, professional development should be a coordinated system, built into teachers' schedules, tied to student needs, funded proportionately with federal, state, and local revenues, and linked to or integrated with a comprehensive performance pay system. Before developing such programs, however, policymakers should attend to four critical factors underlying quality professional development efforts. They recur throughout the literature and collectively form a framework for understanding the intricacies of effective professional development and the role motivation plays in performance pay systems. These factors include (a) theories of adult development and learning, (b) adequate time for professional development, (c) close alignment with student performance, and (d) adequate funding.

Theories/Models of Adult Development and Learning

Designers of teacher incentive programs must consider adult *development* and *learning* theories because they explain growth paths adults follow as they progress through the life cycle. Many developmental models are explained using *stages* and *phases* adults experience as they grow older. A *phase* is a particular time in a process of change or development, "a transitory state between changes in appearance, structure, and character, such as the phases of a man's career" (Webster's Collegiate Dictionary, 1947, p. 744). Conversely, a *stage* is a portion or period of a course of action, "a degree of progression in any pursuit, process, such as the stage of a man's life" (p. 968). Phase theories address a shorter span of time than do stage theories. Examples of adult development phase theories include those described by Levinson (1986) and Sheehy (1977; 1999). Stage theories on the other hand include works by Erikson (1982), Loevinger (1976), and Kohlberg (1969). Mixed models reflect both "transitory states" and "degree of progression" found in phase and stage theories, but importantly, address both developmental and learning principles. Examples of mixed models are described by Chickering and Havighurst (1981), Gould (1978), Lehaman and Lester (1978), and Weathersby (1978).

While phase, stage, and mixed models focus primarily on adult psychosocial and biological development, theories and models of adult learning present concepts and principles that define how adults acquire and process information and the conditions under which they learn. These are usually classified into four groups: behaviorist, cognitive, humanist, and social learning (Diessner & Tiegs, 2001; Merriam & Cafferalla, 1991, 1997). For the most part, these theories are hierarchical or time-based

(Boyatzis, 1993; Boyatzis & Kolb,1993) and provide useful information and guidelines for designing the professional development dimension of a comprehensive teacher incentive program.

While adult development theories provide guidance for effective staff development programs, adult learning theories can do likewise. *Adults as Learners* by Cross (1981), *Learning in Adulthood* by Merriam and Caffarella (1991), and *The Profession and Practice of Adult Learning* by Merriam and Brockett (1997), provide a comprehensive and clear overview of several theories and models alluded to earlier. Likewise, *The Adult Learner* by Knowles et al. (1998) provides one of the most useful models of adult learning with clear implications and practical advice for improving professional development. The Knowles model has practical relevance for designers of professional development programs in schools because it is based on the logical and convincing principles of "andragogy" rather than "pedagogy." Andragogy is the science of teaching adults while pedagogy is the science of teaching children. A key idea reflected in Knowles' model is that because adults develop and learn differently than children, instruction and professional development activities focusing on adult learners should be more learner-centered than teacher-centered. Six principles underpin andragogy:

- *Learner's need to know*. Adults need to know why they need to learn something before undertaking it.

- *Concept of learning*. As the individual grows and matures, his/her self-concept moves from one of dependency to one of increasing self-directedness.

- *Role of the learner's experience*. As the adult engages in an ever-expanding variety of experiences, he/she is more able to relate to new learning experiences.

- *Readiness to learn*. As the individual matures, readiness to learn becomes more dependent on the tasks required for the performance of his/her evolving social role.

- *Orientation to learning*. Adults do not learn for the sake of learning. They learn in order to perform tasks, solve a problem, or live in a more satisfying way.

- *Motivation to learn.* The more potent motivators are internal—self-esteem, recognition, better quality of life, greater self-confidence, self-actualization, and the like. (1998)

Adult learning principles can help designers of professional development activities address the following six questions before implementing a professional development program or inservice activities:

1. To what extent is the staff development program relevant to learner needs?

2. To what extent has the program been personalized as well as individualized; is there an opportunity for self-direction based on personal needs, problems, and interests?

3. To what extent does the program relate to the background of experience possessed by the learner?

4. To what extent does the program provide for active learning on the part of the learners?

5. To what extent does the program provide for assessment and feedback relative to learning and behavioral change? (Webb & Norton, 1999, p. 370)

Additionally, designers of professional development programs would be acting consistently with the "consensus view" of professional development if, according to Elmore (2002), they are "willing to say explicitly what new knowledge and skill educators will learn as a consequence of their participation, how this new knowledge and skill will be manifested in their professional practice, and what specific activities will lead to this learning" (p. 8). These questions and focus points could help structure the design and implementation of professional development activities. Developers may want to regard them as guiding principles on which to build a comprehensive professional development program.

A model by Boyatzis and Kolb (1993) presents a different perspective on adult development and learning. While not as comprehensive as Knowles', it provides a practical framework for aligning professional development activities with student performance. The authors contended that in order "to understand the dynamics of lifelong career development in today's world, we must entertain a non-hierarchical theory in which a specific stage or set of value-based conditions do not dictate the 'best' or most rational place to be" (p. 8). Instead, Boyatzis and Kolb advocated a "recursive" and "non-linear" theory that accommodates the pace and time differences of adults who make changes in jobs and career choices at different ages. They summarized and explained their theory with two postulates and three experiential components. The first postulate states that there are three modes of describing a person's growth and adaptation, while the second postulate states that theory is recursive or becomes clearer and yields more useful information through repeated application. The three modes of growth and adaptation (postulate one) are summarized this way:

Performance—The performance in this mode is preoccupied with successes and the intent is job mastery. Individuals are concerned with job mastery of specific behavioral skills and success in the job. Activities that assist in this mode are behavioral observations such as simulations and critical incidence interviews.

Learning—Growth and adaptation in the learning mode is understood through a focus on learning. Persons in this mode are intent on developing and expanding their capabilities. They have mastered the basics and are looking for novelty, variety or a way to learn and/or generalize their experience. In this mode, methods to appraise should include self-reports and feedback from peers.

Development—Growth and adaptation in the development mode is understood through focus on adult development. A person in this mode is seeking fulfillment of one's purpose in life. The key abilities to focus on are traits and core values that give one purpose, meaning or connectedness in life. Interactive and interpretive methods to involve the respondent in assessing and interpreting the meaning are most helpful in this stage (cited in Boyatzis & Kolb, 1993, pp. 3-5).

The authors have linked these modes to practical dimensions of adult development and learning. The relation to staff development seems clear. The model suggests the importance of ascertaining what mode teachers are in and identifying matching professional development activities.

While there may be other theories and models of adult development and learning, the models presented by Knowles and by Boyatzis and Kolb provide logical and practical frameworks for designing staff development programs for professional educators. Both models offer developers of incentive pay programs both theoretical and practical rational for identifying activities that foster and facilitate professional growth and learning, and opportunities to align salient principles of motivation with teacher pay structures.

Time

Most professional development programs are plagued by a common problem: inadequate time for teachers to meet regularly and acquire necessary knowledge and skills. Most staff development sessions occur during the end of the school day or during planning periods. Joyce and Belitzky (1997) captured the problem:

> Teacher time is at a premium. The designated number of work days is 196, of which 180 are committed to student instruction. Six are usually paid holidays. This leaves 10 days for all activities related to the opening and closing of school, parent conferences, planning school organization, and professional development. Much could be accomplished if there were more time available to teachers for inservice staff development activities. (p. 4)

What staff development experts recommend is a block of time that is regularly scheduled solely for staff development (Joyce & Belitzky, 1997; Lieberman, 1995). This suggestion seems reasonable in light of current practices where adequate time is not allotted for teachers to learn, grow, and change. The National Staff Development Council (NSDC) recommends that "states and districts increase to 25% the time available during the school day for teachers to work together and collaboratively plan lessons and share information" (Sparks & Hirsh, 1999, p. 11). Joyce suggested that about two hours a week of regular staff development activities should be considered (1995, 1997). He further suggested that "a day a month adds up to the same amount of time, but it does not have the same effect as does weekly or bi-weekly embedded time" (p. 4). Odden, on the other hand, noted that funding should be adequate enough to provide teachers with 20 days of professional development and assistance during the school year and "a two- to three-week summer institute (including some pay for all teachers who attend)" (2000b, p. 436). It is imperative that school officials provide sufficient time for teacher development. Researchers are addressing the problem extensively because it has become chronic and must be solved before professional development can be truly effective.[17]

Linkage with Student Achievement

An effective performance pay plan should reflect alignment of professional development with student achievement. This idea reflects the necessity of student outcomes as the measure of successful or unsuccessful staff development activities. This is also the path professional development has taken in most states. In Florida, for example, a new law stipulates that teacher training be designed and conducted on the basis of indicated student needs as measured by the FCAT and Florida Writes!, a test that measures writing proficiency. The statute provides that

> each school district shall design a system, approved by the Department of Education, for the professional growth of instructional personnel that links and aligns inservice activities with student and instructional personnel needs as determined by the school improvement plans, annual school reports, student achievement data, and performance appraisal data of teachers and administrators.... The need for any training activity defined in a teacher's professional development plan must clearly be related to specific performance data for the students to whom the teacher is assigned. (SB 2500)

The Florida School Community Professional Development Act (F.S. 231.600) places the same emphasis on student achievement, stipulating that the school community—including educators, parents, business partners, school advisory councils—should form collaborative relationships to establish coordinated systems of professional development with a principal aim of improving student performance.

Other states have adopted the NSDC's standards and guidelines for staff development (NSDC, 1994). The importance the Council attaches to student achievement is reflected in these standards:

- Set clear and high standards for the learning of all students and then focus on the changes in practice required to achieve student-learning goals.

- Hold superintendents and principals, as well as teachers, accountable for student achievement and the provision of high-quality staff development in their annual performance reviews.

- Invest in teacher learning, ideally allocating at least 10% of their budgets to staff development.

- Review school improvement plans to ascertain that they focus on student learning and specify effective methods for reaching these goals.

- Involve all teachers in the continuous, intellectually rigorous study of the content they teach and the ways they teach it.

- Embed opportunities for professional learning and collaborating with colleagues in the daily schedule of teachers. NSDC advocates that at least 25% of teachers' time be devoted to their own learning. Schools should schedule more time for collaborating with colleagues.

- Provide teachers with classroom assessment and other action research skills that allow them to determine on a regular basis if student learning has been improved because of their new knowledge and skills.

- Recognize the importance of skillful leaders in schools and at the district level who have a deep understanding of instruction, curriculum, assessment, and the organizational factors that affect student learning. (NSDC, 1994, p.6)

The NSDC also advocates that planning and implementing of staff development programs and activities take place within an organizing framework consisting of *content* (researched-based practice), *process* (follow-up), and *context* (leadership support). Collectively, these three components provide a framework for conceptualizing, organizing, and implementing what the NSDC calls "result-oriented staff development."[18] According to Lewis (2002), the American Institute for Research confirmed the NSDC's standards in a recent evaluation study of the federal Eisenhower Professional Development Program.

Funding

States and districts have a history of inadequately funding professional development, and superintendents and school boards have traditionally regarded professional development as a "low budget" item. As Joyce and Belitzky (1997) found, professional development dollars come almost exclusively from state and federal sources. Relegating professional development to the low rungs of the revenue ladder is, however, slowly changing as school officials understand that professional development is a *sine qua non* in any pay plan that focuses on student performance and school-wide reform. Professional development consists of treating teachers as human resources to be developed and professionals who are worthy of financial resources to be invested in their continual growth and development. This is the mantra being espoused by whole-school reformers.

School board and district officials must recognize the importance of regarding and treating teachers as professionals. These officials need to "reconceptualize the role of the teacher as professional," teachers in turn "need to internalize what it means to be truly professional, and school districts and educational leaders should provide the necessary support to help teachers achieve that goal" (Monahan, 1996, p. 47). At this stage of education reform, prudence and visionary leadership demand nothing less.

Odden (2000b) addressed cost estimates for professional development in a *Phi Delta Kappan* article. Focusing on only elementary schools and addressing an ideal as opposed to a real situation, he explained that $60,000 is a "high-end" figure for professional development in a school with 500 students, one principal, 20 teachers, and an assortment of other support personnel. Furthermore, Odden observed, "such a funding level would allow schools to provide their faculties with a two- to three-week summer institute (including some pay for all teachers who attend) and at least 20 days of professional development and assistance during the year" (p. 436). If this sum was used exclusively to provide 20 teachers with professional training and development activities, it would mean an expenditure of only $3000 per teacher, a paltry sum when one considers teachers' needs. Nevertheless, whatever the sum and however funded, performance pay plans should reflect a commitment to sustained professional development support through adequate funding.

Professional Development Models and Approaches

It is important for designers of teacher incentive programs to recognize the linkage between theories and models of adult motivation, learning, and professional development. It is likewise important for them to recognize the necessity of designing and aligning staff development programs with student learning. This idea carries with it a concern for *transfer* of learning, a critical variable in designing professional development activities for performance pay. How can district officials and principals get teachers to apply what they learn in such a way that students achieve at higher levels? When is transfer of learning greatest? These questions are difficult to address. Nevertheless, the literature provides some guidance. Several observers (Cascio, 1998; Ebmeier & Good, 1979; Gage & Berliner, 1998; and Joyce & Showers, 1995; Rouiller & Goldstein, 1993), have suggested that transfer is greatest when teachers or other trainees

- are provided with information about the theoretical base on which new practices are found;
- know that what they are learning is related to what they do on the job;
- are taught principles as opposed to mere content and facts;
- are confident in using their newly learned skills;
- are given opportunity to practice what they have been taught as good teaching behavior;
- implement high quality content that deals with the curriculum, instruction, technology or overall school climate;
- are aware of work situation where demonstration of the new skills is appropriate;
- perceive that their job performance will improve if they use the new skills;
- believe that the knowledge and skills emphasized in the training program are helpful in solving work-related problems.

While there are several professional development models, not all are designed to address principles of transfer. In truth, not all staff development models are comprehensive and stress alignment between teacher performance and student achievement. Some focus only on the process of staff development (Castetter & Young, 2000; Smith, 1998).[19] Others are "one-time in-service training" and "short-term professional development events" and strategies that use a specific procedure to enhance teacher knowledge or develop teaching skills. In each case the focus is on the individual teacher, not the entire school or district. Examples of short-term professional development strategies include mentoring, quality circles, teacher centers, assessment centers, peer-assistant leadership, peer coaching, collaborative curriculum development, portfolio learning, personnel appraisal methods, self-directed learning, and action research.[20] Still others are based on states' support of "infrastructures for technical assistance and professional development, such as Maryland's Regional Staff Development Centers or California's Subject Matter Networks" (Elmore & Furhman, 2001, p. 70). Policymakers should focus on professional development approaches that do not rely solely on traditional practices such as taking additional courses, obtaining certification, or attending inservice conferences and workshops, but which instead focus on reform approaches such as in-class observation, modeling, and active learning, which

> includes opportunities to observe and be observed teaching; to plan classroom implementation, such as practicing simulated conditions and developing lesson plans; to review student work; and to present, lead, and write—for example, present a demonstration, lead a discussion, or write a report. (Birman, et al., 2000, p. 31)

Further, reform approaches should include "strategies that facilitate teacher growth through professional dialogue with colleagues, collaborative curriculum development, peer supervision, peer coaching, and action research" (Monahan, 1996, p. 44).

Professional development techniques, strategies, and approaches that reflect principles of adult development and learning, should also be integral parts of a systemwide professional development program. They do not, however, necessarily constitute comprehensive, systemic professional development (Elmore, 1997; Lewis, 2002; Lieberman & McLaughlin, 1999). Some programs may address process components such as planning, data collection, implementing, and evaluation. Programs may also be the result of a planning process defined with Webb and Norton's five steps:

1. Develop a guiding philosophy.
2. Develop goals and objectives.

3. Plan programs, activities and delivery systems and determine responsibilities.
4. Schedule and deliver plans and programs.
5. Evaluate the process. (1999, p. 361)

Nevertheless, planning processes do not necessarily ensure comprehensive professional development with transfer and student learning as their principal foci. The reality is that many programs neither embrace the philosophy nor do they reflect the standards-driven position taken by the National Staff Development Council (NSDC, 2001) and other professional organizations. Many programs do not have as an ultimate goal the improvement of student learning. NSDC has taken the position that "staff development must shift from counting how many staff participate and whether they enjoyed the session, to determining whether the system is improving student achievement" (2001, p. 2). This is the view being emphasized by researchers and policymakers as they develop or adopt new models of professional development. However, the task of linking professional development with student achievement, especially empirically, is extremely difficult and complex because of the "multivariable syndrome." I am not aware of studies that convincingly demonstrate cause and effect relationships between improved teacher performance resulting from professional development activities and student performance. There are though, professional development models that could serve as examples and seem likely to produce the kind of student achievement results education reformers crave from accountability initiatives.

Exemplars of Comprehensive Professional Development

Three models could serve as exemplars for comprehensive, system-wide professional development approaches that target student achievement as the measure of effectiveness while at the same time addressing the principle of transfer. These models include (a) Joyce and Showers' Student Achievement Through Staff Development Model (1995), (b) Knowles' Human Resources Development Performance and Improvement Model (1998), and (c) the New York City Community School District 2 Model described by Elmore (1997). The following discussion provides an overview of each model or approach to comprehensive professional development.

Model One:
Student Achievement through Staff Development

Joyce and Showers (1995) addressed student achievement relative to comprehensive professional development. Their work was based on extensive research of professional development programs across the country and stressed the wisdom of providing professional growth and learning opportunities to teachers and administrators at the individual level, to faculty at the school level, and to those entrusted with school improvement at the district level. The model offers reasonable hope for improving schools because it focuses on helping professionals use newly learned skills and competencies to influence student performance. Successful programs such as The Schenley Project in Pittsburgh; The Augusta Project in Richmond County, Georgia; and the Ames, Iowa Program, provide opportunities for planning and executing effective professional development programs that result in verifiable student achievement. Conclusions regarding successes of these programs suggest that effective professional development programs that positively affect student achievement have four common characteristics:

- *Content.* First, these programs all focus on content in curriculum, instruction, and technology. As near as we can tell, only content dealing with curriculum, instruction, technology, or the overall social climate of the schools is likely to improve student learning.

- *Implementation.* Content of the highest quality will not change student learning unless it is implemented.

- *Inclusion.* The programs described here involved all the teachers and administrators in particular schools, or in some cases, all the personnel in the school districts where they took place.

- *Goal and Inquiry.* Finally, goals and the understanding about how to achieve them were kept central. (Joyce & Showers, 1995, pp. 55-56)

Hence, successful professional development programs share certain qualities: (a) they emphasize valid curriculum content, quality instruction, and the use of technology, (b) they include implementation of these factors, (c) they require involvement of all personnel at both school and district levels, and (d) they focus on program goals and building an understanding of these goals. While all four of Joyce and Showers' program components seem important, the content and inclusion components add a dimension to professional development lacking in earlier programs, namely the dimension of education reform. A glaring weakness of the model, however, is the absence of pay structures that are aligned with student performance and with the four components. This is a weakness shared by many other programs.

Model Two:
Human Resources Development and Performance Improvement

This model is advocated by Knowles, Holton, and Swanson (1998) and is based on principles of andragogy as well as on the notion that domains of performance should be identified so that performance drivers (e.g., teaching methods) positively influence performance outcomes (e.g., student achievement). The mission of the organization (e.g., helping students learn), the process (e.g., instruction), critical performance subsystems (e.g., teacher teams, work groups, committees), and individuals (e.g., principal, teachers, students, support staff), should all be aligned and working harmoniously. Supporting this framework are the six principles of adult learning mentioned earlier—learners need to know why they need to learn something before undertaking it, self-directedness, role of the learner's experience, readiness to learn, orientation to learning, and motivation to learn.

While the model does not address teacher and student performance specifically, it nevertheless links the key components of motivation, performance, and learning with organizational variables such as mission, process, and outcome. Its biggest advantage seems to be its inclusive focus on the entire organization, or, when applied to education, the entire district. This focus reflects the authors' view that "intervening in only one element of the system without creating congruence in other parts of the system will not lead to systemic change" (Knowles, Holton, & Swanson, 1998, p. 262).

Model Three:
New York Community School District #2

A performance pay system offers the opportunity for comprehensive, systemic professional development to work because it considers the entire school system—from policymakers (school board); superintendent and district staff (those who implement policy at the district level); and principals, teachers, and school staff (those who implement policy at the building level). In short, organizational context, processes, and products are all reflected in a well-designed professional development program such as Community School District #2, New York City Staff Development and Instructional Improvement Model.

Elmore (1997) documented the particulars of professional development in this district with 48 elementary and junior high schools serving a diverse student population of 22,000 (29 % white, 14 % black, 22 % Hispanic, 34% Asian, and less than one percent Native American). The district, led by former Superintendent Anthony Alvarado, "is an exemplar, not so much because it engages in specific professional development activities that other districts do not, but because it does a variety of things in a uniquely systematic way" (p. 3). And just what does District #2 do? It structures professional development around seven principles about the role of comprehensive change:

- Make the highest priority providing high-quality instruction of children.
- Instructional change is a long, multi-state process.
- Shared expertise is the driver of instructional change.
- Focus on system-wide improvement.
- Good ideas come from talented people working together.
- Set clear expectations, and then decentralize.
- Encourage collegiality, caring, and respect.

These principles contribute to system-wide improvement of instruction. They provide the framework within which professional professional development activities are implemented (Elmore, 1997):

- Experienced or "resident teachers" mentor and model effective teaching for a group of "visiting teachers" for three weeks at a time in a professional development laboratory.

- "Adjunct teachers" who substitute for visiting teachers must spend a week or more observing the visiting teacher before taking over the class and a week or more observing the visiting teacher when she returns from a three-week rotation with the resident teacher.

- Instructional Consulting Services uses both outside and district consultants to offer a rich variety of professional development opportunities to teachers in critical areas such as reading and mathematics.

- The superintendent and members of his staff make routine oversight visits to schools. According to Elmore, "the centerpiece of oversight and performance review is the Supervisory Goals and Objectives Process ... which serves as the basis for performance reviews and site visits" (p. 23).

- Teachers, principals, and district staff make myriad visitations to schools and classrooms inside and outside the district.

- Off-site training includes a combination of seminars, summer institutes, and workshops conducted inside or outside the district. These training opportunities focus specifically on subjects germane to instructional improvement.

This district-wide approach to professional development has proven to be effective because of (a) the superintendent's visionary leadership; (b) his ability to hire people who believe in and embody the tenets of leadership and instruction that result in meaningful and measurable learning experiences for children; (c) a commitment to decentralization; (d) the creativity and willingness on the part of teachers and principals to take risks; (e) a resolve to ensure oversight and constant monitoring; (f) the environment or context within which the district is located; and (g) the willingness and foresight of the superintendent to "make professional development visible in the district and to commit the district to spending a specific proportion of the budget (around 3%) as an expression of the priority the district attaches to professional development" (Elmore, 1997, p. 29). While other districts operate under different circumstances and within different contexts, this approach to professional development offers many ideas and opportunities that are worth considering. Granted, obvious differences exist between districts, but some principles and practices may be universal enough to transcend district boundaries.[21] Examples from international settings where professional development programs reflect many of these principles include the Mombassa School Improvement Project in Kenya and (Anderson, 2000) and those programs highlighted by UNICEF (2000).

Those who plan and implement professional development programs may want to remember that professional development programs will not achieve the same level of success with all participants. As Lawler (1998) observed, "In a complex organization, developing organizational competencies is usually a matter of developing the right pattern of competencies and capabilities among different individuals; it is unrealistic to expect every individual to have all the competencies and capabilities that organizations needs" (p. 298). A district professional development program that develops the knowledge and competencies of teachers and principals, who in turn influence student achievement, could be regarded as a success. Such a program recognizes and values teachers' uniqueness and diversity while at the same time contributing to the growth and development of schools as professional communities (Boyatzis, 1993; Lieberman & McLaughlin, 1999). In the final analysis, effective professional development programs are research-driven or consistent with research findings, and reflect those identified by the National Council on Staff Development:

- Results-driven and job-embedded,
- Focused on helping teachers become deeply immersed in subject matter and teaching methods,
- Curriculum-centered and standards-based,
- Sustained, rigorous, and cumulative, and
- Directly linked to what teachers do in their classrooms. (Sparks & Hirsh, 1999, p. 5)

Further, school districts are more likely to develop and implement effective professional development programs if they consider several instructive findings from an evaluation of the large-scale federally funded Eisenhower Professional Development Program:

- Districts that engage in more co-funding of Eisenhower activities with other programs tend to support a greater proportion of reform types of activities than districts that engage in less co-funding, and they tend to provide more opportunities for collective participation.

- In addition, districts that engage in more co-funding tend to engage more extensive continuous improvement efforts and they tend to involve teachers more widely in planning, both of which are related to increased opportunities for active planning.

- Districts that align professional development with standards and assessments are more likely to offer reform types of activities.

- In addition, the districts that align professional development and standards with assessments are more likely than others to engage in continuous improvement, which is related to increased opportunities for active learning. (U.S. Department of Education, 1999, p. ES-13)

The sooner reformers move to design and develop professional development programs that reflect these findings and others mentioned throughout this chapter, the sooner professional development may have the impact envisioned by proponents and supporters of education accountability.

Chapter Summary

Research studies have revealed the inadequacy and ineffectiveness of traditional professional development approaches. Findings from these studies have pointed to reform approaches that appear to be more effective in helping teachers master their craft and become effective change agents in students' lives. What seems desirable is for effective professional development program to be grounded in adult development and learning theories; for them to focus on principles of andragogy as opposed to pedagogy; and be flexible with respect to performance, learning, and development needs of teachers. Further, in order to be truly effective, professional develeopment activities must allow teacher adequate time to learn and apply new knowledge and skills; emphasize transfer of knowledge and skills learned in professional development settings to classroom settings; ultimately influence or affect student achievement; be supported by adequate and sustained funding of all operational costs (including rewards and bonuses); and designed in such a manner that all these critical factors are systemically and holistically aligned. While the literature does not reveal the existence of programs that address all these factors, a few programs such as Community School District #2, New York City Staff Development and Instructional Improvement Model and the Eisenhower

Professional Development Program seem close. In sum, professional development and the five factors addressed in Chapter 2—a systemic, comprehensive approach, teacher motivation, comprehensive assessment, collaboration and collective participation, and adequate funding—provide a foundation and framework for thinking about and implementing performance pay systems that are likely to yield the kind of results in teacher and student performance anticipated by the education and business communities. Examples of these pay systems are addressed in the next chapter.

4

PREVALENT PERFORMANCE PAY PROGRAMS

It is a truism that the private sector dictates changes in education. Indeed, most restructuring efforts and reforms in education occur within a context of change and "radical redesign" created first by business organizations (Fullan, 1993, 1999). Authors such as Hammer and Champy (1993), Carr (1995), Marshall and Tucker (1992), Drucker (1998), Senge (1994), Senge et al. (1999), Bennis (1997), and Covey (1990) have contributed to major reforms in business and industrial organizations, and, indirectly, to a shift from "business as usual" in education to a "fundamental rethinking and radical redesign of ... processes to achieve dramatic improvements in critical, contemporary measures of performance...." (Hammer & Champy, 1993, p. 32). This shift markedly influenced the call to improve schools and student achievement through comprehensive reform that now includes performance pay for teachers. Today more and more states and districts are exploring and "reengineering" their systems along the lines suggested by Drucker (1980, 1998), Lawler (1971, 1998), Hammer and Champy (1993), and other business mavens. Performance pay systems that are linked to standards, teacher performance, and student achievement are among the major new reform initiatives in education. Indeed, the number of districts with pay schemes radically different from the single salary schedule is growing.[22] Evidence from two studies—one by the SREB and the other by the National Center for Education Statistics (NCEE)—support this observation and provide some perspectives.

In 1990, the SREB (1991) surveyed all 50 states to determine what they were doing to link teacher performance to student achievement. The researchers addressed five key questions:

1. Are states linking rewards to performance of teachers and students?
2. Are incentive programs creating new roles for teachers and principals?
3. Are states continuing to fund incentive programs?
4. What has changed in schools because of incentive programs?
5. What is the outlook? (pp. 2)

Results from the study indicated that

- 25 states across the nation were funding teacher incentive programs that include career ladder or mentor programs.

- 10 states had schools incentive programs, including Kentucky, which established a plan in its 1990 legislation.

- States rewarded schools or individual teachers and principals for improvement such as increased student achievement or reduction of dropouts.

- While career ladder programs increased compensation and decreased classroom isolation, differentiated roles were threatening to teachers.

- With the exception of a few states, the proportion of state funding for teacher salaries that was paid through incentive programs was relatively small.

- Few comprehensive evaluations of these incentive programs were conducted. Fewer comprehensive short- and long-term evaluations of incentive programs continue to point to the complexity and difficulty in changing schools (pp. 1-9).

In another national study, the National Center for Education Statistics (1996) surveyed 9,956 public schools and 3,315 private schools and found that

- Thirty-one percent of public schools districts provided step increases on their salary schedules for completing inservice training or college credits.

- One-third of all full-time teachers received additional compensation from their schools or districts during the school year.

- Almost all public school districts (94%) and the majority of private schools (63 %) used schedules to determine teacher salaries in 1993-1994.

- Common types of incentives were cash bonuses (a supplement to the teacher's regular compensation, but no permanent increase in salary), placement on higher steps of the salary schedule, and salary increases that involve some type of reclassification other than a step increase on the salary schedule.

- Relative few public school districts used cash bonuses in 1993-94. Only 7 % offered them for completing additional training, 2% for teaching in fields of shortage, and 2% for teaching in less desirable locations.

- Overall, 31% of public school districts provided step increases on their salary schedules for additional training. The regional differences were striking, with more than 40% of districts in the Northeast and West offering this type of incentive, but only 10 percent in the South.

- Salary increases for additional training were used by 21 percent of public school districts in the Northeast, but by no more than 10 percent of districts in other parts of the country. (pp. 81-86)

These two studies show, among other things, that (a) earlier performance pay efforts were largely restricted to career ladder pay schemes, (b) educators attempted to link teacher performance to student performance, (c) teachers received a relatively small amounts of reward money, (d) cash bonuses, placement on higher steps of the salary schedule, and salary increases without a step increase on the salary schedule constituted the major types of incentives given to teachers, and (e) states and districts failed to use a comprehensive approach to evaluating the effectiveness of incentive programs. These were the salient features of incentive programs during the 1980s and early 1990s. This section of the book, however, addresses the approaches and programs in use today and the features by which they are defined.[23]

Major Compensation and Incentive Approaches

What are the major incentive programs being implemented by districts? What are their advantages and disadvantages? What contribution are they making to the improvement of instruction? How are they contributing to student learning? These questions are addressed in this chapter. The intent is to provide a broad understanding of existing incentive programs and the progress states and districts have made during the past 10 years to document what districts are doing to keep up with demands that schools be held more accountable for student achievement.

Compensation programs can be classified as either *direct* or *indirect*. Direct compensation programs include wages and salaries while indirect compensation addresses employee benefits and services. Education reformers advocate shifting from traditional direct pay structures such as longevity pay and the single salary schedule to alternative ways of rewarding teaching. Odden and Kelley (1997) identified the new compensation approaches as:

- *Skill or competency pay*—for the development of more abstract knowledge or behaviors that are less easily observable than most skills in skill pay.

- *Performance pay*—rewards specific behaviors or outcomes at the individual, team, or organizational level.

- *Gainsharing*—individual, team and/or organizational bonuses are paid as a reward for identification of improvement in organizational processes that lead to increased efficiency.

- *Contingency pay*—makes a portion of pay contingent on the undertaking of specific activities. (p. 54)

Competency pay is similar to Lawler's (1998) skills-based pay where "people are rewarded for increasing their skills and developing themselves." Performance pay corresponds to his notion that rewards should be "based on the performance of the groups and on the performance of the whole organization" (p. 290). Other terms used to classify pay configurations include competency-based pay, contingency-based pay, group-based pay, and school-based pay.

The shift from traditional pay structures such as longevity pay and the single salary schedule to new approaches represents acknowledgement among educators that compensating educators is "viewed as an integral component of efforts to reform and redesign education" (Webb, Norton, & Scott, 1999, p. 419). On the whole, teacher incentive programs proving to be the most acceptable to education officials and teachers can be classified as: (a) programs that provide extra pay and extra responsibility for extra work (*skill/competency-based pay*); (b) programs with monetary incentives for improved performance (*group-based pay*), and (c) programs that offer only *nonmonetary or recognition incentives* such as praise and recognition (Smith, 1998). States that have adopted one or more of these programs are depicted in Table 5. A discussion of the nature and structure of these reward systems as well as their advantages and disadvantages follows.

Knowledge-, Skills-based, and Career Award Programs

Incentive programs that focus on building teacher skills and competencies are called skills-, knowledge-, or competency-based pay programs. In these programs, rewards are given to teachers not because of education and experience, but rather because of knowledge, skills, and competencies they acquire and use in the classroom. According to Odden and Kelley (2002), skills-based program reward four types of skills:

> The first and most critical reward would be depth of expertise in the areas of content, curriculum, and instruction. This would represent the instructional skills needed to be successful in teaching a wide variety of students to high-performance standards. A second set could be those important to nondirect instructional functions, such as curriculum development, professional development, guidance counseling, student advising, and parent outreach. A third set could be management expertise required of teachers in school engaged in site-based management—for example, running meetings, gaining consensus, developing and monitoring budgets, strategic planning, and program evaluation. A fourth would be involvement in professional communities and activities, such as local or regional professional network engaged in curriculum development or instructional

improvement, state and national professional associations—for example, Association for Supervision and Curriculum Development (ASCD) and its affiliates, and content associations such as the National Council of Teachers of Mathematics and its state affiliates—and advocating for students who need social services....(pp. 95-96)

Knowledge- and skills-based pay programs could supplement single salary schedules, "replace either the education or experience component of the current salary schedule, or replace both components" (CPRE, 1995, p. 1). Table 6 shows a district model of a knowledge- and skills-based pay programs. It shows that five career levels (from apprentice to master teacher) can be used to develop a comprehensive knowledge-based program. The focus of the model is on established standards, and based on those standards, moving teachers from lower to higher levels of performance. Compensation and awards, such as Cincinnati's base range of $30,000 to $62,500 (Lewis, 2000), are not linked to earned degrees or longevity on job, but rather to knowledge acquisition and professional expertise.

In their book *Paying Teachers for What they Know and Do*, Odden and Kelley (1997, 2002) discussed four knowledge- and skills-based models. Districts where these models have been adopted in one form or another include the Douglas County, Colorado; Rochester, New York; Manitowoc, Wisconsin; and Cincinnati, Ohio. Each district incorporated skills and competency requirements into the pay structure. They linked pay increases to standards such as professional licensure and certification through the NBPTS and the Interstate New Teacher Assessment Support Consortium.

One of the districts placing emphasis on linking performance pay to National Board certification is Robbinsdale Area Schools in Minneapolis. Robbinsdale gives teachers the opportunity to earn up to $15,000 additional income by submitting "performance portfolios." To receive the award, teachers have to score 100 points by selecting from among the following categories:

Table 5: Districts with Knowledge- and Skills-Based Pay, Group- and School-Based Performance pay Systems

Group/School		Knowledge/Skill	National Board for Professional Standards
Bonus to Staff with No Restrictions	**Funds Granted at School Level with Restrictions**	**Provide Compensation for Knowledge or Credentials**	**Provide Compensation, Fee Support, or Granted Special Standing, e.g. Lead Teacher**
Cincinnati[b]	Boston	Bellevue	Bellevue
Columbus	Minneapolis	Boston	Boston
Denver	Montgomery County	Cincinnati	Cincinnati[a]
Memphis	RochesterDenver		Columbus
Miami/Dade		Miami/Dade	Hammond[a]
New York City		Minneapolis	Los Angeles[a]
Iowa		Rochester	Miami/Dade[a]
		Toledo	Minneapolis[a]
		Westerly	Montgomery County[a]
			New York City[a]
			Pinellas County
			Rochester
			San Diego
			San Francisco
			Toledo[a]
			California, Florida, Maryland and Ohio[c]

a   Provide district-level supplement or cash bonus in addition to that provided by the state.
b   Has moved completely off the traditional salary schedule.
c   States that provide state-funded bonuses or salary supplements.

Adapted with permission from Urbanski and Erskine, *School Reform, TURN, and Teacher Compensation*, in *Phi Delta Kappan,* 81(5), pp. 238-243, January 2000. © 1998 by Phi Delta Kappa International, Inc.

- Certification by the National Board of Professional Standards (50pts)
- Evaluation by principal or supervisor (20)
- Record of past performance (20)
- Participation in district projects (20)
- Knowledge of content areas (10)
- Contributions to teams (20)
- Recognition by professional organizations (10pts)
- Customer-satisfaction information (10pts) (Bradley, 1998)

A six-member committee evaluates the portfolios and identifies teachers eligible for the award. Note the emphasis on the NBPTS standards. Teachers may choose to compile 100 points by omitting the National Board assessment, but to do so makes it more difficult because in order to receive 100 points, they must satisfy requirements for at least six other areas. Obviously, Robbinsdale Areas Schools officials have attached high value to the national certification process.

The Cincinnati Teacher Quality Plan, which approximates the model in Tables 6 and Figure 3, was adopted in May 2000 and since then has drawn much attention because it is the first in the country to "define in a contract what good teaching consists of and to set standards for moving to higher levels of performance" (Lewis, 2000, p. 3). The plan was developed based on what the literature identified as effective teaching. Conditions for acquiring a teaching position or being hired vary from a bachelor's degree and preliminary license for apprentices to obtaining an overall evaluation rating of "4" for a master or accomplished teacher. Teachers have a number of years (2 for apprentice, 5 for novice) to progress to each successive level. As Table 6 and Figure 3 show, factors that could trigger salary increases (in percentages or dollar increases) vary by level and include NBPTS certification and earning dual certification. Moreover, teachers can be awarded incentive pay and bonuses when they enhance their knowledge and competency by developing expertise in technology, writing grants, conducting action research, and assuming various leadership roles.

Table 6: Example of a District's Conceptual Model of a Knowledge- and Skills-based Pay Program

Teacher Category	Conditions for Entry	Max Years in this Category and Years of Experience-based Salary Increases Possible	Other Factors Triggering Salary Increases, Either % or Dollar Amount (Examples for Discussion Purposes)	Factors Triggering Salary Bonuses (Examples for Discussion Purposes)
Master Teacher	Danielson 4	No max years; 3 experience steps	National Board Certification	Microsoft Works
Advanced Teacher	Danielson 3 plus a 4 on Danielson 1 & 3	No max years; 3 experience steps	Approved Masters in an areas of Bd Certification	Writing a grant
Career Teacher	Danielson 3	No max years; 3 experience steps	Subject matter major	Teacher as researcher
Novice	Praxis III Professional License	5 years; 3 experience steps	Dual Certification	Dual Certification
Apprentice	BA, preliminary license, anything with Praxis II	2 years 1 experience step	Shortage area—e.g.math, science, second language	Etc.

Adapted with permission from Allen Odden, *Example of a District's Conceptual Model of a Knowledge- and Skills-based Pay Program,* seminar handout, June 21-23. 1999.

Figure 3: Cincinnati, OH Knowledge- and Skills-Based Salary Schedule.

Cincinnati, OH Knowledge- and Skills-Based Salary Schedule

How are the knowledge and skills measured?

The system has five levels. To move from one level to the next, teachers must show skills and knowledge through some combination of teacher test results, evaluations, and/or formal observations.

Apprentice teacher	Obtain temporary license.
Novice teacher	Pass Praxis III, obtain teaching license, and an overall "2" rating in all domains.
Career teacher	Approved IPDP and an overall "3" for all domains.
Advanced teacher	Approved Master's and an overall "4" in domains 1 and 2, and at least a "3" in the other two domains.
Accomplished teacher	An overall "4" rating on evaluation.

Does the Cincinnati knowledge and skills plan supplement or support the traditional salary structure?

The knowledge and skills plan supplements the traditional salary structure. The new structure has steps with each of the 5 new teacher categories, and has additional bonus pay opportunities within each category.

How much does movement along the knowledge and skills scale pay?

Following is the salary range for each of the five new teacher categories:

Apprentice teacher	$30,000
Novice teacher	$32,000-35,750
Career teacher	$38,750-49,250
Advanced teacher	$52,500-56,250
Accomplished teacher	$60,000-62,500

. . . continued

Figure 3 continued

Following are examples of additional incentive pay opportunities:

Master's degree in content area	$4,600
Ph.D. in education or content area	$9,375
NBPTS Certification	$1,000
Dual certification	$1,250
Technology expertise	$750
Competence Reform Model Training	$750/year for 3 years
Team skills	$750/year for 2 years
Leadership skills	$500/year for 2 years
Specific curriculum training	$500 for 1 year
Content specific	$750/year for 3 years
Lead teacher roles	$5,000-5,500/year

Adapted with permission from Byran C. Hassel (2002), *Better Pay for Better Teaching: Making Teaching Compensation Pay Off in the Age of Accountability*, p. 13, May 2002. © 2002 by Progressive Policy Institute. Source: Odden and Kellor (2000).

Some researchers have equated competency programs such as the Cincinnati plan with mentor teacher plans. For example, Webb and Norton (1999) and Zachary (2000) explained that mentors are experienced teachers who take beginning or inexperienced teachers under their wings, and help them develop subject matter knowledge and instructional competencies. These teachers are usually recognized and compensated for these added responsibilities and new roles. Their mentor duties and responsibilities can include giving advice on developing lesson plans, controlling student behavior, improving classroom management and instructional delivery.

Skills- and competency-based pay programs are also referred to as and equated with career ladder programs. The terms are often used interchangeably. As Webb and Norton suggested, the career ladder may be considered "a form of knowledge or skills-based pay ... [and] are intended to provide both the extrinsic monetary rewards and the intrinsic rewards associated with the 'promotion' structure of the career ladder" (1999, p. 425). They are also characterized by "multiple features such as extra compensation, enlargement of job opportunities, and staff development opportunities to motivate and reward teachers" (Harty, Greiner, & Ashford, 1994, pp. 3-4). However, whereas the career ladder programs of the 1970s and 1980s focused solely on progressive advancement of teachers to higher levels of recognition and monetary rewards, the newer knowledge- and skills-based programs emphasize teacher professional development and student achievement as the primary outcome measures. States and districts have recognized the advantages of linking teacher pay and professional development to student achievement.

Some of the pre-1990s career ladder programs that reflected this linkage were successful. In their report to the SREB entitled *Reflecting on Ten Years of Incentive Programs,* Cornett and Gaines (1994) cited seven states that adopted career ladder programs, most of which proved successful in improving teacher performance and raising student achievement. Among these were Arizona, Indiana, Mississippi, North Carolina, Ohio, Tennessee, and Texas. According to Cornett (1995), student achievement not only increased from instruction delivered within a curriculum structured and defined by career ladder requirements, but student graduation rates increased and drop-out rates decreased. These programs were successful because they focused on building teacher knowledge and skills and getting results through adherence to well defined performance standards and improvement criteria such as student attendance, parental involvement, and reduction of student dropout rates. This is the design reflected in many of the recent knowledge-, skills-based, and career ladder programs such as the plan in Cincinnati, Ohio.

One conclusion that can be drawn from the successes in states with the new career ladder programs is that this approach to performance pay, if planned and implemented well, can be effective in improving professional development and student learning (Odden & Kelley, 1997). One example that corroborates this observation is Arizona's career ladder program. At one time, it was touted as one of the best programs that linked teacher evaluation and student achievement (SREB, 1997). Initiated in the 1980s, the program paid teachers bonuses when students scored at predetermined levels on standardized tests. Several charter schools in Arizona adopted the program and experienced success with it. Because of these successes, some observers (Matthews, 1999) took the position that market-driven models of teacher pay such as Arizona's career ladder program should be adopted in all schools across the country.

However, skills-based and the newer career staffing programs have several disadvantages, many of which were reflected in the unsuccessful pre-1990s career ladder programs. Johnson (1986) noted that because "career ladder plans redefine the formal role and relationships of school personnel, they require more extensive organizational changes than merit pay programs" (p. 72). She identified other factors such as unanticipated costs, teacher opposition, inadequate evaluation, and dissention. Firestone (1994) reported that some of the difficulties associated with developing skills-based incentive programs include difficulty with how to assess and price skills. He argued that instead of developing cultures of learning and providing more opportunities for teacher development, "knowledge-based pay creates incentives for frugal districts to limit teacher learning opportunities because doing so will contain salary costs" (1994, p. 559). These disadvantages are among the reasons some districts prefer other approaches to teacher compensation, such as group-based award systems.

Group-Based/School Award Systems

Standards-based and comprehensive reforms have ignited interest in new ways to compensate teachers. In addition to knowledge- and skills-based programs, reformers have fixed their attention on group-based performance programs, known also as collective pay, school-based reward, school-based performance awards, gainsharing, and collective incentive pay programs. These programs are based on the premise that when an entire school improves, the improvement is due to collective performance, and, as a result, everyone should share reward money. (Interestingly, this is not the position taken by superintendents who negotiate pay-for-performance contracts for themselves. See Lafee, 1999) Furthermore, some educators argue that effective schools are effective not because of one individual's or one group's efforts, but because of the cooperation and combined efforts of both the instructional and noninstructional staff. Consequently, policy researchers and school officials advocate rewarding everyone in the school when gains in student achievement are attained (Firestone, 1994; Harty, et al., 1994; Odden & Kelly, 1997). Sharing gains, according to Mohrman, Galbraith, Lawler, & Associates (1998) and Lawler (1992), encourages collaboration, cooperation, and teamwork, which in turn foster and facilitate collegiality and promote high levels of productivity.

Most existing collective incentive programs are designed around measurable standards such as student achievement, student dropout rate, absenteeism, and teacher attendance. Only those schools within a district that positively influence these factors or produce gains are rewarded with increased monetary reward. The group-based program in Waco, Texas, for example, is based on seven criteria: "five student-related, two staff-related.

The student criteria include: reading, writing, and math scores, student attendance, and drop out rate. The staff-related criteria include employee attendance and staff development and service" (Lenord & Tanaka, 1996, p. 31).

In Dallas, Texas, the school- or group-based performance program is predicated on the philosophy that schools should not be held accountable for the characteristics that students bring to school. The designers of the program reasoned if teachers are not responsible for most of the baggage students bring to school, neither should they be held responsible when that baggage impedes or hinders learning. Concern for fairness resulted in the development and use of two indices to measure school effectiveness—the School Effectiveness Index (SEI) and the Classroom Effectiveness Index (CEI). The CEI measures teacher effectiveness by focusing on how well students perform in individual classrooms. The SEI on the other hand uses three measures: (a) student test results; (b) school-wide attendance, dropout, and promotion rates; and, at the high school level, (c) "participation rates in activities such as AP courses and college entrance tests" (Mendro et al., 1999, p. 3). The program attempts to control for a number of extraneous variables that might influence school effectiveness. Mendro et al. (1999) explained the controls this way:

> Controls at the student level include ethnic/language status, socio-economic status (measured directly by participation in free and reduced lunch, and imputed from block-level census data), and gender. Controls at the school level include percent minority, percent African-American, percent Hispanic, percent LEP, student mobility, school crowding, average socio-economic status (again drawn from Census data), and percent days lost due to teacher vacancies. These control variables are used in a multi-stage regression modeling system that outputs a school score that in effect influence the difference in average achievement on each test for each school from the district average. The scores are then multiplied by the appropriate weight and summed to yield the School Effectiveness Index. (p. 7)

The Dallas system has been touted as one of the fairest because of its emphasis on attributing outcomes to teacher and school efforts and not to extraneous variables such as race, gender, and socioeconomic status. Indeed, the correlation between scores from the SEI and demographic variables is low (Clotfelter & Ladd, 1996; Mendro, et al. 1999; Webster & Mendro, 1995). In addition, monetary rewards resulting from gain scores are based only on the SEI, which is group-based as opposed to the individual-based CEI.

Perhaps the most notable disadvantage of group-based reward programs is the controversy over how reward money is spent and for what purposes. Of the states and districts that have developed these programs, some such as Kentucky have stipulated that the money be used to increase teacher salaries. South Carolina mandated that the money be spent on school improvement initiatives. Districts such as Charlotte-Mecklenburg and Dallas have stipulated that rewards be distributed as bonuses (Odden & Kelley, 1997). In fact, a major criticism of the Texas incentive program has been the insistence on the part of policymakers that reward money be used for bonus pay rather than to increase teacher base pay (Mendro et al., 1999). But one district chose to address this problem head-on. In Coventry, Rhode Island, the school board approved a plan that adds $1,000 to teachers' base pay "if they can demonstrate excellent performance by completing portfolios of their work" (Olson, 1999, p. 18).

However bonus money is spent, there is no existing evidence that indicates a correlation between the effectiveness of programs that award bonuses and those that simply increase the base pay for all teachers. Neither does evidence exists to support the notion that most teachers work harder because they receive bonuses or have extra pay added to their base salary. Some may while others may not. Recall the discussion in Chapter 2 on teacher efficacy and the role it plays in teacher performance.

Group-based pay programs are in vogue partly because of the advantages they offer schools and school districts within the context of comprehensive school reform. Themes emerging from existing programs suggest that these programs address accountability issues in convincing ways and involve the business community through influential committees that use participatory and shared decision-making strategies (Mendro et al., 1999). Furthermore, as Lawler (1990) proffered, when collective incentive programs are combined with effective staff participation,

> collective incentives can increase coordination, teamwork, and sharing of knowledge among staff; raise acceptance of change resulting from new methods and technology because high efficiency leads to bonuses; focus attention on cost saving as well as improved student outcomes; change attitudes among teachers so they demand more efficient management and better planning; and encourage teachers to work smarter rather than harder. (cited in Firestone, 1994, p. 567)

It is likely that the advantages of group-pay systems will motivate more state and district policymakers to adopt them. Since their debut in the 1990s, the list of those advantages has grown. For the moment, one of the biggest issues surrounding group- or school-based pay seems to be whether reward money should be used for one-time bonuses or go towards increasing teachers' base pay (Firestone, 1994; Mendro et al., 1999; Odden & Kelly, 1997; Odden, 2001).

Recognition Incentive Programs

The third category of incentive systems are called nonmonetary or recognition programs. These programs do not provide monetary rewards but rather stress joint goal setting between principals and teachers, comparison of teacher performance with pre-established or targeted performance, and reliance on praise and recognition to motivate and reward teachers (Harty et al., 1994). According to Jung (1984), nonmonetary rewards traditionally used in education include:

- Public recognition: teacher of the year awards
- Peer recognition: designation of master teachers as successful professionals
- Restructuring of the work environment: giving recipients more release time, options to work part-time, more discretion in determining where and what to teach
- Recognition and awards for schools: for example, the Secretary of Education's program of recognition for effective schools (p. 12)

When properly designed and implemented, recognition programs are successful because they rely on immediate feedback. Jung (1984) noted that a recognition program "can be rewarding in and of itself [if it conveys] specific information about performance in a situation where successful performance is valued" (p. 12). Education reformers and proponents of performance pay may want to experiment with developing pay systems that combine performance pay with nonmonetary rewards. Such systems should have a well structured set of incentives based on a variation of meaningful praise and recognition that motivates teachers to teach not for cash rewards, but for what Fullan (1999) calls "moral agency," the joy and satisfaction of knowing they help students learn. Such programs would be consistent with ideas advanced by Jackson, Boostrom, and Hansen (1998) on developing the moral life of the school. They would also be consistent with teacher motivation theory and research findings that identify teacher efficacy (success in helping students learn) as the principal motivating factor in the teaching profession.

Other Incentive Programs

In addition to knowledge-/skills-based, group-based award, and recognition performance systems, other incentive programs and reward structures include merit pay and mentor programs. Because merit pay and career ladder programs of the 1970s and 1980s were addressed in previous sections, and especially because few programs of this type align instruction, evaluation, and student achievement, remarks in this sections will be restricted to differential pay programs, mentor programs, and one incentive program that uses student performance in individual classrooms as the basis for awarding bonuses.

In a recent policy paper on teacher pay, Bryan Hassel (2002) described two differentiated pay programs—one for hard-to-hire teachers and the other for hard-to-staff schools. In the first, teachers in critical subject areas such as math, science, and special education received higher salaries than their colleagues in less critical areas such as language arts, social studies, and physical education. In Utah, for example, math and science teachers receive a one-time signing bonus of $5,000. In the second type of differentiated pay program, teachers receive higher pay after agreeing to teach in schools where most student are from low socioeconomic backgrounds. These are the students who invariably come to school with poor attitudes toward learning and present numerous disciplinary challenges for principals and teachers. New York City exemplifies this second kind of differentiated pay program because teachers who agree to teach high-needs predominantly low income schools are awarded a 15 percent pay raise.

Teachers who participate in mentor programs perform a variety of roles, such as developing lesson plans, observing novice teachers, and helping teachers with classroom management. According to Portner (1998), their primary functions include relating, assessing, coaching, and guiding. Overall, mentor teachers become responsible for nurturing and supporting the professional development of beginning teachers. In return, they are rewarded with a mixture of compensation and release time (Portner, 1998; Webb et al., 1998; Zachary, 2000). In Oldham County, Kentucky, for example, teachers certified by the NBPTS and who "mentor cohort groups of NBC [National Board Candidates] are eligible to receive $500 per person in that group (max. of 5 teachers) and receive an additional $500 [for] teachers in the cohort group who achieve certification" (NBPTS, 2002, p. 1). The Chicago Public Schools award NBC teachers $5,000 who agree to shepherd at least three candidates through the NBPTS process. And in 1998, the Florida Legislature promulgated the Excellent Teaching Program Act, which in addition to paying 90% of the NPBTS fee and providing NBC teachers with 10% salary bonus for the life of the certificate, provided "an additional 10% annual mentoring bonus to NBCT's who agree in writing to provide the equivalent of 12 workdays of mentoring and related services to teachers who may or may not be National Board candidates. Both bonuses are based on 10% of the previous year's statewide average classroom teacher's salary" (NBPTS, 2002, 3).

Another incentive approach unlike those discussed earlier, is a program that rewards teachers based on individual classroom performance, not based on gain scores for an entire school. For example, recently the Denver Classroom Teachers Association approved a trial performance pay program that linked teacher performance to student achievement. It is the first program in the nation that rewards teachers based on how well students do in individual classrooms as opposed to school-wide achievement, group-based pay, or knowledge-based pay. In many respects, this is a true pay-for-performance program because it rewards teachers for their individual efficacy. Teachers (450 of the 4300) in 12 elementary schools will pilot the programs and receive bonuses if they are successful. If the program is successful and eventually adopted, teachers whose students do well on standardized tests such as the Iowa Test of Basic Skills or on tests created by the district will receive salary raises (Denver Teachers, 1999).

Chapter Summary

States and districts are discarding traditional pay systems that have stressed degrees, academic credits, and experience as the bases for teacher pay. Many have instead adopted compensation systems that link rewards and incentives to improved instruction and increased student achievement. While there are many variations of performance pay programs, most can be classified as either (a) knowledge-/competency-based, (b) group or school-based, or (c) recognition- and praise-based. Knowledge-based programs are primarily concerned with rewarding teachers when they acquire knowledge and develop competencies that improve their instruction and ultimately student achievement. Bonuses are given to teachers with or without restrictions, such as allowing teachers to spend bonus money as they please or using it to purchase school supplies. Group or school-base programs, on the other hand, award the entire school or groups of teachers when they contribute to improving student achievement scores on standardized tests. Unlike the competency-based and group-based programs, recognition programs use joint goal setting, performance-by-objectives strategies, and praise to motivate teachers. Other incentive programs include mentor teacher incentive programs and the unique approach of rewarding teachers based on student performance in individual classrooms. While these programs have several disadvantages, presently it seems that they are outweighed by their advantages. The disadvantage that recurs throughout the literature seems to be dissatisfaction among teachers who believe that awards, especially in group-based programs, are inappropriately used to give bonuses instead of being used to increase base pay. Additionally, many educators believe it is unfair for some teachers to receive bonuses while others receive nothing because, they argue, everyone in a school—not just teachers—in one way or another contributes to student achievement.

How should incentive programs be designed? What processes and guidelines should designers follow? What standards of adequacy are appropriate? Chapter 5 examines these questions and attempts to provide some understanding of necessary steps during the design and planning processes.

5

DESIGN AND PLANNING CONSIDERATIONS FOR INCENTIVE PROGRAMS

Assumptions

This chapter addresses design issues and decision-making processes used to develop performance pay systems. The discussion will address the role assumptions, objectives, and standards of adequacy play in constructing an effective incentive program. Lawler's four research-based considerations for designing incentive programs are instructive in this regard because they provide information on which to base assumptions, specify objectives, and develop standards of adequacy that underlie, guide, and evaluate performance pay systems.[24] Lawler observed:

> First, bonus plans are generally better motivators than pay-raise and salary-increase plans because a bonus plan can substantially vary an individual's pay from time to time. Second, approaches that use objective measures of performance are better motivators than those that use subjective measures. Third, group-based and organization wide bonus plans are generally best at producing integration and teamwork. Fourth, group-based and organization wide plans are often the easiest ones to relate to strategic objectives because they are the easiest to tie to performance measures of business success (Lawler, III, 1998, pp. 296-297).

Equally important is Lawler's contention that properly designed pay plans should emphasize open communication as opposed to secrecy, decision making that stresses participation versus hierarchical control, and a structure that reflects decentralization as opposed to centralization. "A decentralized structure," he explains, "allows for local innovation, and for practices that fit with particular businesses and strategies" (1998, 303). The apparent implication for districts is to identify reliable information about pay programs and ground assumptions and operations in democratic values and best practices of leadership and management.

Several assumptions may be drawn from these ideas. According to Jung (1984), assumptions about distribution of teacher skills, interdependence, and learner outcomes are crucial for reforming education through teacher effectiveness, improved student achievement, and performance pay programs. He explained these assumptions in the following way:

Distribution of teaching skills: How is teaching skill assumed to be distributed? Can only a few teachers achieve excellence, or can all teachers? Does the system emphasize identification of a select few or implementation of all?

Interdependence: Is excellent teaching considered primarily an individual activity or a team effort? Can individual teachers produce excellence, or does excellence transcend the individual classroom?

Learner outcomes: Do processes (what teachers do) constitute teaching excellence or are learner outcomes the measure of excellence? Is excellent teaching separable from its results? If learner outcomes are crucial to excellence, how much are they affected by variables like student ability, previous learning, home and family environment, school environment? (p. 9)

Jung's typology suggests that different incentive programs can be developed depending on what assumptions are embraced. In fact, Jung explained, "If system designers examine their assumptions carefully, they can select the most appropriate objectives and strategies" (p. 10). For example, if a design team focuses on distribution of teaching skills and proceeds with the assumption that only a few teachers can achieve excellence, then the program's objectives would identify and encourage these teachers to continue their career in teaching. This would result in only a few teachers being rewarded. On the other hand, if the assumption is that most or all teachers can achieve excellence, the objective of the incentive program would be to "motivate better performance." There would be little need for quotas, and each teacher would have the opportunity to earn the established award. If the assumption is that excellent teaching is largely a group effort, then the objective would be to help all teachers function at high levels of performance with the assistance of an effective professional development program. Standards would be established with all teachers sharing in rewards if all or a predetermined percentage of the standards are met. Gainsharing could function to convince teachers that their individual efforts are important.[25]

Equally important as assumptions for designing incentive programs is the interconnectedness of key elements of the system and the system's objectives. In an informative chapter entitled "Strategic Pay System Design," Lawler, who has perhaps done more to advance the knowledge-base of incentive pay than anyone else, explains that "Pay systems are effective to the degree that there is alignment among the organization's core values, its processes, and its practices and structures" (1998, p. 288).

While Lawler's frame of reference is rooted in business, his ideas can be applied to schools. First, core values of a compensation system in the business world parallel values in education such as excellence, equity, choice, equality, effectiveness, and, spawned by the standards-based movement, measurable outcomes. Second, management processes used in business organizations are similar to leadership and management processes such as communication, decision making, professional development, curriculum development, and performance appraisal. And third, incentive structures and practices in the business world parallel those used in school districts—skill-based pay, group-base pay or gainsharing plans, and nonmonetary plans that rely solely on praise and recognition. Indeed, business and industrial organizations popularized these pay systems long before educators adopted them. The implications here are that effective incentive systems depend on how well district officials and planning teams understand the interplay of values and their influence on school leadership and instructional behavior in schools. Lawler underscored the importance of reward systems being designed with this understanding: "The reward system, in combination with other features of the organization's design, drives the performance of the organization because it influences critical individual and organizational behaviors. Therefore, it must be designed to support the needed organizational behaviors" (1998, p. 287). In sum, when designers of performance pay systems clarify assumptions, develop an understanding of core values, and use appropriate processes, practices and structures, they establish a strong foundation for identifying and selecting goals and objectives, the next critical steps in the design phase of a performance-based incentive system.

Goals and Objectives of Incentive Programs

But what should be the goals and objectives of an incentive system? When restructuring teacher pay systems, the focus should be first on improving teaching quality and ultimately on improving student achievement. With teacher quality as an initial target, accompanying goals could be grouped under two headings: *compositional effects* and *behavioral effects*. According to Hassel,

> With compositional effects, the key questions is how a proposed pay system is likely to effect who enters teaching, who stays over time, and who leaves. With behavioral effects, the key question is how a proposed system is likely to affect the assignments teachers take on, the ways they develop their capabilities over their careers, and the practices they use in classrooms. (2002, p. 9)

Hassel further identified knowledge- and skills-based pay programs in Douglas County, Colorado; Los Angeles; Cincinnati, Ohio; and North Carolina's School-Based Performance Award Program as those improving the composition of the teaching force as well as altering the behavior of teachers. He also identified differential pay programs in Utah and New York City as those improving teacher composition and not altering behavior.

Some standards-based reformers (Harty et al., 1994; Odden, 1999a, 2000a) argue that only two objectives matter when designing incentive pay programs—to improve instruction and increase student achievement. As Lawler (1998) pointed out, however, "research on reward systems suggests that they potentially influence six factors, which in turn have an impact on strategy implementation and organizational effectiveness" (p. 292). These factors are *attraction* and *retention*, *motivation* of *performance*, *skills* and *knowledge*, *culture*, *reinforcement* and *definition of structure*, and *costs*. Several implications can be extrapolated from these objectives and applied to performance programs in schools. Figure 4 displays a synopsis of the six objectives and their implications for education. Conspicuously missing from among the six objectives is student achievement.

Fig. 4 Factors influenced by reward programs.

Attraction and Retention: The more and better a district's rewards and incentives, the higher the quality of teachers it will attract. Of course, the converse may be true. The more teachers are able to feel their rewards are equitable and equal with those in other districts, the more satisfied they will be.

Motivation of Performance: School employees are more likely to be motivated to perform effectively when they "(1) believe that effective performance will lead to outcome, (2) feel that these outcomes are attractive, and (3) believe that effective performance is possible" (Lawler, 1998, p. 294).

Skills and Knowledge: School employees are more motivated to develop the skills and knowledge required by schools when they are rewarded. Consequently, a school incentive program that rewards skills and knowledge that resulting in verifiable student learning will motivate teachers to develop those skills and knowledge.

Culture: A well-designed incentive system helps create and define a school's culture. A pay system that is comprehensive and equitable, will influence beliefs and promote values that in turn will motivate and generate satisfaction among school employees. School-based incentive programs should be developed with participation and cooperation with all concerned parties—superintendent, school board members, district building level staff, principals, teachers, parents, students, and community and business representatives.

Reinforcement and Definition of Structure: A well-designed incentive program helps define, clarify, and reinforce the goals, roles, and formal relationships within schools. Shared decisionmaking enhances and facilitates day-to-day interactions and help to build productive and meaningful relationships. For example, a group-based performance pay system could specify that the major goal of the school is to increase student learning through effective professional development and standards-based achievement. When teachers perform duties and responsibilities in ways that result in increased student learning, they qualify for bonus or incentive pay. The award in turn motivates them to continue their result-oriented behavior, which in turn reinforces participative interactions and contributes to skill enhancement and knowledge acquisition.

Costs: Because reliance on public funding imposes spending constraints on school districts, care must be taken when designing a pay system with predefined reward structures. For this reason, incentive plans should be designed with built-in flexibility, where bonuses, rewards, and nonmonetary incentives come from an array of possible compensations approaches. The incentive system should reflect the reality of shifting economic conditions directly affecting the district's ability to award incentives. All foreseeable constraints and contingencies should be built into the incentive system. Approaches that help account for constraints and contingencies include cost-effectiveness analysis and cost-benefit analysis.

Adapted with permission from Lawler III, *Strategic Pay Systems Designs*, In Susan Mohrman et al., *Tomorrow's Organizations, pp. 286-295.* © 1998 by Jossey-Bass, Inc., Publishers.

This is because Lawler developed the objectives primarily for business and industrial settings. In other words, incentive systems should be designed to attract and retain qualified personnel, motivate and facilitate high performance, develop job-related skills and knowledge, foster organizational culture that supports meaningful and fulfilling interactions, reinforce and define structure, and function cost-effectively.[26]

As we saw in Chapter 2, researchers (such as Johnson, 1986) have argued that it is important for researchers and policymakers to distinguish among incentives that attract teachers (better pay, higher status, extrinsic and ancillary rewards), incentives that retain them (incentive rewards, sense of professional accomplishment), and incentives that improve their practice (solidarity and purposive incentives). This means that designers of incentive programs have other objectives to consider when developing incentive pay programs, namely incentives that attract, retain, and improve teachers.

Objectives provide the direction and focus necessary for developing incentive programs with a high probability of success. They contribute to a strong foundation for developing a performance pay system. Yet, as instructive and helpful as they may be, objectives are among many variables needed to develop an effective performance pay plan, some of which Firestone (1994) articulated when he posed these questions:

- What criteria should be measured and rewarded?
- What comparison among school should be used? Improvement measure?
- An absolute standard measure? The top percentage measure?
- At what organizational level should incentives be established?
- Should all schools be required to participate?
- How should bonuses be funded? Gainsharing? Upfront budget allocation?
- What additional policies will be needed?
- How should decisions about the design of the new pay system be made?
- If consideration is given to combining knowledge-based, group-based, job enlargement, and [nonmonetary] pay systems, how best to choose among these systems?
- How much change does the district want or can support at any one time?
- How best to pay for the incentive system?
- How far can a district go in changing its salary system? (pp. 564-569)

Presumably, the likelihood of developing an effective performance pay program increases when these issues are addressed. But the likelihood may be even higher if appropriate attention is given to aligning core values, assumptions, relevant objectives, processes, practices, and structures. Consequently, what criteria should be addressed to ensure a successful performance pay plan? What standards of adequacy should be considered?

Standards of Adequacy Guidelines

One way of ensuring adherence to all the factors necessary in an effective performance pay program is to organize them in some hierarchal structure and address them systematically. Several researchers and policy analysts have attempted this, but most have provided only abbreviated lists of guidelines that offer only a partial view of incentive pay guidelines. These include guidelines proffered by Duttweiler and Remos-Cancel (1986), Farnsworth et el. (1991), Harty et al. (1994), Odden and Kelley (1997, 2002), SREB (1998), Tucker and Codding (1998); Lawler III (1998),

Odden, Kellor, Heneman, and Milanowski (1999), and Hassel (2002). A synthesis of several of these guidelines is provided in Appendix B.

In their book, *Standards for Our Schools*, Tucker and Codding (1998) observed:

> Almost every piece of [a standard/performance-based system] is in place somewhere in the United States or elsewhere in the world. But nowhere, yet, have all the pieces been put together. Most important, there is not yet anyplace where strong incentives for the students to achieve have been combined with strong incentives operating on the professional staff to help them achieve. When these elements are combined, they will without doubt produce unprecedented gains in student performance. (p. 243)

Since the book was published, several districts have moved closer to putting most of the pieces together. Examples include Florida; Kentucky; Cincinnati, Ohio; Dallas; North Carolina; Douglas County, Colorado; and Manitowoc, Wisconsin. While there are numerous performance pay design models (Milanowski, 2001), few have addressed design guidelines in a comprehensive manner. Duttweiler and Ramos-Cancel (1986), Harty et al. (1994), the SREB (1998), and Odden and Kelley (2002) have provided the most convincing guidelines for designing and planning incentive programs.

Because of the obvious need to account for most of the factors that define a comprehensive performance pay system, and to highlight and underscore what the literature seems to suggest are the most critical factors, this author developed the *Performance Pay Standards of Adequacy Checklist* (PPSAC) illustrated in Appendix A. It shows that most criteria and guidelines necessary for a functional incentive pay system can be grouped under seven headings:

- Preliminary Design and Planning Considerations
- Guiding Assumptions and Agreements
- Student-Focused Considerations
- Instructional Staff Considerations
- Incentives and Sanctions
- Operational Considerations
- Accountability and Evaluation Considerations

Under each heading are subsections followed by several questions that can be checked off as "having been done" or "need to do." While the questions are not exhaustive, combined they provide a comprehensive view of numerous factors that should be considered before, during, and after a performance pay system is planned, implemented, and evaluated. The guidelines were culled and synthesized from the literature on standards-based reform and incentive pay, and from the planning design examples illustrated in Appendix B. Those engaged in the planning phase of these programs should also examine other examples of design guidelines, such as those in the second edition of Odden and Kelley (2002; see especially pp. 206-210).

States and school districts may find the checklist helpful in thinking about the components or factors necessary for an effective performance pay program. It may also help with moving closer toward disproving Tucker and Codding's observation that "nowhere, yet, have all the pieces been put together."

Chapter Summary

Pay-for-performance programs should be guided by appropriate assumptions and objectives. Furthermore, such programs should reflect alignment of assumptions and objectives, which in turn should be aligned with core values, processes, practices, and structures. One way of assuring alignment of these elements is to use a checklist that contains standards and guidelines that could support the design process. However, as useful as checklists may be, they cannot substitute for research evidence that should underpin and inform incentive programs. Presently there is a dearth of empirically derived data on incentive pay programs. Some policy researchers (Odden, 2000a) support this observation and note that there is little research on the outcomes of adopting performance pay programs. But as sparse as empirical studies on performance systems may be, what does existing studies tell us about them? This question is addressed in the following chapter.

6

RESEARCH ON PERFORMANCE PAY PROGRAMS

In a report, *Research Findings on Effective Program Designs and Methodologies*, Packard & Dereshiwsky (1988a) discussed the reasons that contributed to the failure of pre-1990s reform initiatives, especially career ladder incentive programs. Among the key findings was the following:

> Program failures have directly been attributed to the lack of a research base. In the past, adequate collection, analysis, recording and disseminating of empirical observations were not sufficiently generated to provide evidence, which would convince funding bodies to continue support. (p. 2)

The lack of a research base is still evident and a reality today. While many of the standards-based and high-stakes testing programs are data driven (Stringfield, Ross, & Smith 1996), few of the existing incentive pay programs were founded on empirically derived evidence (Odden, 2000a). Nevertheless, reformers are now addressing this deficiency, however slow the process may be. Expectations for systematic research on and evaluation of these initiatives are evident throughout the literature. For example, of the nine components in the Comprehensive School Reform Demonstration Program (CSRDP)—the major reform program sponsored by the U.S.

Department of Education—a focus on research-based methods and strategies is listed first. This emphasis on research evidence communicates the federal government's expectation for data-driven comprehensive school reform, which includes pay systems. It is fitting then, that this section of the book addresses the following questions:

- Do performance pay programs work?
- Do they motivate teachers to perform better?
- Do they improve teachers' performance?
- Do they influence teachers' attitudes in positive ways?
- Do they improve student achievement?
- Overall, is the quality of education in districts with performance pay programs better than those in districts without them?

The aim in addressing these questions is to provide an overview of existing research on performance-based incentive systems and tease out some implications for their design, planning and implementation. The discussion will be restricted to three dimensions of pay programs around which most performance-based research seem to converge—teacher motivation, teacher performance, and student achievement. Since teacher motivation and performance are inextricably linked, they are addressed together.

Research on the Influence of Incentive Programs on Teacher Motivation, Performance, Attitudes, and Attributions

Motivation and Performance

Do incentive programs motivate teachers to improve performance? Most studies on pre-1990s merit pay and career ladder programs suggest they do not (Dorman & Fulford, 1989; Harty et al., 1994; Norton et. al, 1988; Odden and Kelley, 1997). Findings based on research on the newer pay systems, however, are providing mixed results.

Some of the most significant findings from Kelley's study (1999) call attention to what truly motivates teachers. Kelley found that teachers were motivated to perform better when, through their efforts, they changed instructional practices; when student performance was based on clear, focused achievement goals; when there was fear of negative publicity; when meaningful rewards meant a desire for positive public recognition, or the desire to see students achieve; and when there was fear of losing professional autonomy or their jobs. Moreover, these factors had to be buttressed by teachers' own knowledge and skills and by enabling conditions such as curriculum alignment, test-taking skills, professional development, effective leadership from both principals and district officials, and being professionally "in the loop." Together, these elements may be regarded as a model reflecting salient features necessary for developing an effective performance pay system.

In another study on the effects of school-based performance award programs (SBPA) on teacher motivation, Kelley (1998) examined SBPA programs in Kentucky, Charlotte-Mecklenburg, Douglas County, and Maryland. She found that most teachers did not regard monetary rewards as key motivators and concluded that the "direct motivating power of school-based performance bonuses is relatively weak" (p. 316). Similarly, in a recent synthesis paper, Kelley, Melanowski, and Heneman (2001) also noted "that SBPA programs studied did motivate teachers to work toward programs goals. However, increased pressure and stress produced by the program partially offset their positive motivational impact" (p. 11). These findings seem to suggest that teachers are less motivated by the positive aspects (e.g., rewards and bonuses) of incentive programs and motivated more by the negative aspects (e.g., fear).

Other researchers have weighed in on the connection between performance pay programs and teacher motivation. For example, Abelman and Kenyon (1996) conducted four case studies in one high and three elementary schools to ascertain the extent of success after implementing provisions of Kentucky Instructional Results Information System (KIRIS). They found no convincing evidence that rewards served as incentives and motivated teachers and principals to higher performance. As was the case in Kelley's study, what they found was that "fear of sanctions was a stronger motivator than the anticipation of cash rewards" (p. 27). The promise of rewards or the actual rewards played no significant role in getting educators to improve their performance. They concluded that "the basic premise of rewards—that they go to what motivates people—is misaligned with Kentucky's rewards plan" (p. 28). For various reasons, both the reward structure and method of distribution were not adequately addressed by the program and consequently resulted in conflicts that took time from teaching and learning (Abelman & Kenyon, 1996).

Attitudes

The findings by Kelley (1999), Abelmann and Kenyon (1996), however, seem inconsistent with results of another study conducted in Kentucky and Charlotte-Mecklenburg by Heneman and Milanowski (1999). Their study focused on teachers' attitude towards the SBPA programs in those states. After surveying 2,951 teachers (1,150 responded or 39%), they found that receiving a bonus of $1000 and a bonus of $2000 in Kentucky "were among the top three and top five most desirable outcomes, respectively" (p. 335). They also found that "personal satisfaction from improved student performance" and "having students learn new skills" were among other key outcomes. These results supported findings from Kelley's study (1999) that revealed the positive outcomes that motivated teacher to perform better were:

- Personal satisfaction from school meeting goals
- Working cooperatively on curriculum and instruction
- Satisfaction of knowing student performance is up
- Opportunities for professional development
- Having clear schoolwide goals to work toward
- Receiving public recognition for achieving goals
- Having students learn new concepts and skills
- Receiving a pay bonus
- Receiving funds for school improvement. (p. 317)

The negative consequences, however, included embarrassment or public criticism for not meeting goals, loss of professional pride from not achieving goals, and risk of losing their job. What stood out from these studies is that SBPA programs created much stress for teachers, especially those in schools with a large number of students from low socioeconomic backgrounds. The stress attributed to SBPA programs are documented elsewhere (CPRE, 2000; Jones et al., 1999). Overall, though, the major outcomes from these studies were specification and articulation of clear goals, alignment of resources, and a change of teaching practices (Kelley, 1999).

On a larger scale, when national data were examined, teachers gave incentive programs favorable ratings. This was what Boe (1990) found when he used data from the 1988 Schools and Staffing Survey (SASS) by the National Center for Education Statistics to study teacher attitudes relative to incentive programs. SASS is based on a large-scale national sample of 56,242 public and 11,529 private school teachers. The return rates were impressive: 86.4% for public schools and 79.1% for private schools. As Table 7 shows, of the six incentive pay programs public school teachers rated, the majority of teachers (87%) found incentive pay for added responsibilities the most favorable, followed by teaching in high-priority locations (77%), career ladders (70%), and group merit bonus (64%). A smaller number of teachers rated individual merit pay (53%) and teaching in shortage fields (52%) favorable.

Table 7: 1987-1988 School and Staffing Survey Data on Public School Favorability Ratings of Pay Incentives

Pay Incentive Program	Favorability Rating				
	Statistic	Favor		Opposed	
		Strongly	Mildly	Strongly	Mildly
For added responsibilities	Percent	57.8%	28.7%	6.9%	5.7%
	Std. Error	.33	.22	.16	.14
Teaching in shortage field	Percent	23.7%	28.6%	27.0%	20.6%
	Std. Error	.20	.28	.26	.25
Teaching in high-priority location	Percent	40.5%	36.3%	11.0%	12.3%
	Std. Error	.30	.29	.19	.18
Career ladders	Percent	39.1%	30.7%	18.0%	12.2%
	Std. Error	.33	.27	.24	.21
Individual pay	Percent	27.0%	26.2%	30.4%	16.5%
	Std. Error	.31	.29	.28	.20
Group merit bonus	Percent	33.5%	30.1%	21.8%	14.7%
	Std. Error	.28	.29	.24	.18

Adapted by permission from E.E. Boe, (1990). *Teacher Incentive with SASS*, p. 10, University of Pennsylvania.

(It should be noted that a second SASS was conducted during the fall of 1999 but researchers did not ask the same questions as they did in the 1988 survey. It would have been enlightening to contrast findings from both surveys as the first was conducted during the 1970s and 1980s or the era of merit pay and career ladder programs while the second was conducted with some recent knowledge-, skill-, and group-based programs in place.)

What is particularly noteworthy about these national data is that a higher proportion of teachers found group merit bonuses more favorable than individual merit pay. This revelation from a national sample supports similar findings in the literature (Odden & Kelley, 2002). It gives credence to the view that group bonuses serve as better incentives than individual merit pay because individual competition is not a factor in group-based programs.

The findings in Boe's study parallel those in another large-scale study by Norton and Scott (1988). These researchers examined teachers' attitudes in school districts in 28 states. All the data were collected during the same year. After comparing teachers' attitudes toward incentive program in states with performance pay programs to teachers' attitudes in states without such programs, the researcher found that incentive program teachers (IPT) as a group had more positive attitudes toward the programs than did non-IPT districts. IPT teachers also had more positive attitudes about the effects of the incentive program on their motivation than teachers did in districts without. Importantly, IPT teachers as a group viewed the "influence of incentive program on instructional improvement more favorably" (p. 150) than their counterparts in other districts.

The findings in studies by Norton and Scott (1988) and Boe (1990), however, were not consistent with findings from other studies. For example, in the North Carolina study (Jones et al., 1999) discussed earlier, teachers were asked to indicate their beliefs about whether instructional practices had changed since initiation of the program. Among the major findings were the following:

- Teachers spend the majority of the school day preparing students in the basics as defined by the ABC program, including reading, writing, and mathematics.

- The amount of time spent in reading, mathematics, and writing had increased since the implementation of the program.

- Since teachers focus specifically on the information that will be tested, material that involved higher-order thinking and problem solving often falls by the wayside.

- Social studies and science are minimally taught.

- Eighty percent of the teachers indicated that students spend more then 20% of their total instructional time practicing for the end-of-grade tests.

- More than 28% indicated that students spend more than 60% percent of instructional time practicing for tests.

- Sixty-seven percent indicated that they had changed their teaching methods as a result of the ABC program.

- Seventy-seven percent felt that their morale was lower, and 76% stated that they believed that the accountability program would not improve quality of education in their schools.

- More than 76% felt that their jobs were more stressful than before the ABCs program was implemented. (pp. 200-201)

These results show that with respect to impact on teacher performance and beliefs, high-stakes accountability programs could be double-edged swords. On one hand, teachers are spending more time on core content areas like reading, writing, and mathematics. They change their instructional practices to match the dictates of the test. Nevertheless, time spent on core content areas leave little or no time for other subject areas such as social studies and science, a phenomenon referred to as "narrowing." Moreover, the programs reduced teacher morale while increasing anxiety and stress. But there is another side to this issue. For while narrowing of the curriculum does occur (Elmore & Furhman, 2001; Winerip, 2001), other positive outcomes do as well. Elmore and Furhman explained:

> In Kentucky, for example, the accountability system is credited with expanding the content taught to include writing and the humanities. We have seen elementary principals and teachers who are active reformers, as shown by rich examples of student work and many innovative pedagogies. We have also observed high school teachers embracing reform. The teachers in one New York high school accepted the "Regents-exam-for-all" policy enthusiastically. They took personal responsibility for student progress, used data to improve instruction, added instructional time, and

increased professional development. In a Vermont high school, teachers were shocked at low test scores and used state-mandated "action planning" to set ambitious data-driven goals and to emphasize open-end-mathematics questions, to change the algebra sequence, and to broaden the literature curriculum. (p. 69)

(Caution is necessary when interpreting these findings. According to Debray, Parson, and Woodworth (2001), some were based on a study of accountability policies in four high schools in New York and Vermont that "at the time of the study did not involve explicit rewards or sanctions for adults" and therefore raises a question about whether ... findings about school response hold in states that do" (2001, p. 188)).

Attributions

Teachers express different degrees of displeasure with performance pay programs based on their perception of unfairness or inequity in the reward structure. They attribute their success or failure to receive awards or bonuses to what they perceive as circumstances beyond their control or to inequities in the program. A study conducted by the University of Kentucky Institute on Education Reform documented aspects of attribution theory and their linkage with performance pay. Researchers found that "teachers who received rewards were more likely to believe that they could influence student learning. Those who did not receive rewards were more likely to blame factors outside of school for student failure" (cited in SREB, 1997, p. 9). These same teachers were more likely to charge that those receiving rewards cheated. They also were more likely to claim that their failure to receive performance rewards resulted from having to teach without adequate resources, which are necessary for success reflected in student test results.

Research on Performance Pay Programs and Student Achievement

The literature suggests that merit pay and career ladder programs of the 1970s and 1980s were ineffective for myriad reasons, many mentioned earlier in Chapter 2 (Harty et al., 1994; Johnson, 1986; Lortie, 1975; Odden & Kelley, 2002). In one study, Harty et al. (1994) found that "none of the eighteen school districts" they examined that had merit pay and career ladder program "reported significant gains in student achievement"(p. 235). This finding was also echoed by others, including CPRE researchers (Odden & Kelley, 1997). Yet, a closer look reveals that of the two approaches, career ladders seemed the most effective in influencing higher teacher performance and student achievement. Consider the State of Arizona for example.

The Arizona Program

In 1985, the Arizona Legislature piloted a comprehensive career ladder program. The program, which lasted five years, was "to determine if student academic achievement was enhanced through recognizing and developing high levels of teacher performance through a promotion system based on competence" (Packard & Dereshiwsky, 1988b). The system was voluntary. During the first year of the program (1985-86), seven districts joined followed by three the following year and five the next.

A study that spotlighted the program's success—defined strictly as increased student achievement—was conducted by Dickson (1990). Because the program was voluntary for teachers, the study was designed to examine the performance of two groups of students in grades 1, 2, 3, and 4-6: students whose teachers participated in the program (career ladder or CL) and students whose teachers opted not to participate (non career ladder or NCL). The overarching objective of the study was to "track trends in achievement scores" (p. 7). The study compared two samples of teachers (244 in year 1, and 224 in year 2) matched on "class regroupings, school characteristics, grade, and class size." A group of CL teachers ($n = 112$) and a group of NCL teachers ($n = 112$) were compared in year 1 and two similar groups were compared in year 2. Researchers used The Iowa Test of Basic Skills (ITBS), a nationally standardized test that was administered district-wide to students to measure performance in reading comprehension, math, and language.

After using regression analysis and ANCOVA (two robust statistical procedures) to analyze the data, the researcher found "the means for Career Level teachers consistently outpaced those of NCL teachers" (p. 15) by 2 to 6 points. This finding was true for both year 1 and year 2 samples. Although the findings were not significant, the researchers wrote that they saw "a remarkably consistent pattern were CL teachers' scores were higher than those of NCL teachers and higher for higher levels within the CL program itself" (p. 17). These findings were corroborated in other evaluation studies by Packard & Dereshiwsky (1988b; 1990). Examining the program's impact on teacher performance and student achievement, the researchers concluded:

- Students in Phase I CL districts are reaching their learning potentials at a dramatically higher level than they were prior to organizational restructuring & implementation of the CL program, and they are impacting student achievement even more when they are compared to non-CL districts.

- Students taught by CL teachers are making learning gains, which are statistically significant.

- Student achievement depends more on the level of teacher performance than on the number of years teaching.

- CL teachers understand their local, district, and classroom curriculum objectives better than they did before; they are receiving better inservice which is directed toward improved teaching effectiveness; and they are able to see greater student learning in subject(s) they are teaching. (Packard & Dereshiwsky, 1990, p. 52)

Dickson's conclusions and those by Packard and Dereshiwsky seem to suggest that career ladder incentive programs that are well structured—teacher performance is aligned with student performance—can indeed influence student achievement in a positive way.

In their book *Paying Teachers for What They Know* Odden and Kelley (1997, 2002) observed that many districts that implemented career ladder programs "were dropped within a few years" (p. 35) because of inadequate funding, inadequate assessment and mismanagement, opposition by teacher unions, and because they did not produce lasting effects. While this observation seems accurate, it seems that when career ladder programs are planned and implemented as in Arizona during the first years of the program, they are capable of improving both teacher and student performance. Before they achieve result such as those in Arizona, however, they must be structured with some key elements in mind—logical assumptions, relevant objectives, and Lawler's components (core values, processes, practices, structures). The components and guidelines depicted in Appendix A must also be evident throughout the program. Additionally, the program must have long-term commitment and support from both professional educators and policymakers.

The evidence on whether or not recent incentive award programs such as knowledge-based, skills-based, group-based, or gainsharing award systems increase student achievement is mixed and tentative (CPRE, 2001). This is partly due to the short period during which most education incentive programs have been functioning in schools. The uncertainty of the impact of these programs was borne out in a study by the Kentucky Office of Accountability. The researchers found that gains in KIRIS scores "significantly overstate the improvement in student achievement" and that "it is not clear whether any appreciable, generalizable gains in achievement have been produced in some grades and subjects ... the Panel is also unable to determine which of many factors might have caused exaggerated gains on KIRIS" (cited in Abelman and Kenyon, 1996, pp. 28-29).

These findings may not reflect the total picture regarding performance pay programs. Similar to the way evidence from class size studies seems to be converging around acceptable conclusions that students in smaller classes learn more primarily because teachers' efficient use of time enables them to offer better instruction (Finn, 2002; Finn & Achilles, 1999, 2002; Glass & Smith, 1978; Grissmer, et al., 2000; Jacobson, 2001; Molar, et al, 1999; Rice, 1999; Stecher & Bohrnstedt, 2002; Viadero, 2001; Willms, 2000), so too evidence from existing performance-based pay programs seems to indicate that students whose teachers participate in performance pay systems tend to achieve more because of myriad factors that characterize effective instruction as well as an effective incentive program. Research on incentive programs in Kentucky, Dallas, and North Carolina provide some other perspectives.

The Kentucky Program

Kentucky schools are perhaps among the most studied schools in the nation. This is due largely to the well-known case, *Rose v. Council for Better Education, Inc.* (1989), in which the Supreme Court of Kentucky ruled that the state had "failed to establish an efficient system of common schools throughout the Commonwealth." This decision resulted in the Kentucky Educational Reform Act (KERA) and the KIRIS, which together transformed the entire state's K-12 public school system. As a result, districts in Kentucky were among the fist to implement the newer incentive programs and in turn were among the first to attract close scrutiny from policymakers, professional educators, and education researchers from far and wide. During the 1990s, CPRE conducted numerous studies on the way performance-based incentive programs functioned in the state. Carolyn Kelley (1998), a CPRE researcher who may hold the record for conducting empirical studies on the effectiveness of Kentucky's incentive program, conducted many of these studies.

In one of her much cited studies (1998), Kelley examined 16 Kentucky elementary, middle, and high schools that initiated reforms under KERA. Under this act, schools receive one of five status designations depicted in Table 8—reward, successful, improving, decline, or crisis. Schools earn their designation from KIRIS results, the assessment system used to measure student achievement. She found that reward/reward and reward/ successful schools shared common characteristics that accounted for their successful status. First, their curriculum was aligned with assessment instruments and the state curriculum guides. Second, they all incorporated strategies for test taking in their regular instructions. Third, all had highly competent and professionally oriented teachers who were considered to be professionally "in the loop," which meant "they had direct contacts with the accountability program through professional teacher ties and current or past participation of teacher on state committees" (p. 310).

On the other hand, schools designated reward/decline reflected the opposite characteristics. For example, their curriculum was not aligned with assessment instruments and the state curriculum guide, test-taking strategies were emphasized, teachers were generally out of the loop, and "the principal was more of a nurturing figure than a strong instructional leader...." (p. 312). The principals and teachers in these schools were doing everything opposite to what standards-based reform required.

The next group of schools, decline/reward or "turnaround schools," demonstrated remarkable resilience after they were given adequate financial resources, and, most important, a "distinguished educator." This individual had "broad powers" but served as an advisor and expert coach who in addition to advising, answered questions and provided assistance for curriculum and instructional improvement. Kelley reported that of the 53 schools that were in decline, 31 "were in rewards the second cycle and the remaining 22 schools were improving or successful" (p. 313). Evidently, a combination of rewards, sanctions, and assistance contributed to the schools improvement and student performance.

The Dallas Independent School District Program

Unlike Kentucky, where sweeping reform was initiated by the state legislature, the Dallas Independent School District (DISD) performance-based program originated from the school board and several recommendations by a special commission appointed in 1991 to restructure public education. Ladd (1999) designed and conducted an evaluation study to determine the program's impact on student achievement. Recall that findings from this study discussed in Chapter 2 showed that DISD's performance-based program (a) positively impacted the academic performance of white and Hispanic seventh-grade students, (b) provided little or no improvement for Black students, (c) influenced a high turnover rate among principals, (d) influenced a decline in the dropout rate, and (e) increased school attendance. While the program failed to improve learning among all three groups of students, it was partially responsible for increasing the achievement of two student groups and highlighted the need to focus more time and resources on Black students. It would be interesting to know whether extra time and resources have made a difference.

The North Carolina Program

In one of the first comprehensive studies of the North Carolina accountability performance pay program, Jones et al. (1999) examined the program's impact on students. North Carolina's performance-based program, entitled the New ABC of Public Education, is similar to other high-stakes accountability programs in that they have performance levels that are linked to different amounts of bonus money. "Schools are publicly labeled *exemplary, meets expectations,* and *adequate*" (pp. 199-200). Teachers receive bonuses of $1,500 if their schools improve student performance and face the prospect of removal if student performance fell below expectations. Using a survey design, the researchers mailed questionnaires to a stratified random sample of 470 teachers, of which 230 or 50.2% responded.

Table 8: Rewards and Sanctions Associated with the Kentucky Accountability Program

Status	Program Outcome	Effect
Reward	Exceeds accountability goals	Monetary award
Successful	Meets accountability goals	No effect
Improving	Above baseline, below goal	Transformation plan
Decline	Less than 5 points below baseline	Distinguished educator Improvement funds Transformation plan
Crisis	5 or more points below baseline	Distinguished educator with broad powers Loss of job security Improvement funds Transformation plan

Adapted with permission from Corwin Press, Inc., *Educational Policy*, Vol. 12, No. 3, p. 307. © 1998 Corwin Press, Inc.

When asked to assess how the program had affected students, 28% of the respondents "indicated that they felt their students were more prepared for learning and 15% indicated that their students had more confidence, 61% felt their students experienced more anxiety, and 24% felt that their students were less confident." A substantial number, 48.4%, "indicated that the ABC program has a negative impact on students' love of learning" (p. 201).

While these data do not have the same degree of credibility as those from experimental, quasi-experimental, and gain-score studies, they provide perceptual evidence that supports the view that performance-based incentive programs positively affect student learning. Results from studies such as these, however, are suspect because opinions and perceptions are far less reliable than outcome measures such as achievement scores, which are seen as preeminent measures of effectiveness by comprehensive school reformers. Self-report data or teachers' perceptions of a program's impact on student performances do not by themselves build a convincing case for validity and legitimacy.

In a well-designed study from North Carolina, Smith and Mickelson (2000) examined the impact of Charlotte-Mecklenburg School System's (CMS) comprehensive reform initiative on student learning. While this study did not address performance pay directly, it gives some perspective on the effectiveness, or in this case, ineffectiveness of comprehensive school reform approaches. The researchers compared CMS's comprehensive reform initiative implemented during the 1991-1992 school year with two other North Carolina districts and the state as a whole. The two districts used as comparison groups did not experience any of the reform initiatives (high standards, benchmark goals, increased principal autonomy, and high-stakes testing) instituted in CMS. After analyzing a large data set, the researchers concluded:

> We found little evidence to support claims of distinctive success of CMS's reform program in improving student outcomes. Although CMS may be able to claim progress in improving participation and success in AP courses and some other higher level courses, the school district's progress on other broader indicators of secondary school outcomes—SAT scores, dropout rates, core high school courses—largely paralleled those in comparison districts. Moreover, CMS's progress in improving reading and math proficiency in Grades 3-8 lagged behind that of the comparison school systems. While some of these lags were small, they were consistent and widespread, which helps explain why CMS generally underperformed the comparison districts in these crucial subject areas by a larger margin at the end of the time period we examined than at the beginning. (p. 121)

To date, results from this CMS study and results from the Arizona, Kentucky, and DISD programs present some of the most credible evidence on the effectiveness of performance pay programs. To varying degrees, these programs show that incentive programs linking teacher performance and rewards to student achievement do indeed influence student learning in positive ways. Based on evidence from Texas (Ladd, 1999), however, most of the influence seems to benefit students from high socioeconomic backgrounds. Whether these observations will be supported as more studies are conducted will become more evident in time.

While performance pay studies such as one conducted by Jones et al. (1999) in North Carolina are useful, school leaders in other districts should be cautioned against attaching the same degree of importance to them as they do to studies such as to those conducted in Arizona, Kentucky, and Dallas. This observation holds true for case studies conducted by CPRE researchers. According to CPRE, case studies have been conducted on school-based performance award programs in Boston, Charlotte-Mecklenburg, Cincinnati, Dallas, Kentucky, Philadelphia, San Fernando, California; and case studies on knowledge- and skills-based pay programs have been conducted in Cincinnati, San Fernando, and Douglas County, Colorado. While these case studies and several CPRE survey studies "provide contextual information and specific design features" (CPRE, 2001, NP) that can help in the development of incentive programs, they do not provide the reliable data policymakers need when making adoption decisions. Case studies and survey studies are good beginnings, but it is worth noting that performance pay systems will survive and play a role in transforming public education only so long as educators and policy researchers are able to build a critical mass of incontrovertible empirical evidence, similar to what medical researchers did when they established a convincing link between nicotine and lung cancer.

Chapter Summary

An adequate research base does not exist for district and school-based performance pay programs. This is partly due to the recency of these programs in schools. It is much too early for conclusive results from these programs as most of them are still in their nascent stage. Additionally, insufficient research has been conducted on those that are fully functional. The evidence is too sparse and tentative for conclusive results that could inform policy development. Moreover, as Kelley, Heneman, and Milanowski (2001) admitted, attributing any increase in student performance to incentive programs "require a leap of faith that the program itself was the key policy variable that produced the student achievement gains. In all three of these contexts, there were multiple types of policy interventions initiated at the federal, state, and school levels that could have influenced student performance gains in important ways" (p. 3).

Nevertheless, emerging research on existing programs in states such as Kentucky and Texas seems to indicate that well-designed incentive programs do affect student performance in positive ways. When the impact of incentive systems on teacher motivation and performance is considered, the evidence presents a mixed picture. Some results show performance pay programs motivate teachers to perform at higher levels of proficiency while others indicate the programs do not. Yet when teacher attitudes are considered, most studies indicate that teachers regard performance pay favorably. Favorable ratings of performance pay programs do not deter teachers and principals from expressing displeasure with them. Many educators are displeased with the heavy emphasis placed on high-stakes tests as primary measures of success or failure. Others tend to attribute their success in receiving or failure to receive performance awards or bonuses to factors beyond their control and to perceived inequities in the program.

On the whole, after examining the history, major arguments for and against, the critical variables, emerging research on existing programs, and design and decision-making processes used to develop performance pay programs, what grand conclusions are evident? This question is the focus of the next chapter.

7

CONCLUSIONS AND OBSERVATIONS

In the concluding chapter of *Policy Studies for Educational Leaders*, Fowler (2000) observed that the dominant values driving education reform include economic growth, freedom, and excellence. She defined freedom as choices that some groups in the community want parents to have, and excellence as the "way to produce a workforce better able to compete in the global economy" (p. 345). These seem to be the major values promoted by some proponents of school reform. Other reformers and policymakers, however, want reform efforts to emphasize equality and equity. On a larger scale, school reform with its myriad waves and models is about protecting, preserving, and promoting these values.[27]

It is argued here that comprehensive school reform includes performance pay programs that provide excellent opportunities to preserve and promote values embraced by all segments of the education community. On one hand, these programs could be integrated into existing whole-school standards-based approaches. On the other hand, they could be regarded as vehicles for "reengineering" education or unifiers that link all facets of comprehensive reform into united, coherent wholes. The components and factors necessary for effective incentive pay programs are numerous, as revealed in Appendices A and B. However, the most critical appear to be these: (a) a comprehensive, systemic approach to reform; (b) attention to what motivates teachers; (c) effective professional development with adequate time for learning and application; (d) reliable assessment of teacher and student performance; (e) credible holistic evaluation of program processes and outcomes; (f) participation and collaboration among interested parties; and (g) adequate funding. Additionally, emerging research findings should also play a central role in the design and development of performance pay programs.[28] This chapter addresses conclusions relative to each of these seven factors and to the emerging role research should play in the design and development of performance pay systems. In each case, the discussion will be framed within the context of considerations that are most likely to result in effective performance pay programs that positively and substantially influence comprehensive reform.

Conclusion 1: Performance pay systems are likely to succeed if they are integral parts of comprehensive, systemic school reform efforts.

As discussed in Chapter 1, the major components of comprehensive reform include (a) a focus on student performance, (b) schools as the unit of performance, (c) continuous improvement strategies, (d) inspections, (e) accountability categories, (f) public reporting, and (g) consequences attached to performance levels. Performance pay systems should have incentives and rewards that influence performance levels. Pay systems should be structured in a way that provides teachers, principals, and noninstructional staff with tangible evidence that their efforts are appreciated and valued. The system should reflect adherence to standards of adequacy such as those outlines in Appendices A and B. In essence, a comprehensive performance pay program should:

1. reflect preplanning considerations,
2. reflect critical assumptions and agreements,
3. reflect clear goals and objectives,
4. be student focused,
5. emphasize professional development,
6. be driven by reliable research and assessment data,
7. be holistically accountable to students, parents, the community, and taxpayers,
8. characterized by appropriate incentives and awards that are aligned with teacher motivational needs,
9. have sanctions that are consistent and equitable,

10. have long-term, adequate and continual funding,
11. be administered and managed in an effective manner,
12. be legally defensible,
13. reflect adherence to change theory and principles such as Fullan's "moral purpose" and "change agency," and
14. be designed and implemented on the bases of valid and reliable results from well-executed evaluation and empirical studies.

Conclusion 2: Performance pay programs are likely to succeed if collaboration is encouraged and nurtured.

The more participants are consulted and treated as equals, the more likely they are to accept and support a performance pay program. Recall that this is the lesson the Denver School System learned after its initial attempt to institute an incentive program without input from teachers. The plan was adopted the second time after extensive collaboration with the Denver Classroom Teacher Association. School officials and policymakers should focus on developing "collaborative cultures" that reflect the five characteristics Fullan (1999) advocated. In essence, collaborative cultures

- foster diversity while trust-building,
- provoke anxiety and contains it,
- engage in knowledge creation (tacit to explicitly, explicitly to explicit),
- combine connectedness with openendednness, and
- fuse the spiritual, political and intellectual. (p. 37)

Together these characteristics provide "deep meaning" that translates into enriching and productive experiences for everyone. They enhance the environment and make it conducive to creativity and meaningful productivity.

Conclusion 3: Performance pay programs are likely to succeed if attention is given to what motivates teachers.

Familiarity with motivational theories could help developers of performance pay systems keep the "moral purpose" and "change agency" horses in front of the compensation and reward cart. To do this, there are five research-driven themes to consider: First, theories of motivation can be categorized according to content theories or process theories. Content theories focus on what energizes and motivates human behavior while process theories focus on how motivation occurs. Second, rewards to motivate teachers can be classified as *extrinsic* (e.g., income, prestige, and power over others), *intrinsic* (psychic, internal and intangible, e.g., pride and satisfaction when students learn), and *ancillary* (good working condition, professional growth opportunities, retirement benefits). Third, of all the intrinsic rewards that can be identified in teaching, professional efficacy ranks first. There seems to be no deeper satisfaction teachers can experience while teaching. Fourth, teachers base their decision to continue or leave teaching on the lack of or insufficiency of both extrinsic and ancillary rewards. The implication here is that while some teachers may continue teaching because of professional efficacy, in the end they too may leave because of inadequate pay or the absence of opportunities for meaningful professional growth and development. The economic boom of the 1990s made leaving attractive for many, and, once the and post-September 11th security difficulties and the corporate-related financial scandals abate, another climate of prosperity may beckon other educators to do likewise. Fifth, theories developed by Alderfer (1972), Csikszentmihalyi (1990), Locke & Latham (1995), and Ozcan (1996) appear to be among the most practical with clear implications for designing performance pay programs.

Conclusion 4: Performance pay programs are likely to succeed if school officials make continual professional development an indispensable part of the program.

The literature is replete with studies that highlight the ineffectiveness of professional development programs. As we saw in Chapter 3, the reason for most ineffective professional development programs include (a) lack of coordination with other programs aimed at improving instruction, (b) failure to bring about change in the absence of continuity in training, (c) focus on changing behavior with no provision for collaborative learning, (d) weakness in design, and (e) insufficient time to participate in knowledge and competency-building activities. Furthermore, some observers find professional development to be "sporadic and rudimentary" while others "regard it as insufficient and ineffective." The literature also suggests that workers in business organizations and private schools receive more professional development opportunities than do public school teachers. According to some researchers (e.g., Monahan, 1996), contemporary systems of incentives and rewards encourage teachers to engage in more traditional and outdated forms of professional development. But what seems to be the major culprit of ineffective professional development is insufficient time for teachers to engage in meaningful growth and development activities and to transfer and apply what they learn.

Fortunately, there are ways to solve most of these problems. Some of the most practical approaches seem to be: (a) using adult development and learning theories such as Knowles' andragogy and Boyatzis' postulates and experiential typology to guide the design and planning process; (b) providing a regularly scheduled block of time for professional development during the school year and opportunities during summer months where teachers are paid to attend; (c) aligning professional development activities and student performance (consider the approach used in Florida where results from the state-wide achievement test (FCAT) dictate the kind of training teachers receive); (d) providing adequate and sustained funding; and (e) adopting professional development models and approaches such as those suggested by Joyce and Showers (1995), Knowles et al. (1998), and Elmore (1997, 2002). Other models such as those advocated by Sparks and Loucks-Horsley (1989), as well as professional development principles and research-driven guidelines articulated by the NCSD and the Eisenhower Professional Development Project, can help build and support an effective system-wide professional development program. These are among the factors that seem to be working in places such as New York Community School District #2, where the entire school system, including the school board and the central office, is involved in and responsible for professional development. Professional development activities pervade the entire district. They are embedded in the district's philosophy, they are the way of life, and they are how things are done around there. While caution is justified with adapting initiatives designed and intended for particular environments, some initiatives are worth emulating. The conceptualization and practice of professional development in District #2 appeals to reason, common sense, and gut instinct, all of which seem to communicate the same message—follow the yellow brick road.

Conclusion 5: Performance pay programs are likely to succeed if they are aligned with a credible and reliable process of teacher and student performance assessment.

High-stakes tests are integral to comprehensive school improvement. These tests drive school reform and, in so doing, define what student achievement is and is not. They are indicative of the quality of instruction provided in each school and the extent to which entire districts are effective in increasing student achievement.

The consensus among policy researchers, policymakers, and education officials suggests that schools will become truly effective when curriculum development, professional development, teacher performance assessment, and measures of student performance are aligned with performance pay systems. This means the following: First, the curriculum should be designed with standards and benchmarks that encourage and challenge students to think, solve problems, and make good decisions (see Figure 1 in Chapter 2). Second, teachers should be given opportunities to increase their knowledge, develop skills and competencies in their subject areas, and transfer new skills and competencies to the classroom in ways that influence student learning. Third, teacher performance should be assessed from two perspectives—one using what I call *first level* assessment strategies such as portfolios, teacher tests, peer evaluation, TQM, and the other using *second level* assessment techniques such as high-stakes student achievement tests similar to the Texas Assessment of Academic Skills, the Stanford Achievement Test used in California, Virginia Standards of Learning, and the Florida Comprehensive Assessment Test. (For more on first level or authentic alternative assessment, see pp. 278-279 of Hodge & Jones, 2000.) Fourth, teachers should be compensated and rewarded based on results from first level assessment as well as results from second level assessment. The incentive approaches discussed in Chapter 4 exemplify comprehensive systems where most of these components are integrated and aligned. Note that comprehensive assessment approaches like those developed by the Interstate New Teacher Assessment and Support Consortium, ETS's PRAXIS program, and the NBPTS are examples of first level assessment approaches that are used by some districts for making decisions about teacher qualifications and readiness to move between pay levels. A well-designed performance pay program should reflect both first and second level assessment and, most importantly, should reveal a tightly woven tapestry of standards, benchmarks, professional development activities, compensations, rewards, and incentives.

Conclusion 6: Performance pay programs are likely to succeed if decisions about their design, development, implementation, and continuance are based on reliable data derived from comprehensive program evaluation.

During the current era of education reform, conventional wisdom and accepted practice advocate comprehensive evaluation of all reform initiatives. The framework for evaluation includes the following components: standards and benchmarks, curriculum development, professional development, teacher assessment, and student assessment. Districts have a smorgasbord of first level assessment approaches with which to evaluate their comprehensive reform programs. The most prevalent seem to be professionally developed approaches by Interstate New Teacher Assessment and Support Consortium, the National Board for Professional Teaching Standards, PRAXIS by the Educational Testing Service, and the Danielson standards that are linked to PRAXIS III. Some districts have also recognized the effectiveness of portfolios and action research as performance assessment approaches. To conduct second level assessment of student performance, virtually all states have developed or adopted a standardized test similar to the Texas Assessment of Academic Skills, Arizona's Instrument to Measure Standards, Michigan Education Assessment Program, and the Florida Comprehensive Assessment Test.

While both first and second level assessment conducted by districts can be used to help gauge the effectiveness of school reform—which should include performance pay systems—they are limited in their ability to address all aspects of a comprehensive reform. This is where quantitative and qualitative approaches to evaluation can contribute to ensuring accountability. Examples of quantitative approaches that can assay comprehensive reform include models by the Joint Committee on Standards for Educational Evaluation, Stufflebeam's CIPP Model (1974), and New American Schools (Stringfield, Ross, & Smith, 1996). Qualitative approaches on the other hand have included case studies, focus groups, and "fourth generation" designs that comprise standards of adequacy such as credibility, transferability, generalizability, and conformability. Combining first and second level assessment strategies with quantitative and qualitative evaluation designs could create a systematic, robust approach for ensuring accountability in comprehensive school reform.

Conclusion 7: Performance pay programs are likely to succeed if they are funded adequately over a long period.

The do-more-with-less philosophy espoused by some in policy-making positions is a direct call to uphold efficiency as a central value in school reform. Not too many people can make convincing arguments against promoting efficiency. After all, it is among our most cherished values. Yet, while it is true that doing more with less is feasible in some instances, it is not so in others. The simple truth is that if teachers are being held accountable for increasing both their own and students' performance, they should expect to be compensated and rewarded in substantial ways that signal respect for them as professionals. Incentive pay systems need money to make them what they are—motivational forces in the lives of teachers.

Whether the debate is for an overarching philosophy based on equity or one based on adequacy and accountability, discussants must always return to the question of how best to fund performance pay programs. Cost structures have been advanced for both comprehensive school reform and performance pay plans (see Odden, 1999b, 2000a, 2000b, 2001). These structures seem reasonable given the complexity of traditional funding formulas (see Chapter 4 in Wood & Thompson, 1996). Whether or not these approaches are more effective, school officials should avoid an over reliance on funding incentive programs from outside or private sources. The experience in Dallas is instructive because it suggests that money promised by the business community could be reduced or eliminated at anytime. Full-state funding, as implemented in South Carolina, may be among the most effective and sustained ways to finance performance pay programs. As detailed in a recent paper by Milanowski (2001), however, reallocation is the funding approach preferred and used by most districts adopting performance pay programs.

Conclusion 8: Performance pay programs are likely to influence teacher performance and student achievement if emerging research findings are used in their design and development.

Do incentive programs affect student achievement? Do they influence teacher performance? Emerging empirical evidence suggests some do.

Since most states are only in the "beginning stages of implementing" performance-based incentive programs, it is far too early to say conclusively that what works in the business community (see Lawler, 1998) and in some school districts will work in the majority of the country's 14,891 districts. Evidence on performance pay systems will have to accumulate over time to demonstrate conclusively whether students whose teachers participate in performance pay programs are motivated to higher levels of performance. This may occur because these programs reflect respect for teachers as professionals and emphasize the importance of student achievement as the primary measure of success.

Nevertheless, on examination of a small number of research studies on performance pay systems, six emerging themes are evident:

- First, it appears that student performance is being impacted in profound ways by comprehensive education reform that includes performance pay programs. As scanty and inconclusive as the data may be, research suggests that some incentive programs do influence student learning.

- Second, teacher performance is being impacted in positive ways that are in turn positively influencing student achievement.

- Third, while there are instances of increased teacher performance and positive student achievement, in other instances teacher morale has decreased and their stress levels have increased with no appreciable student gains.

- Fourth, while gains in student achievement are evident in the core content areas of reading and math, curricula are being narrowed and instruction in other courses such as science and social studies are being de-emphasized or ignored all together.

- Fifth, despite narrowed and de-emphasized subjects, positive outcomes such as content expansion, innovative pedagogies, the embracement of reform by many teachers, and an increase in the use of action planning are documented in the research literature.

- Sixth, both "policy-based incentives" (e.g., incentive pay) and "inherent incentives" (e.g., positive student feedback, increased student performance) are important to teachers, but only inherent incentives give teachers real and lasting satisfaction. An implication here is that performance pay systems should be structured more around inherent incentives and less so around policy-based incentives.

Some Final Observations

While this book has focused on research on performance pay systems, education reformers and policymakers may want to consider some emerging issues and conditions that could slow or derail whole-school reform, and especially the performance pay movement. The most obvious of these conditions is an economy that provides career alternatives to teachers who may be attracted to less stressful, demanding, and far better paying employment.[29] (While some economists now see an economy that is growing stronger, others see a weak economy that teeters between recession and depression.) Additionally, stricter licensing requirements demanded by comprehensive reformers may discourage prospective teachers from entering the teaching profession. The dynamics of both these realities compound and exacerbate the current teacher shortage crises.

Second, emerging evidence has begun to paint an unsettling picture of the true impact of high-stakes testing and comprehensive reform programs such as Success for All, Roots and Wings, and other programs advanced by New American Schools. Attention to this evidence is important because many districts and schools use these reform models to address the rigor and particulars of whole-school reform. The programs serve as mechanisms through which districts and schools align standards, curriculum, instruction, professional development, teacher assessment, and student performance. Importantly, these programs are used to achieve the kinds of student performance outcome data that help determine whether schools receive passing or failing grades and whether teachers receive rewards and bonuses.

The three major complaints against comprehensive reform programs are these: (a) they make only a dent in the performance of children from impoverished and low socioeconomic backgrounds because school intervention comes too late in these students' development, (b) the programs are not as effective as proponents claim because while they raise the achievement level of students from high socioeconomic backgrounds, they invariably raise the dropout rate among low SES students, and (c) research conducted on these programs is suspect because of inadequate designs, faulty methodology, and because the original designers, who conducted most of the research on these programs, have much to gain from touting positive outcomes. A tide of disparagement can be discerned in either positions taken or research conducted by, among others, Carpenter (2000), Bracey (1998, 2002), Goertz (2001b), Herman (1999), Hoover (2000), Orlich (2000), Smith and Mickelson (2000), Traub (2000), Wong and Meyer (1998), Walberg and Greenberg (1999), and several others documented on the Internet, in particular http://www.alt-sfa.com/, a site devoted to collecting and cataloging reports and empirical evidence that refute claims made by apologists and proponents of the New American Schools.[30]

From a policy perspective, some observers (Fowler, 2000; Weiss1992) would contend that these criticisms represent nothing more that a liberal backlash against ideologies and policies advocated and championed by business and religious conservatives, which is what happens when high-stakes tests mask deficiencies in minority student achievement. This masking in turn contributes to higher dropout rates among minority students than their white counterparts. This is what one researcher (McNeil, 2000a, 2000b) found when she examined the Texas accountability system and discovered evidence that teaching to the test undermined or detracted from real learning. There may be an element of truth to her claim as conservatives and rightwing ideologues have a "self-interested, commercial vision" (Bracey, 2002, p. 185) and champion and emphasize choice, standards, high-stake testing, and public grading—the quality and efficiency values that are dear to this group. The New Politics Liberals and "Neolibralists," on the other hand, believe in improving education also but not at the expense of sacrificing equality and equal access to quality education for all children (Fowler, 2000). It would seem that liberals (those who Bracey would say have a "communal, democratic vision") have found some convincing wedge issues and valid points of contention. By articulating unintended consequences of standardized testing, and the inadequacies of evaluation and research methodologies employed by supporters of standards-based reform, they send a message that not all that glitters amidst comprehensive school reform is gold.

In criticizing the way new standards-driven programs are evaluated and studied, the "New Politics Liberals" are also questioning conservatives' foundation of credibility and legitimacy. The ideologies of special interests are evident in the advancement and implementation of recent initiatives, as well as in their criticisms. This view was articulated by Bracey (2000) who suggested that "the movement toward high-stakes testing is not about education; it is about power and control and ideological agendas" (p. 92). This brings to the fore the whole business about whose agenda is driving education reform and for what ultimate purpose. In the end, do children really matter? Should the ultimate aim of comprehensive reform with its performance pay appendage be to privatize and marketize education? And, with Fullan's (1993, 1999) admonition that "moral purpose" or making a meaningful difference in students' lives should be the principal focus of change in education, are reformers truly concerned about this seemingly lofty goal? From the discussion in preceding chapters, it appears that comprehensive reform, including the integration of performance pay systems, answers the first question in the affirmative, the second in the negative, and the third in the affirmative.

The third issue is the misalignment between federal, state, and local reform policies. While policymakers and practitioners envision a coherent, seamless accountability system, the reality is quite different. Margaret Goertz (2001a) explained the issue when she wrote:

> ... although the intent of federal legislation was to create single and "seamless" accountability systems that would treat all schools equally, only 22 states had single or "unitary" accountability systems in place in 2000-01. A congressionally mandated review panel concluded that the variability that results from flexibility in the Title I legislation confound[s] efforts to target resources at low performing schools....The flexibility/uniformity tradeoff extends to the local level as well. The more discretion states give their districts to create standards, set performance goals, or develop accountability policies, the greater the variation in local policy and practice. (p. 64)

While some disjointedness and misalignment are inevitable during school comprehensive reform efforts, reformers should continually advocate and work towards more uniformity in expectations, standards, outcomes, and overall accountability.

The fourth issue has to do with growing displeasure with standardized high-stakes testing, arguably the centerpiece and most salient component of comprehensive school reform. This unpopularity has been most recently documented in New York (Winerip, 2001) and in the 32nd and 33rd Annual Phi Delta Kappa/Gallup Poll of the Public's Attitudes Toward the Public Schools (Rose & Gallup, 2000; 2001), a scientifically valid and reliable survey. Appendix C shows five questions taken from the most recent polls conducted in 2000 and 2001. Of the five, four reflect a general displeasure with the dominant role standardized testing plays in current reform efforts. Question #1 shows that while 20% of the public in 1997 believed too much emphasis was placed on testing in the public schools, this figure increased to 30% in 2000 and 31% in 2001, a 10 and 11 point increase, respectively. Responses to this question also show that while 48% of the public in 1997 believed about the right amount of emphasis was placed on testing in public schools, the proportion decreased to 43% in 2000, a five-point reduction. Questions 2, 3, and 4 are equally revealing about what the public thinks about testing. First, these questions show that the public does not agree with the purpose for which standardized tests are used. Instead of using tests to measure how much students have learned, a convincing majority in 2000 (65%) and 2001 (66%) believed they should be used to determine the kind of instruction students need in the future. Second, the majority in 2000 (68%) believed that the best way to measure student achievement is not solely by standardized tests, but rather in-class activities and homework. In 2001, this percentage decreased slightly to 65%. Additionally, while 13% of the public believed that a single standardized test is the best way to measure student academic achievement, 41% believed schools should use a combination of standardized and teacher-designed tests. A similar proportion (44%) believed portfolios of students' work and other demonstrations of academic competence should be emphasized over standardized tests. No comparisons could be made with data from the 2001 poll as this question was omitted during the survey.

In a broader sense, growing evidence suggests that the accountability movement has spawned a host of challenges that must be confronted if whole-school reform is to be truly effective. Many of the challenges are explained by researchers and policy analysts in *From the Capitol to the Classroom: Standards-Based Reform in the States, the One Hundredth Yearbook of the National Society for the Study of Education* edited by Susan Fuhrman (2001). In addition, Elmore and Fuhrman (2001) articulated several other challenges in "Holding Schools Accountable: Is It Working?" a *Phi Delta Kappan* article. Among them: (a) accountability or performance requires changes in schools' internal capacities for instruction; (b) capacity matters, but not much is being done about it; (c) stakes matters, but we need to know more about how they matter; and (d) the expectations underlying performance-based accountability systems are often unclear to the public, to students, and to school systems.[31]

The final observation brings us once again to the merit and worth of teacher incentive or performance pay programs. Do they affect student performance? Does the American public support them? Let us examine these two questions once again with the goal of clarifying the role money, salary, compensation, reward, and incentives play in improving education.

The last question was partially addressed in the Phi Delta Kappan/Gallup Poll mentioned earlier and in the data shown in Appendix C (see Question 5). When asked, "How closely should a teacher's salary be tied to his or her students' academic achievement?" (Rose & Gallup, 2000, p. 54), an overwhelming majority (60%) said "very or somewhat closely tied," 25% said "very closely tied," and 35% said "somewhat closely tied." These responses were different for 12% of the respondents who said "not very closely tied" and 24% who said "not at all tied." Clearly, these data indicate substantial support among the public for linking teacher pay to student performance.

But while the public supports this linkage, does this mean that incentive pay systems necessarily affect student achievement in meaningful and measurable ways? Do they influence higher student achievement? Obviously, these questions were not and could not be addressed in the Kappan/Gallup Poll because they require a more robust quantitative research design (true experimental) than a survey. To date, much of the research on performance pay systems conducted by CPRE and others has yielded results that show that they

- provide clear goals for teachers, administrators, and policy makers and thus help teachers channel their efforts toward these priorities;
- leverage other resources, including professional development, to support these goals;
- produce outcomes many teachers view as positive, including monetary rewards and opportunities to see student performance improve, to collaborate with other teachers, and to participate in meaningful professional development; and
- improve school performance. (Odden, 2001, p. 89)

However, most of these findings were based on studies conducted with nonexperimental research designs that lack the robustness of true experimental designs. Therefore, what we are left with are uncorroborated, inclusive, and dubious findings of whether these programs are directly and unquestionably responsible for improving student performance. It seems likely that we will always be hostage to the "multivariable syndrome," the idea that student performance is influenced not only by a single or a few factors, but rather by a multitude of variables among which performance pay is but one, albeit an important one.

While empirical evidence from true experimental designs is scanty, as we saw in Chapter 6, some existing studies suggest performance pay programs do positively influence student achievement, and this is despite Nelson's (2001) pronouncement that pay-by-results programs will result in "a loss of trust in the learning community, the ascendance of competition and corresponding breakdown of cooperation in and among schools, and, most significantly, the corruption of genuine improvement efforts" (p 386). This is also despite somber results from a RAND study (Grissmer, et al., 2000) that found, among other things, no correlation between higher teacher salaries and student performance. But results from this study should be interpreted circumspectly because (a) it only addressed NAEP student achievement data from 1990 to 1996, the period when comprehensive reform initiatives and performance pay programs were in their embryonic stages, and (b) it did not directly investigate the newer knowledge-, competency-, and group-based performance pay programs. From all indications, then, and with respect to their impact on teacher and student performance, we have to accept that fact that the jury is still out on performance pay systems, but we must also acknowledge that there are indications that some jurors are leaning towards an affirmative vote. In fact, at this juncture in the whole-school reform movement, our conclusion about performance pay programs must be similar to the General Accounting Office's conclusion about whether government-financed school voucher programs improve student performance: "Studies have found both higher achievement and little or no difference, but none of the findings can be considered definitive" (U.S. General Accounting Office, 2001, p. 27).

It is uncertain whether definitive studies will ever surmount the multivariable syndrome. What is certain is that the education community must continue with reform initiatives that directly or indirectly influence classroom instruction and student achievement in profound, substantive, and measurable ways. Because performance pay systems are system-wide, attempts to align most of their critical factors while focusing on teacher and student outcomes may contribute to reducing the risks to this country identified and articulated almost two decades ago by the National Commission on Excellence in Education. Whether they are given the chance to succeed or fail on their own merit will largely depend on whether researchers can provide convincing evidence that they affect student achievement. Furthermore, success or failure will likewise hinge on whether competing interests or individuals and groups with the "communal, democratic vision" and those with the "self-interested, commercial vision" are able to suspend ideological and political sabotaging activities—as well as their cacophony of criticisms—that invariably doom education initiatives that do not support and advance their particular agendas. At some point self-interests must give way to what is best for instruction and learning.

APPENDIX A

STANDARDS OF ADEQUACY CHECKLIST FOR DESIGNING PERFORMANCE PAY SYSTEMS

I.
Preliminary Design and Planning Considerations

A. First Steps: The Planning Team, Participation, and Trust Building

___1. Are the right people involved in planning and designing the performance pay system (PPS)?
___2. Are representatives from all interested parties included in the design and planning task force or committee?
___3. Are members of the design or planning task force or committee duly selected by the people they represent?
___4. Are they the legitimate representatives of the groups they purport to represent?

B. Readiness

___1. Are member of the design team familiar with research on performance-based pay systems?
___2. Are they making planning and design decisions based on credible research findings?
___3. Did the planning team examine PPS programs that have been implemented elsewhere?

___4. Have they identified what has and has not worked?
___5. Were teachers and administrators surveyed to discover what they would support?

II.
Guiding Assumptions and Agreements

A. Philosophy, Vision, and Mission

___1. What philosophy serves as the foundation of the program?
___2. What vision guides the program?
___3. What is the program's mission?

B. Assumptions

___1. What assumptions does the planning team hold about:
   a. Bonus, pay-raise, and salary-incentive plans?
   b. Group-based versus knowledge- and competency-based plans?
   c. Objective and subjective measures of performance?

___2. How are teaching skills assumed to be distributed?
   a. Can only a few teachers achieve excellence, or can all teachers?
   b. Does the system emphasize identification of a select few or implementation of all?

___3. Is excellent teaching considered primarily an individual activity or a team effort?
   a. Can individual teachers produce excellence, or does excellence transcend the individual classroom?
   b. If excellence transcends the classroom, how is it defined and articulated?

___4. Do processes (what teachers do) constitute teaching excellence or are learner outcomes the measure of excellence?

___5. Is excellent teaching separable from its results?

___6. If learner outcomes are crucial to excellence, how much are they affected by variables like student ability, previous learning, home and family environment, school environment?

C. Goals and Objectives

What are the goals and objectives of the Program?

___1. To provide the staff with the means of achieving instructional improvement and professional development?
___2. To provide an incentive for professional growth?
___3. To provide a means of recognizing and rewarding teacher performance?
___4. To attract to the community teachers whose knowledge, skills, and professional dedication are markedly above average?
___5. To provide an incentive for talented teachers to remain in teaching in the district?
___6. To raise student achievement scores?
___7. To attract teachers with instructional specialties to teach in the district?
___8. To provide an incentive for teachers to teach in particular areas of the district or with special student groups?

D. A Comprehensive and Systemic Approach

___1. Is the approach used to plan the performance pay system comprehensive and systemic?
___2. Does it show alignment among *effective leadership, teacher performance, the curriculum, standards,* and *student achievement*?
___3. Were new role definitions for teachers and administrators established?
___4. Does the program reflect restructuring the organization of the schools and district in order to accommodate the new role definitions?

III.
Student-Focused Considerations

A. Student Achievement Standards and Outcome Indicators

__1.   Were student achievement standards developed with considerable input from a variety of sources? Are they:
    __a.   Concise and understandable?
    __b.   Rigorous and challenging?
    __c.   Reasonable and attainable?
    __d.   Focused and organized by grade level or course?
    __e.   Measurable whenever possible?
    __f. Reliable and valid for accountability purposes?
    __h.   Aligned directly to content standards?
    __i.   Useful for school improvement?
    __j.   Operationally feasible?
    __g.   Do they have a clear purpose?

__2   In addition to student achievement, what other outcome indicators are used to measure program success?
    __a.   Dropout rates?
    __b.   Retention rates?
    __c.   Customer satisfaction (as measured by periodic survey of satisfaction of parents, students, teachers, other faculty, the general community, employers, higher education admissions officers, and other interested parties)?

B. Student Performance Assessment

__1.   What performance should be assessed?
__2.   Does the PPS address student assessment in a comprehensive manner?
__3.   Are standards realistic and reflect what students really need to know to function in a global environment?
__4.   Are the measures (tests) used to gauge student progress valid and reliable?
__5.   Are the measures aligned with clear goals, a well structured and relevant curriculum, and effective instructional practices?

___6. What types of teacher performance assessment procedures are used?
___7. Are teacher performance assessment linked to specific award amounts?

IV.
District and Instructional Staff Considerations

A. Professional Development

___1. Is the PPS aligned with a professional development component (PDC)?
___2. Does the plan reflect adherence to content and process theories of motivation?
___3. Does the plan provide for intrinsic, extrinsic, and ancillary rewards?
___3. Does the plan provide opportunities for teachers to develop and become motivated through professional efficacy?
___5. Is the PDC coordinated with other programs aimed at improving instruction?
___6. Does the PDC provide for collaborative learning among teachers?
___7. Does the PDC provide adequate time for effective staff development through regular structured interaction?
___8. Does it reflect a clear linkage with student achievement?
___9. Does it reflect adherence to the National Staff Development Council's standards classified as content (research-based), process (follow-up), and context (e.g., leadership)?
___10. Is the PDC supported by adequate funding from federal, state, and local agencies?
___11. Does the PDC reflect knowledge of adult development and adult life cycle stages and phases?
___12. Does it reflect adherence to adult learning theories such as Boyatzis' modes of growth and adaptation theory and Knowles' andragogy theory? If so,
    ___a. To what extent does the PDC address the needs of teachers who are at the performance mode? The learning mode? The development mode?
    ___b. To what extent is the PDC relevant to learner needs?

      _c.   To what extent has the program been individualized?
      _d.   To what extent does it provide opportunity for self-direction based on personal needs, problems, and interests?
      _e.   To what extent does the program relate to the background of experience possessed by the learner?
      _f.To   what extent does the program provide for active as opposed to passive participation?
      _g.   To what extent does the program provide for assessment and feedback?

_10. Does the PDC reflect adherence to the motivation-leaning-development cycle?

_11. To what extent does the program ensure transfer of learning?

_12. Is the PDC consistent with principles and processes reflected in other effective comprehensive professional development plans such as Knowles's Human Resources Development Performance and Improvement Model, Joyce and Showers Professional Performance Model, or the New York City Community School District #2 model?

_13. Is professional development integrated throughout the school system and part of of the day-to-day work throughout the district?

B. Teacher Performance Assessment

_1. Does the PPS address teacher assessment in a comprehensive manner?

_2. Are standards realistic and reflect what teachers really need to know to function effectively in the classroom?

_3. Are the measures used to gauge teacher progress valid and reliable?

_4. Are the measures aligned with clear goals, a well-structured and relevant curriculum, effective instructional practices, and effective professional development opportunities?

C. Principal Performance Assessment

_1. Does the PPS address principal assessment in a comprehensive manner?

_2. Are standards realistic and reflect what principals really need to know to function effectively in the school leaders?

___3. Are the measures used to gauge principal progress valid and reliable?
___4. Are the measures aligned with clear goals, a well-structured and relevant curriculum, effective leadership practices, and effective professional development opportunities?

D. District Staff Assessment

___1. Does the PPS address teacher assessment of district staff in a comprehensive manner?
___2. Are standards realistic and reflect what the district staff really needs to know to function effectively in the central office?
___3. Are the measures used to gauge district staff progress valid and reliable?
___4. Are the measures aligned with clear goals, a well-structured and relevant district-wide strategic plan, effective professional practices, and effective professional development opportunities?

E. Superintendent Assessment

___1. Does the PPS address superintendent assessment in a comprehensive manner?
___2. Are standards realistic and reflect what a superintendent really needs to know to function effectively in the district?
___3. Are the measures used to gauge superintendent progress valid and reliable?
___4. Are the measures aligned with clear goals, a well-structured and relevant district-wide strategic plan, effective leadership practices, and effective professional development opportunities?

F. School Board Assessment

___1. Does the PPS address school board assessment in a comprehensive manner?
___2. Are standards realistic and reflect what school board members really need to know to function as policymakers?
___3. Are the measures used to gauge school board progress valid and reliable?

___4. Are the measures aligned with clear goals, a well-structured and relevant district-wide strategic plan, effective policy making practices, and effective professional development opportunities?

V.
Incentives and Sanctions

A. Incentives and Awards

___1. What types of extrinsic, intrinsic, and ancillary incentives and awards are appropriate for teachers in the district?
___2. How large should the awards be?
___3. Should every recipient receive the same size reward?
___4. What proportion of a teacher's compensation should be linked to performance?
___5. Should merit increase be in addition to cost-of-living or other across-the-board adjustment?
___6. How long should the performance period be?
___7. When should the awards be given?
___8. Who should be eligible for awards?
___9. Should individual or group incentives (or a combination) be used?
___10. Should participation be voluntary?
___11. Should persons other than teachers be included?
___12. How many persons should be able to receive awards? Should there be some from or quota?
___13. Is the formula setting the performance targets for release of reward funds calibrated so that a smaller gain in each successive year will trigger the rewards and so that the cumulative gains over a fixed and common period of years will bring all schools up to the desired standard by a certain date?
___14. Is the formula setting performance targets designed so that schools are not able to improve their chances of reaching the targets by forcing poor-performing students to leave school or by not counting them in the student performance data?
___15. To what extent is the program competitive with other school districts and, as much as possible, with other public agencies and the private sector?

___16. To what extent is nondirect compensation a built-in feature of the program?

B. Sanctions

___1. When sanction are used, are they:
   a. Fair, consistent, and equitable?
   b. Based on clear rules?
___2. Are sanctions:
   a. Based on absolute standards?
   b. Focused on performance and not personality?
   c. Focused on producing results?
   d. Able to develop the ability of school staff to plan and achieve continued improvements toward high standards?

VI.
Operational Considerations

A. Funding

___1. Can state and districts pay for development costs, administration costs, the rewards, and for the additional efforts needed to implement the system properly?
___2. Can they continue to pay the costs in the future?
___3. Does the PPS reflect a shift from concern for equity to concern for adequacy, accountability, and verifiable results?
___4. Does it reflect a clear distinction between the federal, state, and local roles in funding?
___5. Is it funded with an "up-front" allocation as opposed to relying on outside funding?
___6. Does it reflect a long- as opposed to a short-term commitment on the part of the state and the district?
___7. Is the financial support adequate and stable enough to sustain the program?
___8. In addition to or in place of full state funding, does the plan reflect other strategies of funding such as class size reduction, the employment of instructional facilitators, tutors, and mentors, and

emphasize professional development programs that focus on student achievement as the primary outcome measure?

B. Program Management and Administration

__1. The program has a system for managing and administering its day-to-day activities?
__2. Is the effort to evaluate, train, reward, keep records, and design new jobs reasonable?
__3. Is state and school district staff capable of handling this effort?
__4. Can the plan be modified to suit individual school needs?
__5. Can it be changed if it is not working?
__6. Has a process for communication been established?

C. Legal Aspects

__1. Is the program nondiscriminatory, defensible, and legal?
__2. Do the procedures for judging and rewarding teachers met required standards of fairness?
__3. Has the program been examined for its legal implications?

D. Planned Change and Implementation Considerations

__1. Have group approaches to planned change been considered? For example: Role analysis? Intergroup problem solving? Process consultation? Survey feedback? Strategic Planning?
__2. Have methods and procedures that reduce resistance to change been considered? For example: Participation? Communication? Support?
__3. Have program participants received adequate training or preparation to carry out the planned change?
__4. Are supervision, support, and guidance available to assist those making changes?
__5. Has sufficient time been allowed to develop the plan, train personnel, field-test the assessment system, and implement the plan on a pilot basis?
__6. Has sufficient time been allowed to revise, institutionalize, and evaluate the effectiveness of the plan?

___7. Was a cost-benefit analysis conducted on each component making up the performance-based pay system?
___8. Was a cost-effectiveness analysis conducted on the program?

VII.
Accountability and Evaluation Considerations

A. Comprehensive Program Evaluation

___1. Does the PPS have a comprehensive program evaluation process?
___2. Does it reflect quantitative standards developed by the Joint Committee on Standards for Educational Evaluation, e.g., utility, feasibility, propriety, and accuracy?
___3. Does it reflect qualitative standards, e.g., credibility, transferability, dependability and conformability?
___4. Does the program provide feedback to administrators?
   a. Group summary comparisons?
   b. Group match reports?
   c. Evaluator analysis?
   d. Analysis of the evaluation items?
   e. Database comparisons?

B. Continuous, Sustained Evaluation

___1. To what extent will the program be continually monitored and reviewed to ensure internal consistency and equity?
___2. Does the program have both a formative and summative evaluation component?
___3. Does the program include a process for revising the system based on the results of the evaluation and experience?

APPENDIX B

SEVEN EXAMPLES OF DESIGN AND DECISION MAKING PROCESSES FOR PERFORMANCE PAY PROGRAMS

Example 1
Strategies for Designing and Planning an Effective Performance-Based Incentive System

Adapted from Duttweiler, P. C., & Ramos-Cancel, M. L., (1986). *Perspectives on performance-based incentive plans.* Austin, TX: Southwest Educational Development Laboratory. Reprinted with permission of Southwest Educational Development Laboratory.

Questions

1. *Effectiveness*: How likely is it that the proposed system will achieve the state's or school districts' goals?
2. *Acceptability*: Does the plan allow for meaningful teacher participation? Is the plan acceptable to parents and the community?
3. *Legal Defensibility*: Do the procedures for judging and rewarding teachers meet required standards of fairness?
4. *Manageability*: Is the effort to evaluate, train, reward, keep records, and design new jobs reasonable? Are state and school district staffs capable of handling this effort?
5. *Affordability?* Can state and districts pay for the development costs, the administration costs, the rewards. and for the additional efforts needed

to implement the system properly? Can they continue to pay the costs in the future?
6. *Flexibility*: Can the plan be modified to suit individual school needs? Can it be changed if it is not working?
7. *Evaluation*: How can the effectiveness of the plan be assessed?

Steps

1. Involve the Right People
2. Conduct the right research
   a. Investigate the various kinds of programs that have been tired.
   b. Discover what has and what hasn't worked.
   c. Survey teachers and administrators to discover what they will support.
3. Define the Goals of the Incentive Plan
   a. To provide the staff with the means of achieving instructional improvement and professional development.
   b. To provide an incentive for professional growth.
   c. To provide a means of recognizing and rewarding teacher performance.
   d. To attract to the community teachers whose knowledge, skills, and professional dedication are markedly above average.
   e. To provide an incentive for talented teachers to remain in teaching in the district.
   f. To raise student achievement scores.
   g. To attract teachers with instructional specialties to teach in the district.
   h. To provide an incentive for teachers to teach in particular areas of the district or with special student groups.
   i. To provide an incentive for teachers to perform duties in addition to their regular classroom duties.
   j. To develop a cadre of professionally outstanding teachers who, while spending the majority of their time in the classroom, will be a part of the instructional-leadership and decision-making structure of the school and district.
4. Design a Program to Meet Your Goals
   a. Decide on Type and Amount of Incentives
   b. Establish New Role Definitions for Teachers and Administrators When Developing Career-Ladder Plans

c. Restructure the Organization of the School and District in Order to Accommodate the New Role Definition in a Career-Ladder Plan
   d. Develop and Test the Performance-Evaluation System
   e. Include a Strong Staff Development and Inservice Component
   f. Develop a Management System
   g. Include a Process for Evaluating the Effectiveness of the Program
   h. Include a Process for Evaluating the Effectiveness of the Program
   i. Include a Process for Revising the System Based on the Results of the Evaluation and Experience
5. Establish a Budget and Identify Funding Sources
6. Determine the Legality of Your Program
7. Establish a Process for Communication
8. Put the Plan Into Action
9. Evaluate the Program and Refine It

Follow-up Questions for Planners and Implementers

1. Has the research and literature on such plans been reviewed?
2. Is the incentive plan consistent with other school goals?
3. Is the financial support adequate and stable enough to sustain the program?
4. Have all the stakeholders been involved in the development? Is there sufficient ownership of the plan?
5. Are there too many simultaneous changes? Is there an orderly progression to change so that the participants will feel comfortable and secure?
6. Has the program been pilot tested?
7. Have the people involved received adequate training or preparation to carry out the planned change?
8. Are supervision, support, and guidance available to assist those making changes?
9. Are the incentives and rewards adequate?
10. Have all those who will be affected by the program been involved in developing the assessment system?
11. Is there a system of communication that keeps everyone informed— teachers, administrators, school board members, parents, teachers, and the community?
12. Is professional growth and leaning given a prominent place in the plan?
13. Has the pan been examined for its legal implications?

14. Has sufficient time been allowed to develop the plan, train personnel, field-test the assessment system, implement the plan on a pilot basis, revise, institutionalize, and evaluate the effectiveness of the plan?
15. Is there a mechanism to document and evaluate the effects of the plan and to revise or modify as indicated?

Example 2
The AIM Design Guidelines for an Effective Merit Pay Program

Adapted with permission from Farnsworth, Briant, et al., *and Designing and Implementing a Successful Merit Pay Program for Teachers*, in *Phi Delta Kappan,* 73(4), pp. 321-324, December 1991. © 1991 by Phi Delta Kappa International, Inc.

1. Develop criteria to measuring teaching excellence
2. Establish evaluation procedures
3. Provide feedback to teachers
4. Provide feedback to administrators
   a. Group summary comparisons
   b. Group match report
   c. Evaluator analysis
   d. Analysis of the evaluation items
   e. Database comparisons
5. Set merit pay plan
   a. Voluntary participation
   b. Significant economic rewards
   c. Equitable rewards
6. Career development
7. Manage AIM with CAPE software
   a. Data input
   b. Merit pay calculations
   c. Teacher reports
   d. Management reports

Example 3
Major Issues for School Districts when Considering Teacher Incentive Plans

Adapted with permission from Harty and Ashford, *Issues and Case Studies in Teacher Incentive Plans* (2nd ed.), p. 6, 1994. © 1994 by the Urban Institute.

1. What should the objectives of the plans be?
2. What types and sizes of awards should be used?
   a. What types of awards should be used?
   b. How large should the awards be?
   c. Should every recipient receive the same size reward?
   d. What proportion of a teacher's compensation should be linked to performance?
   e. Should merit increase be in addition to cost-of-living or other across-the-board adjustment?
   f. How long should the performance period be?
   g. When should the awards be given?
3. Who should be eligible for awards?
   a. Should individual or group incentives (or a combination) be used?
   b. Should participation be voluntary?
   c. Should persons other than teachers be included?
   d. How many persons should be able to receive awards? Should there be some from or quota?
4. How should teacher performance be evaluated?
   a. What elements should be evaluated?
   b. What types of teacher performance evaluation procedures should be used?
   c. How should teacher evaluations be linked to specific awards amounts?
5. Other incentive design issues.
   a. To what extent can and should the teacher evaluation procedures also be used to identify ways to improve teacher performance?
   b. To what extent should information on who receives the awards be promulgated?
   c. To what extent should teachers and teachers' association participate in the design and implementation of the plan?

d. How much advance planning and preparation time is needed?
   e. What is the appeal process?
   f. What preconditions are needed for success?
6. What issues should be addressed after the plan is implemented?
   a. Will the program be adequately funded each year?
   b. What provisions were made for subsequent evaluation and revision of the plan?
   c. What additional activities and resources are needed to operate the plan?
7. What special issues are associated with career ladder plans? Knowledge-based plans? Group-based plans?
8. What are the issues and potential benefits associated with nonmonetary performance-by-objectives plans?
9. What should be the role of the state government?

Example 4
Guidelines for Ensuring Accountability from Performance-Pay Programs

Adapted with permission from Southern Regional Education Board, *Getting Results: A Fresh Look at School Accountability*, pp. 2-25, 1998.

1. Content and student achievement standards.
   a. Developed with considerable input from a variety of sources
   b. Concise and understandable
   c. Rigorous and challenging
   d. Reasonable and attainable
   e. Focused and organized by grade level or course
   f. Measurable whenever possible
2. State testing should be:
   a. Reliable and valid for accountability purposes
   b. Have a clear purpose
   c. Be aligned directly to content standards
   d. Useful for school improvement
   e. Be operationally feasible
3. Professional development should be:
   a. Aligned with content standards and assessment
   b. Focused on results in student achievement

c. Flexible and responsive to school needs
   d. Accessible and convenient
   e. A part of the day-to-day work in schools
   f. Adequately funded
   g. Coordinated among local schools, higher education and state agencies
4. Accountability reporting and report cards should:
   a. Focus on student achievement and reduction results
   b. Be useful for school improvement as part of a total accountability system
   c. Be concise and understandable for a variety of audiences
   d. Provide timely and accurate information
   e. Show trends
   f. Give schools-, district-, and state-level information
   g. Include data on groups of students within schools when appropriate
5. Rewards, sanctions and targeted assistance should be:
   a. Fair, consistent and equitable
   b. Based on clear rules
   c. Balanced with one another
   d. Based on both absolute standards and improvement
   e. Supported with adequate and sustained financial resources
   f. Focus on producing results
   g. Develop the ability of school staff to plan for and achieve continued improvements toward high standards.

Example 5
Guidelines for Building a Strong State or District Accountability Performance-Pay Program

Adapted from Tucker and Codding, of *Standards for our Schools: How to Get Them, Measure Them, and Reach Them, pp. 238-243.* © 1998 by Jossey-Bass, Inc., Publishers. This information is used by permission of John Wiley & Sons, Inc.

1. Choose the student performance standards you will use.
2. Choose the indicators that will be used to drive the incentive system and the measures of progress you will use.
   a. Measures of student performance against the standards

b. Dropout rates
c. Retention rates
d. Customer satisfaction (as measured by periodic survey of satisfaction of parents, students, teachers, other faculty, the general community, employers, higher education admissions officers, and other interested parties.
3. Develop incentive systems (systems of rewards and consequences) that will motivate students to reach the student performance standards.
4. Develop incentive system (systems of rewards and consequences) for school faculty and other district employees that will reward those who contribute to improved student performance and provide consequences for those who fail to do so.
    a. Engage a highly qualified academic probation manager for each school
    b. Require that the staffing plans, hiring, budget, and program plan of a school on academic probation be approved by the probation manager.
    c. Authorize the probation manager to recommend the expedited dismissal of any member of the staff of a school on probation, subject to the laws and regulations.
    d. Require every school on academic probation to select an approved external technical assistance provider or school reform network to affiliate with and to use the assistance that organization or network provides.
    e. Authorize the probation managers to recommend the reconstitution of any school on academic probation.
5. Create a reward system for the schools that are contributing to substantial year-to-year improvements in the performance of the whole student body.
    a. The reward should go not to individual faculty members but to the whole faculty and are based on the performance of the whole student body.
    b. The rewards are based on the progress that the school makes against its earlier performance, rather than on reaching a fixed target that is the same for all schools.
    c. The rewards can be added to the school budget or distributed as a cash bonus to the faculty and staff of the school, a decision to be made by the faculty and staff.

d. The formula setting the targets for the release of reward funds is calibrated so that a smaller gain in each successive year will trigger the rewards and so that the cumulative gains over a fixed and common period of years will bring all schools up to the desired standard by a certain data.
e. The formula setting the targets is designed so that schools are not able to improve their chances of reaching the targets by forcing poor-performing students to leave the school or by not counting them in the student performance data.
f. The formula setting the targets, though heavily weighted toward student performance indicator data, also includes some weighing for school's customer satisfaction data (parent and, at the secondary level, students).

Example 6
Design and Administration Elements of a School-Based Performance Award Program

Adapted from Odden, Kellor, Heneman, & Milanowski, *School-Based Performance Award Programs: Design and Administration Issues Synthesized from Eight Programs*, August 1999. © 1999 by Consortium for Policy Research in Education, pp. 238-243.

1. Identify the dimensions of school performance: academic achievement and non-academic achievement including subjects and/or grade levels.
2. Measure the performance dimensions
3. Calculate the change or improvement
4. Make the change calculation fair
5. Determine the amount of change required to qualify for an award
6. Set levels and types of awards
7. Fund the program
8. Enable conditions/supports for the program
9. Plan for formative and summative evaluation of the program
10. Develop an effective program design proves itself

Example 7
Performance Award and Template Questions

Adapted with permission from Consortium for Policy Research in Education, *Performance Award and Template Questions*, 2000, http://www.wcer.wisc.edu/cpre/teachercomp/tchrcomp/designtemp.htm.© 1999 by Consortium for Policy Research in Education.

Category 1: Objectives and Readiness

- Why do performance awards?
- How did you decide to do performance awards? Who decides?
- How did you determine your readiness for performance awards?

Category 2: Goals

- What should students know and be able to do?
- Who should decide the goals?
- Which content areas?
- What is the weighting of different content areas? Other performance indicators?
- What is the weighing of content versus other performance indicators?
- How are measures combined to produce a total school score or index?
- Are current or absolute performance levels used in calculating a school score?
- Does the testing system keep track of subgroups of students (e.g., by race, income or gender)?

Category 3: Measurement of Performance

- What is the measurement method?
- Are there existing or new measures used?
- What data are there now? What data are needed?
- How will benchmark data be created?
- Reliability and validity of the assessment?
- What is the minimum participation rate for assessment?
- Do you use individual or cohort student scores?
- Do you use cross-sectional or longitudinal test score data?

- Which students are assessed?
- How does the system adjust for the following students: Low income? Limited English
- Proficient? Disabled/Handicapped? Mob

Category 4: Targets for Performance Improvement

- Who participates in setting targets for the district and each school?
- Do you use numerical targets or percentage improvement targets?
- Is improvement required for different subgroups of students? If so, which subgroups?
- Are different targets set for different measures, such as each content area, topics within content
- areas, non-academic areas?
- What is the time frame for improvement?
- How difficult are the targets (e.g., easy to accomplish, a real stretch)?
- How are the targets communicated?
- How and when are targets revised?

Category 5: Awards

- Who decides the nature of the awards?
- Is the award determined by how many are eligible or is it a fixed amount?
- Who is eligible to receive awards?
- What is the size of the monetary awards?
- How are the monetary awards distributed?
- Is it a one-time bonus or an increase in base pay?
- Are there conditions for eligibility?
- Are other awards (non-monetary) used?
- Is there a predetermined formula to qualify for an award?
- If so, what is the formula used?
- Is there a set amount awarded if the improvement target is met or exceeded?
- Does the amount vary depending on the number of schools eligible?
- Is there room for discretion with the formula, and if so, how much and by whom?
- How was the formula determined?

Category 6: Funding

- What is the source of the funding (e.g., state, district, private)?
- Is it a new appropriation or a reallocation of existing money?
- Is there a commitment to one year or multiple years?
- What is the total amount of funding? Is it linked to a target (e.g., 2% of base payroll)?
- How is the money appropriated?
- How will this be communicated to teachers?
- What are the plan's start-up costs?
- How will best practices be funded?

Category 7: Best Practices Supporting Performance Improvement

- Have the best practices that help achieve goals been identified and shared?
- What is the role of the state or district in promoting best practices?
- How should best practices be documented so they can be improved over time? How do you disseminate best practices information?

Category 8: Implementation, Monitoring, and Evaluating

- What were the steps to implementation?
- Did you pilot first or do full-scale implementation?
- Was implementation voluntary?
- How long does it take to go from design to implementation?
- What is the monitoring and evaluation plan?
- What is the nature of the evaluation plan?
- How can the information be used to improve the performance award?
- Is there information that needs to be collected now to support future evaluation?

APPENDIX C

THE PUBLIC'S ATTITUDE TOWARDS STANDARDIZED TESTING AND TYING TEACHERS' SALARY TO STUDENTS' ACADEMIC ACHIEVEMENT FOR 2000[a] AND 2001[b]

1. Is there too much emphasis on achievement testing in the public schools in your community, not enough emphasis on testing, or about the right amount?

	National Totals		
	1997 %	2000 %	2001 %
Too much emphasis	20	30	31
Not enough emphasis	28	23	22
About the right amount	48	43	44
Don't know	4	4	3

2. Should the primary use of tests be to determine how much students have learned or to determine the kind of instruction they need in the future?

	National Totals	
	2000 %	2001 %
Determine how much students have learned	30	30

Determine the kind of instruction needed	65	66
Don't know	5	4

3. In your opinion, which is the best way to measure student academic achievement—by means of test scores or by classroom work and homework?

	National Totals	
	2000	2001
	%	%
Test scores	26	31
Classroom work and homework	68	65
Don't know	6	4

4. Which is the best way to measure student academic achievement?

	National Totals
	2000
	%
Single standardized test	13
Combination of standardized and teacher-designed tests	41
Portfolios of students' work and other demonstrations of academic competence	44
Don't know	2

5. In your opinion, how closely should a teacher's salary be tied to his or her student's academic achievement?

	National Totals
	2000
	%
Very or somewhat closely tied	60
Very closely tied	25
Somewhat closely tied	35
Not very closely tied	12
Not at all tied	24
Don't know	4

[a]Adapted with permission from Rose and Gallup, *The 32nd Annual Phi Delta Kappa/Gallup Poll of the Public's attitudes towards the Public Schools,* in *Phi Delta Kappan,* 82(1), pp. 41-58, September 2000. © 2000 by Phi Delta Kappa International, Inc.

[b]Adapted with permission from Rose and Gallup. *The 33rd Annual Phi Delta Kappa/Gallup Poll of the Public's attitudes toward the Public Schools,* in *Phi Delta Kappan,* 83(1), pp. 41-58, September 2001. © 2001 by Phi Delat Kappa International, Inc.

NOTES

1. In their study, Smylie and Smart (1990) found that while teachers diametrically opposed merit pay programs (64% against), they strongly supported career ladder programs (66% for). These findings were consistent with those from the School and Staffing Survey conducted in 1988 by the National Center for Education Statistics.
2. Similar sentiments were expressed by British teachers who "do not want pay for performance partly because they allege [that] high quality performance cannot be recognized" (Tomlinson, 1996).
3. While the phrase standards-based has come to define the accountability movement, it should be noted that for two decades some researchers were calling for outcome-based education, which was largely responsible for focusing attention on linking student outcome to whatever happened in schools. Spady (1988) was among the ardent advocates of this idea. He is responsible for explicating the key features and components of outcome-based education in several works. See for example *Outcome-based instructional management: A sociological perspective* (Spady, 1981), *Organizing for results: The basis of authentic restructuring and reform* (Spady, 1988), and *Beyond traditional outcome-base education* (Spady & Marshall, 1991).
4. The work by Zemelman, Daniels, and Hyde (1998) defines standards for each subject area, including writing, mathematics, science, social science, visual arts, music, dance, and theatre. But what distinguish this treatise on standards from several others are case studies that illustrate the standards being discussed. The authors also outlined practical and useful strategies at the end of each chapter teachers may find helpful while planning and executing instructional units.
5. A fuller description of the linkage between expectancy, equity, job enrichment theory, and teacher pay programs was described by Johnson (1986, pp. 55-61). For example, she noted that while expectancy and equity theory provided some justification for merit pay and career ladder programs, job

enrichment supported differentiated staffing and career ladder programs. Milanowski (2001) also explained the linkage in a recent synthesis paper. See especially pages 2-6. Additionally, a description of the linkage between contingency, expectancy, social dilemma, participative management theory, and incentive programs is described by Odden and Kelley (1997, pp. 58-79).

6. Johnson (1986) identified another set of rewards called "solidarity" and "purposive" rewards that, she contends, "seem to provide incentives for educators. Solidarity rewards are those that are derived 'from the act of associating' while purposive rewards are derive 'from the stated ends of the association.' For example, solidarity rewards might include the congeniality of cooperative work with colleagues while purposive rewards might include the satisfaction of committing oneself to school improvement or the well-being of disadvantaged students" (p. 72).

7. Ozcan (1996) posited eight propositions that provide insight for designing teacher incentive programs. They are: (a) The greater the opportunities to earn economic rewards, the greater will be teacher motivation. (b) The greater the opportunities to earn honorific rewards [recognition, praise, accolades), the greater will be teacher motivation. (c) The greater the opportunities to earn political rewards—decision making power and a sense of ownership of teaching—the greater will be teacher motivation. (d) The greater the opportunities to earn intrinsic rewards the greater will be teacher motivation. (e) The greater the opportunities to earn mean rewards—necessary vehicles to earn intrinsic and extrinsic rewards—the greater will be teacher motivation. ((f) The greater the consistency between reward—opportunities and teachers' beliefs about teaching—the greater will be teacher motivation. (g) The greater the consistency between reward-opportunities and teachers' social group values, the greater will be teacher motivation. (h) The greater the objectivity of the feedback coming from the assessment and evaluation of teachers' performance, the greater will be teacher motivation. (p. 44)

8. Ozcan noted: "teachers de-emphasize the importance of extrinsic-economic resources, despite the necessity of these rewards in their survival and self-realizations struggle." He refers to this behavior as "an anomaly" and discusses several reasons for it: (1) ... because of the prevailing social values which favor service to society over the pursuit of personal extrinsic rewards (Lortie, 1975), teachers cannot express their real ideas. (2) ... teachers prefer respect and power more than salary. (3) ... in a society with normative values, current research methods and instruments used to measure the attitude of teachers might be inappropriate. (pp. 13-14)

9. See other articles in the May 1999 issue of *Phi Delta Kappan* that address performance assessment. See especially "A Short History of Performance Assessment: Lessons Learned" by Madaus and "Performance Assessment and Education Reform" by Edward Haertel.

10. For more information on how performance-based assessment has been successfully implemented at a college, by a state, and by the National Board for Professional Teaching Standards, see Milanowski and Young, (1999, pp. 2-10).
11. Some districts, such as Coventry, Rhode Island, "allow individual teachers to earn $1,000 on top of their base pay if they can demonstrate excellent performance by completing portfolios of their work" (Olson, 1999, p. 19).
12. Useful instruments for assessing teacher performance include the Teacher Performance Assessment Instrument (TPAI) (Capie & Cronin, 1986) and the Meritorious Teacher Program (MTP) FORM Instrument used in Dade County, Florida. Computers are also being used to help with teacher evaluation. See for example Chapter 16—Use of Microcomputers in Teacher Evaluation—by Peterson (1995).
13. See for example Texas (Lemann, 1999), Florida (Florida DOE, 1999a), Kentucky (Kelley, 1998), and North Carolina's (Jones et al., 1999) supposed positive experience and results using the standards and testing approach.
14. Some researchers have cautioned proponents of other evaluation approaches that do not emphasize alignment of standards, curriculum, and tests. They claim, for example, that "systems using 'alternative' methods of assessment such as student portfolios and open-ended responses are more likely to have problems with measurement error than those based on standardized tests (Milanowski, 1999, p. 344). But in his study of the role of measurement error and school achievement data, Milanowski found that "results of applying the measurement consistency information provided by the Kentucky Department of Education (KDE) to a sample of 1,032 Kentucky schools do not support the claim that the lack of consistency in accountability categorization of schools across cycles is largely due to measurement error" (1999, p. 357). For an in-depth understanding of the testing movement and its unintended consequences, see Nicholas Lemann's (1999) *The Big Test: The Secret of the American Meritocracy.*
15. To see non-incentive pay programs that successfully involved parents and families in schools, educators may want to consult Rioux and Berla's book, *Innovations in Parent and Family Involvement* (1993). In it, the authors document and analyze over 50 programs in pre-, elementary, middle, high, district, and community schools the employed effective parent-involvement approaches.
16. Garris and Cohn's model is illustrated in this funding formula:
DA = Rev x [1+(S x Rate/3}] x DADM, Where:
DA = District Allocation
Rev = Revenue Per Pupil (a flat grant)
DADM = District Average Daily Membership
S = Efficiency Coefficient

Rate = Selected rate (for study, .3, .2, & .1) (1996, p. 118)
17. See ERIC Digest ED40025 entitled "Making Time for Teacher Professional Development" for a list of references on this subject. See also the National Staff Development Council standards (www.nsdc.org/standards.htm)
18. The NSDC's standards and guidelines for staff development are located at http://www.nsdc.org/library/standards2001.html
19. Other examples of process models include the Readiness-Planning-Training-Implementation-Maintenance Model, the Concerned Based Adoption Model, and coaching application discussed in Jones and Walters (1994, pp. 161-162).
20. See Webb & Norton, 1999, pp. 359-359, for a general description of these strategies, which Monahan (1996) calls "contemporary professional development strategies that facilitate teacher growth." Also see Showers (1984), Joyce and Showers (1995, pp. 117-124), and Hargrove (1995) for particulars on peer coaching; Glatthorn (1987) for particulars on cooperative professional development; Darling-Hammond (1994) for particulars on professional development schools; Cushman (1999) for particulars on portfolios; Lieberman (1999) for particulars on professional communities peer supervision; Arhar, et al. (2001) for particulars on action research; Sparks and Loucks-Horsley (1990) for five theories and research-driven models of professional development; and Elmore (2002) for particulars on large-scale comprehensive professional development.
21. Elmore identified several themes and issues that emerged from the strategy used to develop professional development in District #2. They may provide guidance and insight for others wishing to adapt the professional development principles and activities used in District #2. They include: (1) Phased introduction of instructional changes are organized mainly around content areas; (2) The boundaries between management of the system and the activities of staff development are intentionally blurred; (3) There is a complex and evolving balance between central and school-site autonomy; (4) district administrators are unapologetic about exercising control in areas that are central to the success of the strategy; (5) there is consistency of focus on the implementing the strategy over time; (6) the strategy gives high priority to standards and assessment; (7) focus on schools that, for one reason or another, have lagged behind others in the district in instructional improvement; (7) move instructional improvement strategy more explicitly to the next grade level that needs it (Elmore, 1997, pp. 25-38).
22. See Olson (1999) for a description of other districts following the same path and recent increases in the number of performance pay programs. Also see CPRE's website (www.weer.wisc.edu/cpre) and AASA's website (www.aasa.org) for districts using the new compensation models. For private sector companies using group-based pay programs, see Firestone (1994, p. 560).

23. See pp. 415-419 of Webb and Norton (1999) for a full discussion of internal and external factors that influence teacher compensation, e.g., supply and demand, ability and willingness to pay, cost of living, prevailing wages, collective bargaining, and government regulations.
24. See Lawler's description of different design options for reward structures (1998, pp. 288-293).
25. A related group of assumptions was provided by Abelmann and Kenyon (1996). They contended that several assumptions are demonstrated when implementing SBPA programs.
26. One study compared a pay-for-knowledge (PFK) compensation system in a manufacturing plant with a non-PFK in a subsidiary of another manufacturing plant of the same subsidiary. Researchers for the *Compensation and Benefits Magazine* found that while the PFK facility produced better quality products, had lower absenteeism levels and accident rates, there was no significant difference in productivity between the two plants relative to cost efficiency. See *Reliability and Validity of Pay-for-Knowledge Compensation Systems* at Internet site: http://www.snc.edu/socsci/chair/336/payforkn.htm. See also Gupta, Schweizer and Jenkins (1987).
27. For a listing of these waves and approaches, see Futrell (1989), Murphy (1990), Stringfield et al. (1996), and Lunenberg and Orstein (2000).
28. A summary of other findings based on research conducted by CPRE workers on skills- and knowledge-based program can be seen at CPRE web site.http://www.weer.wisc.edu/cpre/teachercomp/PROJECT/FINDINGS.HTM.
29. The economy may appear to be improving, but there are signs that not all is well. For example, the latest G.D.P. report form the Commerce Department revealed "less than 3 percent appears to lie ahead for most, of not all, of this year" (Uchitelle, 2002, p. Bu 4). This does not bode well since, according to Uchitelle, "less than 3 percent is insufficient to generate enough jobs to keep down the unemployment rate or enough tax revenue to maintain public spending at the state and local levels—among other ills" (p. 4). In addition, many companies have laid off thousands of employees (McGinn & Naughton, 2001; Shiller, 2001) and states have reduced expenditures because of lower projected tax revenues. Not surprisingly, states that earmarked funding to enhance education, including teacher incentive pay, are now planning to reduce or eliminate them altogether. Among the states are Iowa, North Carolina, Alabama, Mississippi, Tennessee, South Carolina, Ohio, Michigan, Kansas, Wisconsin, Missouri, and Florida ("States left scrambling ..." 2001).
30. It should be noted here that Slavin and Madden (2000) responded to their detractors. In "Research on Achievement Outcomes of Success for All," a *Phi Delta Kappan* article, the authors argued that critics such as Pogrow (2000), Walberg and Greenberg (1999), "primarily based their criticisms on a subjective conclusion reached in a single study" (p. 39). But in a rebuttal,

Pogrow maintained that the mountain of data presented by Slavin and Madden did not answer the questions he raised originally.)
31. As an example, evaluation results on the effectiveness of Florida's A+ Accountability Program are mixed. As George (2001) pointed out, studies commissioned by Florida state officials (Green, 2001) and a study by an independent scholar (Camilli & Buckley, 2001), show conflicting results.

REFERENCES

Abelman, C. H., & Kenyon, S.B. (1996). *Distractions from teaching and learning: lessons from Kentucky's use of rewards.* Paper presented at the meeting of the American Educational Research Association, New York, NY.

Adams, J. S. (1964). Equity in social exchange. In L. Berkowitz (Ed.), *Advances in experimental social psychology* (pp. 267-299). New York, NY: Academic Press.

Airasian, P.W. (1991). *Classroom assessment.* New York: McGraw-Hill.

Alderfer, C. P. (1972). *Existence, relatedness, and growth.* New York, NY: Free Press.

Alexander, K., & Alexander, D. M. (2001). *American public school law* (5th ed.). Belmont, CA: Wadsworth Group.

American Evaluation Association. (2002). *Position statement on high stakes testing in prek-12 education.* Retrieved April 14, 2002, from http://www.eval.org/hst3.htm.

Anderson, S. E. (2000, March). *A coordinated district consultant/teacher center approach to school-based teacher development: The Mombasa School Improvement Project.* Paper presented at the Annual Meeting of the Comparative and International Education Society, San Antonio, Texas.

Andrews, H.A. (1997, April). *TQM and faculty evaluation: Ever the twain shall meet?* (ERIC Document Reproduction Service No. ED 408 004)

Angelo, T. A., & Cross, K.P. (1993). *Classroom assessment techniques: A handbook for college teachers.* San Francisco, CA: Jossey-Bass.

Area Center for Educational Enhancement. (1998). *Seeing the linkages.* Tallahassee, FL: Author.

Argyris, C. (1957). *Personality and organization.* New York, NY: Harper and Row.

Arhar, J. M., Holly, M. L., & Kasten, W. C. (2001). *Action research for teachers: Traveling the yellow brick road.* Upper Saddle, NJ: Merrill/Prentice Hall.

Arthur, G., & Milton, S. (1991). The Florida teacher incentive program. *Educational Policy, 5* (3), 266-278.

Atweh, B., Kemmis, S., & Weeks, P. (1998). *Action research in practice: Partnership for social justice in education.* London: Routledge.

Ballou, D., & Podgursky, M. (1997). *Teacher pay and teacher quality.* Kalamazoo, MI: W. E. Upjohn Institute for Employment Research.

Ballou, D., & Podgursky, M. (1998). Teacher recruitment in public and private Schools. *Journal of Policy Analysis and Management, 17* (3), 393-417.

Bennis, W. (1997). *Managing people is like herding cats: Warren Bennis on leadership.* Provo, UT: Executive Excellence Publishing.

Berends, M. (1999). *Assessing the progress of new American schools: A status report.* Santa Monica, CA: RAND.

Birman, B. F., Desimone, L., Porter, A. C., & Garet, M. S. (2000). Designing professional development that works. *Educational Leadership, 57(8),* 28-33.

Blair, J. (2001, May). Iowa approves performance pay for its teachers. *Education Week,* 1-5. Retrieved from http://www.educationweek.org.

Bleach, K. (1999). *The induction and mentoring of newly qualified teachers: A new deal for teachers.* London: David Fulton.

Block, J., Everson, S., & Guskey, T. (Eds.). (1995). *School improvement programs.* New York: Scholastic.

Boe, E. E. (1990, April). *Teacher incentive research with SASS.* Paper presented at the meeting of the American Educational Research Association, Boston, MA.

Boudreau, J. W., Sturman, M. C., Trevor, C.O., & Gerhart, B. (1999). *Is it worth it to win the talent war: Using turnover research to evaluate the utility of performance- based pay.* (Working Paper #99-06). Ithaca, NY: Center for Advanced Human Resource Studies, Cornell University.

Boyatzis, R. E. (1993). Beyond competencies: The choice to be a leader. *Human Resources Management Review, 3* (1), 1-14.

Boyatzis, R., & Kolb, D. (1993). *Performance, learning and development as modes of growth and adaptation.* Unpublished manuscript.

Bracey, G. W. (1998). TIMSS, rhymes with 'dims,' as in 'witted.' *Phi Delta Kappan, 81* (9), 686-687.

Bracey, G. W. (2000). Literacy in the information age. *Phi Delta Kappan, 82* (1), 91-92.

Bracey, G. W. (2002). *War against America's public schools: Privatizing schools, commercializing education.* Boston: Allyn and Bacon.

Bradley, A. (1998, February). A better way to pay. *Education week.* Retrieved June 5, 1999, from www.edweek.com.

Brandenburg, I. J. (1992). *The special incentive programs.* Brooklyn, NY: Office of Research Evaluation and Assessment, Research Unit, New York City Public Schools.

Bryk, A., Sebring, P., Kerbow, D., Rollow, S., & Easton, J. (1998). *Charting Chicago school reform.* Boulder, CO: Westview Press.

Capie, W., & Cronin, L. (1986, April). *How many teacher performance criteria should there be?* Paper presented at the annual meeting of the American Educational Research Association, San Francisco, California.

Carlson, R. (1996). *Reframing and reform: Perspectives on organization, leadership, and school change.* White Plains, NY: Longman.

Carpenter, W. A. (2000). Ten years of silver bullets: Dissenting thoughts on education reform. *Phi Delta Kappan, 81* (5), 383-389.

Carr, D.K., & Johansson, H. J. (1995). *Best practices in reengineering: What works and what doesn't in the reengineering process.* New York: NY: McGraw-Hill.

Cascio, W. F. (1998). *Applied psychology in human resources management* (5th ed.). Englewood Cliffs, NJ: Prentice-Hall.

Castetter, W., & Young, I. P. (2000). *The human resource function in educational administration* (7th ed.). Upper Saddle, NJ: Merrill.

Chickering, A. W., & Havighurst, R. J. (1981). The life cycle. In A. W. Chickering and Associates (Eds.), *The modern American college: Responding to the new realities of diverse students and a changing society.* San Francisco: Jossey-Bass.

Childs, T. S., & Shakeshaft, C. (1986). A meta-analysis of research on the relationship between educational expenditures and student achievement. *Journal of Educational Finance, 12,* 249-264.

Cicchinelli, L. F., & Zoe, B. (1999). Evaluating for success. *Comprehensive school guide for districts and schools.* Aurora, CO: McREL.

Cleland, D., & King, W. R. (Eds.) (1969). *Systems, organization analysis, management.* New York: McGraw-Hill.

Clotfelter, C. T., & Ladd, H. F. (1996). Recognizing and rewarding success in public schools. In H. Ladd (Ed.), *Holding schools accountable: Performance based reform in education.* (pp.23-63). Washington, D.C.: The Brookings Institution.

Conley, D. (1993). *Road map to reconstructing. Policies, practices and the emerging vision of schooling.* Eugene, OR: ERIC Clearinghouse on Educational Management.

Consortium for Policy Research in Education. (2000). *Teacher compensation system.* Madison, WI: Author. Retrieved December 14, 2000 from http://www.wcer.wisc.edu/cpre/tcomp/

Consortium for Policy Research in Education. (2001). *Emerging findings in teacher compensation.* Madison, WI: Author. Retrieved January 29, 2001 from http://www.wcer.wisc.edu/cpre/tcomp/research/general/findings.asp#ksbp

Cornett, L. M. (1995). Lessons from 10 years of teacher improvement reforms. *Educational Leadership, 52* (5), 26-30.

Cornett, L. M., & Gaines, L. M. (1994). *Reflecting on ten years of incentive programs: The 1993 career ladder clearinghouse survey.* Atlanta, GA: Southern Regional Education Board.

Cornett, L. M., & Gaines, G. F. (2002). *Quality teachers: Can incentive policies make a difference?* Atlanta, GA: Southern Regional Education Board.

Conway, C. (1998). *Strategies for mentoring.* New York: John Wiley & Sons.

Covey, S. (1990). *The 7 habits of highly effective people: Powerful lessons in personal change.* New York, NY: Simon and Schuster.

Cross, K. P. (1981). *Adults as learners.* San Francisco: Jossey-Bass Publishers.

Csikszentmihali, M. (1990). *Flow: The psychology of optimal experience.* New York, NY: Harper-Collins Publishers.

Cushman, K. (1999). Educators making portfolios: First results from the national school reform faculty. *Phi Delta Kappan, 80* (10), 744-750.

Danielson, C. (1996). *Enhancing professional practice: The framework for teaching.* Alexandria, VA: Association for Supervision and Curriculum Development.

Darling-Hammond, L., Wise, A., & Pease, S. (1983). Teacher evaluation in the organizational context: A review of the literature. *Review of Educational Research, 53* (3), 285-328.

Darling-Hammond, L. (1994). *Professional development schools: Schools for developing a profession.* New York: Teachers College Press.

Darling-Hammond, L. (1997). *The right to learn: A blueprint for school reform.* San Francisco, CA: Jossey-Bass.

DeBray, E., Parson, G., & Woodworth, D. (2001). Patterns of response in four high schools under state accountability policies in Vermont and New York. In S. H. Fuhrman (Ed). *The Classroom: Standards-Based Reform in the States* (pp. 170-92). Chicago: Chicago, IL: University of Chicago Press.

DeMitchell, T. A., & Carroll, T. (1999). Educational reform on the bargaining table: Impact, security and tradeoff. *West's Education Law Reporter, 134* (3), 675-693.

Denver teachers accept plan linking pay to performance. (1999, September). *The New York Times,* p 23.

Dickson, L. (1990). *Student achievement and career ladder status.* Paper presented at the meeting of the American Educational Research Association, Boston, MA.

Diessner, R., & Tiegs, J. (Eds.) (2001). *Notable selections in human development* (2nd ed.). Guilford, CT: McGraw-Hill.

Dorman, A., Fulford, N. (1989). *Incentives closeup: Profiles of twenty-one teacher incentive programs.* Elmhurst, IL: North Central Regional Educational Laboratory. (ERIC Document Reproduction Service No. ED 327 927)

Dorman, A., & Fulford, N. (1990). (Eds.). *Teachers incentives from the inside: Five studies by teacher-researchers.* Elmhurst, IL: North Central Regional Educational Laboratory. (ERIC Document Production Service No. 327 928)

Drinkard, J. (1999, September). Bush would tie schools' scores to federal funds. *USA Today,* p. 6A.

Drucker, P. (1980). *Managing in turbulent times.* New York, NY: Harper and Row.

Drucker, P. (1998). *Managing in a time of great change.* New York, NY: Plume.

Duttweiler, P. L., & Remos-Cancel, M. L. (1986). *Perspectives on performance-based incentive plans.* Austin, TX: Southwest Educational Development Laboratory.

Duval County Development Task Force. (1999). *Professional development: A new vision, a new system for high quality student work.* Jacksonville, FL: Author.

Dwyer, C. A. (1994). *Development of the knowledge base for the Praxis III classroom performance assessment criteria.* Princeton, NJ: Educational Testing Service.

Eastburn, R. A. (1986). Developing tomorrow's managers. *Personnel Administrator, 31* (3), 71-76.

Ebmeier, H., & Good, T. L. (1979). The effects of instructing teachers about good teaching on the mathematics achievement of fourth grade students. *American Educational Research Journal 16(1),* 1-6.

Educational Testing Service. (1995). *Praxis III: Classroom performance assessments-orientation guide.* Princeton, NJ: Author.

Eisner, E. W. (1999). The uses are limits of performance assessment. *Phi Delta Kappan, 80* (9), 658-660.

Eisner, E. W. (2001). What does it mean to say a school is doing well? *Phi Delta Kappan, 82* (5), 367-372.

Elam, S. M., & Gallup, A. M. (1989). The 21st annual Gallup/Phi Delta Kappan poll of the public's attitudes toward the public schools. *Phi Delta Kappan, 71* (1), 41-54.

Elmore, R. F. (1997). *Investing in teacher learning: Staff development and instructional improvement in community school district #2, New York City.* New York, NY: National Commission on Teaching and America's Future.

Elmore, R. F., & Fuhrman, S. H. (2001). Holding schools accountable: Is it working? *Phi Delta Kappan, 83(1),* pp. 67-72.

Elmore, R. F. (2002). *Bridging the gap between standards and achievement: Imperatives for professional development in education.* Washington, D.C.: The Albert Shanker Institute.

Erikson, E. H. (1982). *The life cycle completed: Review.* New York: Norton.

Farnsworth. B., Debenham, J. & Smith, G. (1991). Designing and implementing a successful merit pay program for teachers. *Phi Delta Kappan, 73* (4), 320-325.

Finn, J. D., & Achilles, C. M. (1999). Tennessee's class size study: Findings, implications, misconceptions. *Educational Evaluation and Policy Analysis, 21*(2), 97-109.

Finn, J. D. (2002). Small classes in American schools: Research, practice, and politics. *Phi Delta Kappan, 83* (7), 551-560.

Firestone, W. (1994). Redesigning teachers salary systems for educational reform. *American Educational Research Journal, 31*(3), 549-574.

Firestone, W. A., Mayrowetz, D., & Fairman, J. (1998). Performance-based assessment and instructional change: The effects of testing in Maine and Maryland. *Evaluation and Policy Analysis, 20* (2), 93-113.

Fisher, R., & Ury, W. (1991). *Getting to yes: Negotiating agreement without giving in.* (2nd ed.). New York: Penguin.

Florida Association of District School Superintendents. (1999). *HRMD: Systems guidelines in Florida's school districts* (3rd ed.). Tallahassee, FL: Author.

Florida Department of Education. (1999a). *Florida's system of school improvement and accountability.* Tallahassee, FL: Author.

Florida Department of Education (1999b). Gallagher sets legislative priorities: New initiatives to boost teacher status. *Monday Report, 34* (3), 1.

Florida Department of Education. (2000). *System guidelines in Florida's school districts* (3rd ed.). Tallahassee, FL: Author.

Fowler, F. C. (2000). *Policy studies for educational leaders: An introduction.* Upper Saddle River, NJ: Merrill.

Frazer, J. (1998). *Teacher to teacher: A guidebook for effective mentoring.* Portsmouth, NH: Heinemann.

Fuhrman, S. H. (Ed.). (1993). *Designing coherent education policy: Improving the system.* San Francisco, CA: Jossey-Bass, Inc.

Fuhrman, S. H. (1999). *The new accountability.* Philadelphia, PA: Consortium for Policy Research in Education.

Fuhrman, S. H. (Ed.). (2001). *From the capitol to the classroom: Standards-based reform in the states.* Chicago, IL: National Society for the Study of Education.

Fuhrman, S. H., & Odden, A. (2001). A special section on school: Introduction. *Phi Delta Kappan,* 83(1), 59-61.

Fullan, M. (1993). *Change forces: Probing the depths of educational reform.* New York, NY: Falmer Press.

Fullan, M. (1999). *Change forces: The sequel.* New York, NY: The Falmer Press.

Futrell, M. H. (1989). Mission not accomplished: Education reform in retrospect. *Phi Delta Kappan, 71* (1), 9-14.

Gage, N. E., & Berliner, D. (1998). *Educational psychology* (6th ed.). Boston: Houghton Mifflin.

Garris, J. M., & Cohn, E. (1996). Combing efficiency and equity: A new funding approach for public education. *Journal of Education Finance, 22,* 114-134.

Gay, L. R., & Airasian, P. (2000). *Educational research: Competencies for analysis and application* (6th ed.). Upper Saddle, NJ: Merrill.

General Accounting Office. (2001). *School vouchers: Publicly funded programs in Cleveland and Milwaukee.* (GAO-01-914). Washington, DC: U.S. Government Printing Office.

George, P. S. (2001). A+ accountability in Florida? *Educational Leadership, 59(1)*, 28-32.

Gielen, E. (1995). *Transfer of training in a corporate setting.* Enschede, the Netherlands: University of Twente.

Giunta, A. (1999, June 18). Denver proposal unacceptable. (*USA Today*, p. 25A.

Glass, G. V., & Smith, M. L. (1978). *Meta-analysis of research on the relationship of class size and achievement.* Eugene, OR: Far West Laboratory for Educational Research and Development.

Glatthorn, A. (1987). Cooperative professional development: Peer-centered options for teacher growth. *Educational Leadership, 45* (3), 31-35.

Goertz, M. E. (2001a). Redefining government roles in an era of standards-based reform. *Phi Delta Kappan, 83*(1), pp. 62-66.

Goertz, M. E. (2001b). Standards-based accountability: Horse trade or horsewhip? In S. H. Fuhrman (Ed.), *From the capital to the classroom: Standards-based reform in the states* (pp. 39-59). Chicago: National Society for the Study of Education.

Goertz, M. E., Duffy, M., & LeFloch, K. C. (2001). Assessment and accountability systems in 50 states: 1999-2000. Philadelphia: Consortium for Policy Research in Education, University of Pennsylvania.

Gould, R. (1978). *Transformations: Growth and change in adult life.* New York: Simon & Schuster.

Grissmer, D., Flanagan, A., Kawata, J., & Williamson, S. (2000). *Improving student achievement: What NAEP test scores tell us.* Retrieved January 17, 2000, from http://www.rand.org/publications/MR/MR924/

Guba, E., & Lincoln, Y. (1989). *Fourth generation evaluation.* Newbury Park, CA: Sage.

Guskey, T. R. (1999). Moving from ends to means. *Journal of Staff Development, 20* (2), 48.

Gupta, N., Schweizer, T. P., & Jenkins, Jr., G. D. (1987). Pay-for-knowledge compensation Plans: Hypotheses and survey results. *Monthly Labor Review, 110* (10), 40-43.

Hall, G. E., Caffarella, E., & Burtlett, E. (1997). *Assessing implementation of a performance pay plan for teachers: Strategies, findings and implications.* Paper presented at the meeting of the American Educational Research Association, Chicago, IL.

Hamilton, M. L. (1995). Relevant readings in action research. *Action in Teacher Research, 16* (4), 79-80.

Hammer, M., & Champy, J. (1993). *Reengineering the corporation: A manifesto for business revolution.* New York, NY: Harper-Collins Publishers.

Hanushek, E. A. (1989). The impact of differential expenditures on school performance. *Educational Researcher, 18* (4), 45-51; 62.

Hargreaves, A., & Fullan, M. (2000). Mentoring in the new millennium. *Theory Into Practice, 39 (1),* 50-56.

Hargrove, R. (1995). *Masterful coaching.* San Francisco, CA: Jossey-Bass.

Harty, H. P., Greiner, J. M., & Ashford, B. G. (1994). *Issues and case studies in teacher sensitive plans* (2nd ed.). Washington DC: The Urban Institute Press.

Hassel, B. C. (2002). *Better pay for better teaching: Making teacher compensation pay off in the age of accountability.* Retrieved July 9, 2002, from www.ppionline.org

Hawley, W. D. (1985). The limits and potential of performance-based pay as a source of school improvement. In H. C. Johnson, Jr., (Ed), *Merit, money and teachers' careers: Studies on merit pay and career ladders for teachers* (pp. 3-21). Washington, D.C.: Univ. Press of America.

Heneman III, H.G., & Milanowski, A. T. (1999). Teachers' attitudes about teacher bonuses under school-based Performance and Programs. *Journal of Personnel Evaluation in Education, 12* (4), 327-341.

Herman, J. L. (1997). *Large-scale assessment in support of school reform: Lessons in the search for alternative measures.* Los Angeles: Center for the Study of Evaluation, University of California.

Herman, R. (1999). *An evaluator's guide to school-wide reform.* Washington, DC: American Association of School Administrators, American Federation of Teachers, National Association of Elementary School Principals, National Association of Secondary School Principals, National Education Association, American Education Research Association.

Herzberg, F. (1966). *Work and the nature of man.* Cleveland, OH: World.

Heubert, J., & Hauser, R. (Eds.). (1999). *High stakes: Testing for tracking, promotion, and graduation.* Washington, D.C.: National Academy Press.

Hibbard, K. M. (1996). *A teacher's guide to performance-based learning assessment.* Alexandria, VA: Association for Supervision and Curriculum Development.

Hodge, W., & Jones, J. (2000). Evaluating the role of waivers in systemic school reform. *Evaluation and Program Planning, 23* (1), 267-279.

Hoover, R. L. (2000). *Forces and factors affecting Ohio proficiency test performance: A study of 593 Ohio school districts.* Youngstown, OH: Youngstown State University.

Howey, K., & Vaughn, J. (1983). Current patterns of staff development. In G. Griffin (Ed.), *Staff development* (pp. 92-117). Chicago: Univ. of Chicago Press.

Ingvarson, L., Chadbourne, R., & Culton, W. (1995). *Implementing new career structures for teachers: A study of the advanced skills teacher in* Australia. Paper presented at the meeting of the Annual meeting of the American Educational Research Association, San Francisco, CA.

Interstate New Teacher Assessment and Support Consortium. (1995). *Next steps: Moving towards performance-based licensing in teaching.* Washington, D.C.: Council of Chief State School Officers.

Jackson, P. W., Boostrom, R. E., & Hansen, D. T. (1998). *The moral life of schools.* San Francisco, CA: Jossey-Bass.

Jacobson, L. (2001). Wis. Class-size study yields advice on teachers' methods. Retrieved April 13, 2002 from http://www.edweek.org/ew/ewstory.cfm?slug=19sage.h20

Jipson, J., & Paley, N. (2000). Because no one gets there alone: Collaboration as co-mentoring. *Theory Into Practice, 39 (1)*, 36-42.

Johnson, Jr. H. C. (1985). *Merit, money and teachers' careers: Studies on merit pay and career ladder for teachers.* Lanham, MD: University Press of America.

Johnson, S. M. (1986). Incentives for teachers: What motivates, what matters. *Educational Administration Quarterly, 22* (3), 54-79.

Johnson, S. M. (1990). *Teachers at work: Achieving success in our schools.* New York: Basic Books.

Joint Committee on Standards for Educational Evaluation (1994). *The Program evaluation standards.* Thousand Oaks, CA. Sage.

Jones, J. J., & Walters, D.L. (1994). *Human resources management in education.* Lancaster, PA: Technomic.

Jones, M. G., Jones, B. D., Hardin, B., Chapman, L., Yarbrough, T., & Davis, M. (1999). The impact of high-stakes testing on teachers and students in North Carolina. *Phi Delta Kappan, 81* (3), 199-203.

Jordan, H. R., Mendro, R. L., & Weerasinghe, D. (1997). *Teacher effects on longitudinal student achievement: A preliminary report on research on teacher effectiveness.* Paper presented at the meeting of the National Evaluation Institute, Indianapolis, IN.

Joyce, B., & Showers, B. (1988). *Student achievement through staff development.* White Plains, N.Y.: Longman, Inc.

Joyce, B., & Showers, B. (1995) (2nd ed.). *Student achievement through staff development.* White Plains, N.Y.: Longman, Inc.

Joyce, B, & Belitzky, A. (1997). *The Florida department of education 1997 staff development evaluation study.* Tallahassee, FL: Florida Department of Education.

Jung, S. M. (1984). *Guidelines for evaluating teacher incentive systems.* Denver, Colorado: Education Commission of the States.

Kelley, C. (1998). The Kentucky school-based performance award program: school-level effects. *Educational Policy, 12* (3), 305-324.

Kelley, C. (1999). The motivational impact of school-based performance awards. *Journal of Personnel Evaluation in Education, 12* (4), 309-326.

Kelley, C., Heneman, H., & Milanowski, A. (2001). *School-based performance awards: Research findings and future directions.* Manuscript submitted for publication.

Kerchner, C. T., Koppich, J. E., & Weeres, J. G. (1997). *United mind workers: Unions and teaching in the knowledge society.* San Francisco: Jossey-Bass Publishers.

King, J. A. (1994). Meeting the educational needs of at-risk students: A cost analysis of three models. *Educational Evaluation and Policy Analysis, 16* (1), 1-19.

King, B. (1991). Thinking about portfolios with assessment center exercises: Examples from the teacher assessment project. *Teacher Education Quarterly, 18* (3), 31-40.

Knopp, R., & O'Reilly, R. R. (1978). *Job Satisfaction of teachers and organizational effectiveness of elementary schools.* (ERIC Document Reproduction Service No. ED 177 719).

Knowles, M., & Associates. (1984). *Andragogy in action.* San Francisco, CA: Jossey-Bass.

Knowles, M. S., Holton III, E.F., Swanson, R. A. (1998). *The adult learner* (5th ed.). Houston, TX: Gulf Publishing Co.

Kohlberg, L. (1969). Stage and sequence: The cognitive-developmental approach to socialization. In D. A. Goslin (Ed.), *Handbook of socialization theory and research.* Chicago, IL: Rand McNally.

Kottkamp, R., Provenzo, E. F., & Cohn, M. M. (1986). Stability in a profession: Two decades of teacher attitudes, 1964-1984. *Phi Delta Kappan, 67(8),* 559-567.

Krueger, A. B. (1998). Experimental estimates of education production functions. *Quarterly Journal of Economics, 114*(2), 497-532.

Krueger, A. B. (2000). *Economic considerations and class size.* Working paper 447, Industrial Relations Section, Princeton University. Retrieved June, 2002, from www.irs.princeton.edu/pubs/working_papers.html

LaBoskey, V. K. (2000). Portfolios here, portfolios there... Searching for the essence of 'educational portfolios.' *Phi Delta Kappan, 81* (8), 590-595.

Ladd, H. F. (1999). The Dallas school accountability and incentive program: An evaluation of its impacts on student outcomes. *Economics of Education Review, 18,* 1-16.

Ladd, H., & Hansen, J. (1999). *Making money matter.* Washington, D.C.: National Academy Press.

LaFee, S. (1999, February). Pay for performance. *The School Administrator,* 1-7.

Lawler E .E., III. (1971). *Pay and organizational effectiveness: A psychological view.* New York: McGraw Hill.

Lawler, E. E. III. (1990). *Strategic pay: Aligning organizational strategies and pay systems.* San Francisco, CA: Jossey-Bass.

Lawler, E. E., III. (1992). *The ultimate advantage: Creating the high involvement organization.* San Francisco: Jossey-Bass.

Lawler III, E. E. (1998). Strategic pay systems design. In S. A. Mohrman, J. R Galbraith, E. E. Lawler, III, & Associates. *Tomorrow's organization: crafting winning capabilities in a dynamic world* (pp. 286-305). San Francisco, CA: Jossey-Bass.

Lehaman, T., & Lester, V. (1978). *Adult learning in the context of adult development.* Empire State College Series. Saratoga Springs: Empire State College.

Lemann, N. (1999). *The big test: The secret history of the American meritocracy.* New York, NY: Farrar, Strauss and Giroux.

Lenord, D., & Tanaka, L. (1996, May). Should teacher pay be based on student achievement? *NEA Today, 14* (9), 31-134.

Levin, B., & Young, J. (1998). International educational reform: From proposals to results. *Alberta Journal of Educational Research, 44* (1), 91-93.

Levin, H. M. (1983). *Cost-effectiveness: A primer.* Beverly Hills, CA: Sage.

Levine, R. A., Solomon, M. A., Gerd-Michael, H., & Wollmann, H. (Eds.). (1981). *Evaluation research and practice: Comparative and international perspectives.* Beverly Hills, CA: Sage Publications.

Levinson, D. J. A. (1986). A conception of adult development. *American Psychologist, 41* (1), 3-13.

Lewis, A. C., & Barnett, B. (1999). *Figuring it out: Standards-based reform in urban middle grades.* New York, NY: Edna McConnell Clark Foundation.

Lewis, A. C. (2000). Parochialism and performance pay for teachers. *Phi Delta Kappan, 82* (1), 3-4.

Lewis, A. C. (2002). School reform and professional development. *Phi Delta Kappan, 83(7),* 488-489.

Lieberman, A. (1995). Practices that support teacher development: Transforming conceptions of professional learning. *Phi Delta Kappan, 76* (8), 591-596.

Lieberman, A., & McLaughlin, M. (1999, January). *Professional development in the United States: Policies and practices.* Paper presented at the meeting of the International Conference on New Professionalism in Teaching, Stanford, CA.

Lindblom, C. E. (1959). The science of muddling through. *Public Administration Review, 20,* 79-88.

Little, J. W. (1993). *Teachers' Professional development in a climate of reform.* New York, NY: National Center for Restructuring Education, Schools, and Teaching.

Locke, E. A., & Latham, G. P. (1995). *A theory of goal setting and task performance.* (2nd ed.). Englewood Cliffs, NJ: Prentice-Hall.

Lockwood, R., & McLean, J. (1993, November). *Educational funding and student achievement.* Paper presented at the mid-south educational research association annual conference.

Loevinger, J. (1976). *Ego development: Conception and theories.* San Francisco: Jossey-Bass.

London, M., & Smither, J. (1999). Empowering self-development and continuous learning. *Human Resource Management, 38* (1), 3-15.

Lortie, D. (1975). *School teacher: A sociological study.* Chicago, IL: University of Chicago Press.

Lunenburg, F. C., & Ornstein, A. C. (2000). *Educational administration: Concepts and practices* (3rd ed.). Belmont, CA: Wadsworth.

Ludwig, J., & Bassi, L. J. (1999). The puzzling case of school resources and student achievement. *Education Evaluation and Policy Analysis, 21* (4), 385-403.

McClernon, T. R., & Swanson, R.A. (1995). Team building: An experimental investigation of the effects of computer-based and facilitator-based interventions on work groups. *Human Resource Development Quarterly, 6*(1), 39-58.

McGinn, D. (1999, September 6). The big score. *Newsweek Magazine,* pp. 46-51.

McGinn, D., & Naughton, K. (2001, February). How safe is your job? *Newsweek,* pp. 36-38; 39,42-43.

McNeil, L. (2000a). *Contradictions of school reform: Educational costs of standardized testing.* New York, NY: Falmer Press.

McNeil, L. M. (2000b). Creating inequalities: Contradictions of reform. *Phi Delta Kappan, 81* (10), 728-734.

Mak, K. (2000, April). *Effects of expectations, homework, discipline, and home environment on the TIMSS performance of consortium students.* Paper presented at the meeting of the American Educational Research Association in New Orleans, LA.

Malen, B., Ogawa, R. T., & Kranz, J. (1989, May). *What do we know about school based management? A case study of the literature—a call for research.* Paper presented at the Conference on Choice and Control in American Education, Madison, University of Wisconsin-Madison.

Marshall, R., & Tucker, M. (1992). *Thinking for a living: Education and the wealth of nations.* New York, NY: Basic Books.

Martin, M. O., & Kelly, D. L. (Eds.). (1996). *Third international mathematics and science study: Technical report.* Chestnut Hill, MA: Boston College.

Maslow, A. (1970). *Motivation and personality* (Rev. ed.). New York, NY: McGraw-Hill.

Matthews, Jr. M. (1999, April 10). Better way to raise teachers' salaries. *Investor's Business Daily,* p. A-24.

May, W. T. (1993). Teacher-as-researchers or action research: What is it, and what good is it for the art education? *Studies in Art Education, 34* (2), 114-26.

Mendro, B., Olivarez, R., Maureen, P., Milanowski, T., Kellor, E., & Odden, A. (1999, January). *A case study of the Dallas public school-based performance award program.* Paper prepared for the Consortium for Public Research in Education, Madison, Wisconsin.

Merriam, S. B., & Caffarella, R. S. (1991). *Learning in adulthood: A comprehensive guide.* San Francisco: Jossey-Bass.

Merriam, S. B., & Brockett, R.C. (1997). *The profession and practice of adult education: An introduction* (1st ed.). San Francisco, CA: Jossey-Bass.

Michaels, J, W., & McCulloh, D. H. (1976). *Effects of differentially rewarding groups on cooperative task performance and satisfaction.* (Report No. 211, NE-C-00-3-0114). East Lansing, MI: National Center for Research on Teaching and Learning. (ERIC Document Reproduction Service No. ED128676)

Milanowski, T. (1999). Measurement error or meaningful change? The conspiracy of school achievement in two school-based performance award Programs. *Journal of Personnel Evaluation in Education, 12* (4), 343-363.

Milanowski, T., & Young, P. (1999). *Evaluating teaching skills: Lessons from performance-based teacher assessment.* Madison, WI: CPRE Teacher Compensation Project.

Milanowski, T. (2001). *Varieties of knowledge and skill-based pay designs: A comparison of seven new pay systems for K-12 teachers.* Madison: University of Wisconsin-Madison, Wisconsin Center for Education Research, Consortium for Policy Research in Education.

Minorini, P., & Sugarman, S. (1999). School finance litigation in the name of educational equity: Its evolution, impact, and future. In H. Ladd, R. Chalk, & J. Hansen. (Eds.). *Equity and adequacy in education finance: Issues and perspectives* (pp. 34-71). Washington, DC: National Academy Press.

Mitchell, D. E., Ortiz, F. I., & Mitchell, T. K. (1983). *Work orientation and job performance: The cultural basis of teaching rewards and incentives.* Riverside, CA: University of California.

Mitchell, S. (1995). *New pay: Compensation as a strategic tool.* Annapolis Junction, MD: National Alliance of Business.

Mizell, H. (1999). Link staff learning to student learning. *Journal of Staff Development, 20* (2), 47.

Mohrman, S. A., Galbraith, J. R., Lawler III, E. E, & Associates. (1998). *Tomorrow's organization: Crafting winning capabilities in a dynamic world.* San Francisco, CA: Jossey-Bass.

Molar, A., Smith, P., Zahoriky, J., Palmer, A., Halbach, A., & Ehrle, K. (1999). Evaluating the SAGE program: A pilot program in targeted pupil-teacher reduction in Wisconsin. *Educational Evaluation and Policy Analysis, 21* (2), 165-177.

Monahan, T. C. (1996). Do contemporary incentives and rewards perpetuate outdated forms of professional development? *Journal of Staff Development, 17* (1), 44-47.

Mungazi, D. A., & Kay, W. L. (1997). *Educational reform and the transportation of Southern Africa.* Westport, CT: Praeger.

Murphy, J. (1990). *The educational reform movement of the 1980s.* Berkeley, CA: McCutchan.

Murphy, J. (1991). *Restructuring schools: Capturing and assessing the phenomena.* New York, NY: Teacher's College Press.

Murphy, J., & Hallinger, P. (1993). *Restructuring schooling: Learning from ongoing efforts.* Newbury Park, CA: Corwin Press.

Murray, S. L. (1986). *Considering policy options for testing teachers.* Portland, OR: Northwest Regional Educational Laboratory.

National Assessment for the Progress of Education. (2000). *The nation's report card.* Available: http://www.odedodea.edu/testing/naep/.

National Board for Professional Teaching Standards. (1996). *National board certification sampler.* Southfield, MI: Author.

National Board for Professional Teaching Standards. (2001). *Accomplished teachers taking on new leadership roles in schools.* Retrieved May 22, 2002, from http://www.nbpts.org/about/news_center/20010419.html

National Board for Professional Teaching Standards. (2002). *General information about national board certification.* Retrieved July 7, 2002, from www.nbpts.org/standards/nbcert.cfm

National Center on Education and the Economy. (1996). *The America's Choice Design.* Rochester, NY: Author.

National Center on Education and the Economy. (1998). *New Standards Performance Standards.* Rochester, NY: Author.

National Center for Education Statistics. (1996). *School and staffing in the United States: A statistical profile, 1993-1994* (NCES 96-124). Washington, D.C.: U.S. Government Printing Office.

National Commission on Excellent in Education. (1983). *A nation at risk.* Washington, DC: U.S. Department of Education.

National Commission on Excellence in Education. (1993). *Meeting the challenge: Present efforts to improve education across the nation.* (Report No. SP0238217). Washington, DC: National Commission on Excellence in Education. (ERIC Document Reproduction Service No. ED 240 114)

National Staff Development Council. (2001). *Standards for staff development.* Oxford, OH: Author.

Nelson, W. (2001). Timequake alert: Why payment by results is the worst 'new' reform to shake the educational world. *Phil Delta Kappan, 82* (5), 384-389.

Newman, F. N. (1993). Beyond common sense in educational restructuring: The issues of content and linkage. *Educational Researcher*, 22 (2), 4-13, 22.

Norton, M., & Scott, H. W. (1988). Incentive pay programs: Does participation change viewpoints? *Clearing House, 62(4)*, 149-151.

Oakley, K. (1998). The performance assessment system: A portfolio assessment model for evaluating beginning teachers. *Journal of Personnel Evaluation in Education, 11* (4), 323-341.

Odden, A. (1999a, June). Teacher quality: The rule of new forms of compensation. *Education Weekly, 28* (41), 1.

Odden, A. (1999b). *Creating school finance policies that facilitate new goals.* CPRE Policy Brief. Philadelphia, PA: Consortium for Policy Research in Education.

Odden, A. (1999c). *Example of a district's conceptual model of a knowledge- and skill-based pay program.* Madison, WI: Consortium for Policy Research in Education.

Odden, A. (2000a). New and better forms of teacher compensation are Possible. *Phi Delta Kappan, 81*(5), 361-366.

Odden, A. (2000b). The costs of sustaining educational change through comprehensive school reform. *Phi Delta Kappan, 81*(6), 433-438.

Odden, A. (2001). The new school finance. *Phi Delta Kappan, 83*(1), 85-91.

Odden, A., Archibald, S., & Tychsen, A. (1999). *Reallocating resources to support higher student achievement: How five schools did it.* Madison, WI: Consortium for Policy Research in Education.

Odden, A., & Busch, C. (1998). *Financing schools for high performance: Strategies for improving the use of educational resources.* San Francisco: Jossey-Bass.

Odden, A., & Kelley, C. (1997). *Paying teachers for what they know and do.* Thousand Oak, CA: Corwin Press.

Odden, A., & Kelley, C. (2002). *Paying teachers for what they know and do* (2nd ed.). Thousand Oak, CA: Corwin Press.

Odden, A., & Kellor, E. (2000). *How Cincinnati developed a knowledge- and skills-based salary schedule.* Madison, WI: Consortium for Policy Research in Education.

Odden, A., Kellor, E., Heneman, H., & Milanowski, A. (1999). *School-based performance programs: Design and administration issues synthesized from eight programs.* Madison, WI: Wisconsin Center for Education Research Consortium for Policy Research in Education. Retrieved October 15, 1999, from www.wcer.wis.edu/cpre.

Odden, A., & Picus, L. O. (2000). *School finance: A policy perspective* (2nd ed.). New York: McGraw-Hill.

Olson, L. (1999, October 13). Pay-performance link in salaries gains momentum. *Education Weekly*, 7 (7), pp. 1, 18.

Orlich, D. C. (2000). Education reform and limits to student achievement. *Phi Delta Kappan*, 81, (6), 468-472.

Ozcan, M. (1996, April). *Improving teacher performance: Towards a theory of teacher motivation.* Paper presented at the meeting of the American Educational Research Association Annual Meeting, New York, NY.

Packard, R. D., & Dereshiwsky, M. I. (1988a). *Study of the effects of a career ladder intervention program with focus on the production and outcomes in student achievement.* Paper presented at the meeting of the Arizona Educational Research Association, Phoenix, AZ.

Packard, R. D., & Dereshiwsky, M.I. (1988b). *Research findings on effective program designs and methodologies: Evaluating state and local program impact on professional development and improved student outcomes.* Flagstaff, AZ: The Arizona Career Ladder Research and Evaluation Project, Center for Excellence in Education.

Packard, R. D., & Dereshiwsky, M.I. (1990). *Final accumulative results and transfer of knowledge of the Arizona career ladder research and evaluation project.* Flagstaff, Arizona: Northern Arizona University Center for Excellence in Education.

Parsons, T. N. (1951). *The social system.* New York, Free Press of Glencoe.

Peterson, K. D. (1995). *Teacher evaluation: A comprehensive guide to new directions and practices.* Thousand Oaks, CA: Corwin Press, Inc.

Picus, L. O. (1998). Rethinking equity—there are alternatives. *School Business Affairs,* 64 (4), pp. 3-8.

Pogrow, S. (2000). Success for all does not produce success for all. *Phi Delta Kappan, 82* (1), 67-80.

Popham, W. J. (1971). Performance test of teaching proficiency: Rationale, development, and validation. *American Educational Research Journal, 8* (1), 105-117.

Popham, W. J. (1995). *Classroom assessment: What teachers need to know.* Neablam Heights, MA: Allyn and Bacon.

Popham, W. J. (1988). The dysfunctional marriage of formative and numerative teacher evaluation. *Journal of Personnel Evaluation in Education, 1,* 269-273.

Portner, H. (1998). *Mentoring new teachers.* Thousand Oaks, CA: Corwin Press.

Quinn, D. (2000, April). *A first estimate of the ses effect on the consortium's TIMSS Performance.* Paper presented at the meeting of the American Educational Research Association, New Orleans, LA.

Ravitch, D. (1995). *National standards in American education: A citizen's guide.* Washington, D.C.: Brookings Institution.

Ravitch, D. (2000). *Left back: A century of failed school reforms.* New York: Simon & Schuster.

Reese, C. M., Miller, K. E., Mazzeo, J., & Dossey, J. A. (1997). *NAEP 1996 mathematics report card for the nation and the states.* Washington, DC: National Center for Education Statistics.
Reynolds, R. J., & Cruz, J. (1998). Reform of preservice teacher education: Doomed to failure. *International Journal of Education Reform, 7*(2), 122-128.
Rice, J. K. (1999). The impact of class size or instructional strategies and the use of time in high school mathematics and science courses. *Educational Evaluation and Policy Analysis, 21,* (2), 215-229.
Rioux, W. J., & Berla, N. (1993). *Innovations in parent and family involvement.* Princeton, NJ: Eye on Education.
Rose, L. C., & Gallup, A. M. (2000). The 32nd annual Phi Delta Kappa/Gallup poll of the public's attitudes toward public schools. *Phi Delta Kappan, 82* (1), 41-58.
Rose, L. C., & Gallup, A. M. (2001). The 33rd annual Phi Delta Kappa/Gallup poll of the public's attitudes toward public schools. *Phi Delta Kappan, 83* (1), 41-58.
Rose v. Council for Better Schools, 790 S.W.2d 186 (KY, 1989).
Ross, S. (2000). *How to evaluate comprehensive school reform models.* Arlington, VA: New American Schools.
Ross, S. M., Anderson, R., Bassoppo-Moyo, T., Bol, I., Buggery, T., Dietrich, A., Grehan, A., Hacker, D., Henry, D., Lowther, D., Maxwell, S., McNeils, M., Pace, J., Phillipens, L., Rich, L., Smith, L., Troutman, A., Wasson, R., & Weddle, K. (1997). *Evaluating of new American school designs: 1996-1997.* Report prepared for Memphis City Schools. Memphis, TN: Center for Research in Educational Policy, the University of Memphis.
Rouiller, J. Z., & Goldstein, I. L. (1993). The relationship between organizational transfer climate and positive transfer of training. *Human Resource Development Quarterly, 4*(4), 377-390.
Saavedra, R., & Kwan, S. (1993). Peer evaluation in self-management work groups. *Journal of Applied Psychology, 78* (3), 450-462.
Sanders, W.L., & Horn, S. P. (1995). The Tennessee value-added system (TVAAS): Mixed model methodology in educational assessment. In A.J. Shinkfield & D. Stufflbeam (Eds.). *Teacher evaluation: Guide to effective Practice* (pp.337-350). Boston: Kluwer.
Sanders, W. L., & Rivers, J. C. (1996). *Cumulative and residual effects of teachers on future student academic achievement.* Research Progress Report. Knoxville: University of Tennessee Value - Added Research and Assessment Center.
Seiler, J. A. (1967). *Systems analysis in organization behavior.* Homewood, IL: Irwin and Dorsey.

Senge, P. (1994). *The fifth discipline: The art and Practice of the learning organization.* New York, NY: Doubleday Books.

Senge, P., Kleiner, A., Roberts, C., Roth, G., & Ross, R. (1999). *The dance of change.* New York, NY: Doubleday Books.

Senge, P., Cambron-McCabe, N., Lucas, T., Smith, B., Dutton, J., & Kleiner, A. (2000). *Schools that learn: A fifth discipline fieldbook for educators, parents, and everyone who cares about education.* New York, NY: Doubleday.

Seyfarth, J. T. (1996). *Personnel management for effective schools.* Boston, MA: Allyn and Bacon.

Shanahan, T. (1998). On the effectiveness and limitations of tutoring in reading. *Review of Research in Education, 23,* 217-234.

Sheehy, G. (1977). *Passages: Predictable crises of adult life.* New York, NY: Bantham.

Sheehy, G. (1999). *Understanding men's passages: Discovering the new map of men's lives.* New York: Ballantine Books.

Shiller, R. J. (2001, February 4). The mystery of economic recessions. *The New York Times,* p. Wk 17.

Shore, T., Shore, L, M., & Thorton, III, G. (1992). Construct validity of self and peer evaluations of performance dimensions in an assessment center. *Journal of Applied Psychology, 77*(1), 42-54.

Slavin, R. E., Madden, N.A., Dolan, L.J., Wasik, B.A., Ross, S.M., Smith, L.J., & Dianda, M. (1996). Success for all: A summary of research. *Journal of Education for Students Placed at Risk, 1*(1), 41-76.

Slavin, R. E., & Madden, N. A. (2000). Research on achievement outcomes of success for all: A summary and response to critics. *Phi Delta Kappan, 82*(1), 38-40; 59-66.

Showers, B. (1984). *Peer Counseling: A strategy for facilitating transfer of training.* Eugene, ER: Center for Educative Policy and Management.

Smith, R. E. (1998). *Human resources administration: A school-based perspective.* Larchmont, NY: Eye on Education.

Smith, S. S., & Mickelson, R. A. (2000). All that glitters is not gold: School reform in Charlotte-Mecklenburg. *Educational Evaluation and Policy Analysis, 22*(2), 101-27.

Smylie, M. A., & Smart, J, C. (1990). Teacher support for career enhancement initiative: Program characteristics and effects on work. *Educational Evaluation and Policy Analysis, 12(2),* 139-155.

Southern Regional Educational Board (1991). *Linking performance to rewards for teachers, principals, and schools,* Atlanta, GA: Author.

Southern Regional Education Board. (1997). *Accountability in the 1990s: Holding schools responsible for student achievement.* Atlanta, GA: Author.

Southern Regional Education Board. (1998, October). *Getting results: A fresh look at school accountability.* Atlanta, GA: Author.

Spady, W. G. (1988). Organizing for results: The basis of authentic restructuring and reform. *Educational Leadership, 49* (2), 4-10.
Spady, W. G., & Marshall, K. (1991). *Beyond traditional outcome-base* Education. *Educational Leadership, 49* (2), 67-72.
Sparks, D., & Loucks-Horsley, S. (1990). Models of staff development. In W. R. Houston (Ed), *Handbook of research on teacher education* (pp. 234-250). New York: Macmillan.
Sparks, D., & Hirsh, S. (1999). *A national plan for improving professional Development.* Retrieved October 22, 1999, from http://www.nsdc.org/library/NSDCPlan.html
Stake, R. (1998). Some comments on assessment in U.S. education. *Education Policy Analysis Achieves, 6,* (14). Retrieved October 16, 1999, from http://epaa.asu.edu/epaa/v6n14.html.
States left scrambling as revenues fall short. (2001, February 9). *The Florida Times Union*, p. A-4.
Stecher, B. M., & Bohrnstedt, G. W. (2002). Class size reduction in California: Findings from 1999-00 and 2000-01. Retrieved April 13, 2002, from http://www.classize.org/summary/99-01/index.htm
Stiggins, R. J. (1994). *Student-centered classroom assessment.* New York: McMillan Publishing Company.
Stringfield, S., Ross, S., & Smith, L. (1996). *Bold plans for school restructuring: The new American school designs*. Mahwah, NJ: Erlbaum.
Stufflebeam, D. L. (1974). *Educational evaluation and decision making.* Bloomington, IN: Phi Delta Kappa.
Stufflebeam, D. L. (1998). Conflicts between standards-based and post-modernist Evaluations: Toward rapprochement. *Journal of Personal Evaluation in Education, 12* (3), 287-296.
Stufflebeam, D. L. (2002). *Evaluation models.* San Francisco, CA: Jossey-Bass.
Swanson, C. B., & Stevenson, D. L. (2002). Standards-based reform in practice: Evidence on state policy and classroom instruction from the NAEP assessments. *Educational Evaluation and Policy Analysis, 24(1),* 1-27.
Swanson, R. A., & Holton III, E. F. (Eds.). (1997). *Human resource development research handbook: Linking research and Practice.* San Francisco, CA: Berrett-Koehler Publishing.
Tomlinson, H. (1996). Performance related pay and professional development. In S. L. Jacobson, E.S. Hickcox, & R. B. Stevenson (Eds.), *School Administration: Persistent dilemmas in preparation and practice* (pp. 101-110). Westport, Connecticut: Praeger.
Traub, J. (2000, January 16). Schools are not the answer. *The New York Times Magazine,* pp. 52-57; 68; 81; 90-91.

Tucker, M. S., & Codding, J. B. (1998). *Standards for our schools: How to set them, measure them, and reach them.* San Francisco, CA: Jossey-Bass Publishers.

Tyack, D. B. (1990). Restructuring in historical perspective: Tinkering toward utopia. *Teachers College Record, 92* (2), 170-179.

Tyack, D., & Cuban, L. (1995). *Tinkering toward utopia: A century of public school reform.* Cambridge, MA: Harvard University Press.

Uchitelle, L. (2002, May 5). Despite appearances, economy is still shaky. *The New York Times*, p. BU4.

UNICEF. (2000). Curriculum report card. Working Paper Series, Education Section. Programme Division. New York, NY: Author.

Urbanski, A., & Erskine, R. (2000). School reform, TURN, and teacher compensation. *Phi Delta Kappan, 81*(5), 367-370.

U. S. Department of Education. (1995). *Educational programs that work* (21st ed.). Washington, D.C.: Author.

U. S. Department of Education. (1998, May 22). *The comprehensive school reform demonstration program (CSRD): Selected profiles of early state implementation efforts.* Washington, DC: United States Department of Education. Retrieved November 3, 1999, from http://www.ed.gov/offices/OESE/compreform/profiles.html

U.S. Department of Education. (1999). *Designing effective professional development: Lessons from the Eisenhower program.* (Executive Summary, Doc #99-3). Washington, D.C: Author.

U.S. General Accounting Office. (2001). *School vouchers: Publicly funded programs in Cleveland and Milwaukee.* Washington, D.C.: Author.

Viadero, D. (1998, March 4). U.S. seniors near bottom in world test. *Education Week, 4,* p. 1.

Viadero, D. (2001, April 25). Smaller classes in L.A. seen lifting test scores, especially among poor. *Education Week*, p. 8.

Von Bertalanffy, L. (1968). *General systems theory.* New York: Braziller.

Vroom, V.H. (1964). *Work and motivation.* Malabar, FL: Krieger Publishing Co.

Wainer, H. (1993). Does spending money on education help. *Educational Researcher, 22(9),* 22-24.

Walberg, H. J., & Greenberg, R. C. (1999). Educators should require evidence. *Phi Delta Kappan, 81* (2), 132-135.

Weathersby, R. (1978). Life stages and learning interests. In *The adult learner: Current issues in higher education.* Washington, D.C.: American Association of Higher Education.

Webb, N. M., Nemer, K. M., Chizhik, A. W., & Sugrue, B. (1998). Equity issues in collaborative group assessment: Group composition and performance. *American Educational Research Journal, 35* (4), 607-621.

Webb, L. D., & Norton, M. S. (1999). (3rd ed.). *Human resources administration: Personnel issues and needs in education.* Upper Saddle River, N.J.: Merrill/Prentice-Hall.

Webster, W. J., & Mendro, R. L. (1995). Evaluation for improved school level decision-making and productivity. *Studies in Educational Evaluation, 21(4),* 261-399.

Weick, K. E. (1966). The concept of equity and perception of pay. *Administrative Science Quarterly, 11*(3), 414-439.

Weiss, C. (Ed.). (1992). *Organizations for policy analysis.* Newbury Park, CA: Sage.

Wells, C. (2000). *Pay for performance: Current views and practices.* Unpublished manuscript.

Wenglinsky, H. (1998). *How educational expenditures improve student performance and how they don't.* Princeton, NJ: Educational Testing Service.

Whitehead, M. M. (2000). *Do teacher salaries make a difference?: Tennessee teachers' salaries and student achievement in the year 2000.* Franklin, TN: Tennessee Valley Educators for Excellence. Retrieved January 22, 2001, from the World Wide Web: http://www.dpo.uab.edu/~tnmarie/tnsal00.htm

Wholey, J. S., Hatry, H. P., & Newcomer, K. E. (Eds.) (1994). *Handbook of practical program evaluation.* San Francisco, CA: Jossey-Bass Publishers.

Wiegman, J., & Binnie, D. (1985). Attitudes toward merit pay for instructional personnel: A survey of Florida public district policy makers and administrators. *Florida Educational Research and Development Council, Inc., Research Council Bulletin, 19*(2), 1-64.

Wiggins, G. (1998). *Educative assessment: designing measurements to inform and improve student performance.* San Francisco, CA: Jossey-Bass.

Wiggins, G. (1999). *Assessing student performance: Exploring the purpose and limits of testing.* San Francisco, CA: Jossey-Bass.

Willms, J. D. (2000, April). *Standards of care: Investments to improve children's educational outcomes in Latin America.* Paper presented at the Year 2000 Conference of Early Childhood Development sponsored by the World Bank, D.C.

Wilson, G. (1985, April). *The Florida master teacher program.* Paper presented at the Annual Meeting of the American Educational Research Associations, Chicago, IL.

Winerip, M. (2001, November 18). *Never mind the inventive curriculum: One size fits all.* The New York Times, p. A27.

Wise, A. E. (1984). *Teacher evaluation: A study of effective practices.* Santa Monica, CA: RAND Corporation.

Wong, K. K., & Meyer, S. J. (1998). Title I schoolwide programs: A synthesis of findings from recent evaluation. *Educational Evaluation and Policy Analysis, 20* (2), 115-136.

Wood, R. C., & Thompson, D.C. (1996). *Educational finance law: Constitutional challenge to state aid plan—an analysis of strategies* (2nd ed.). Topeka, KA: National Organization on Legal Problems of Education.

Wright, S. P., Horn, S. P., & Sanders, W. L. (1997). Teachers and classroom context effects on student achievement: Implications for teacher evaluation. *Journal of Personal Evaluation in Education, 11*(1), 57-67.

Zachary, L. J. (2000). *The mentor's guide: Facilitating learning relationships.* San Francisco, CA: Jossey-Bass.

Zemelman, S., Daniels, H., & Hyde, A. (1998). *Best Practice: New standards for teaching and learning in America's schools.* Portsmouth, NH: Heinemann.

INDEX

A

Abelman, C. H., and Kenyon, S. B. (1996), 101, 102, 109, 165, 167
Adams, J. S. (1964), 17, 167
Airasian, P. W. (1991), 26, 167
Alderfer, C. P. (1972), 16, 19, 120, 167
Alexander, K., and Alexander, D. M. (2001), 39, 167
American Evaluation Association (2002), 24, 167
Anderson, S. E. (2000), 49, 65, 167
Andrews, H. A. (1997, April), 25, 167
Angelo, T. A. and Cross, K. P. (1993), 27, 167
Argyris, C. (1957), 18, 167
Arhar, et al (2001), 164, 167
Arhar, J. M., Holly, M. L. and Kasten, W. C. (2001), 27, 167
Arthur, G. and Milton, S. (1991), 5, 167
Atweh, B., Kemmis, S. and Weeks, P. (1988), 27, 168

B

Ballou, D., and Podgursky, M. (1997), 37, 39, 168
Ballou, D., and Podgursky, M. (1998), 49, 168
Bennis, W. (1997), 69, 168
Berends, M. (1999), 3, 30, 168
Birman, B. F., Desimone, L., Porter, A. C., and Garet, M. S. (2000), 48, 49, 59, 168

Blair, J. (2001), 40, 168
Block, J., Everson, S., and Guskey, T. (1995), 8, 168
Boe, E. E. (1990), 4, 102–103, 104, 168
Boudreau, J. W., Sturman, M. C., Trevor, C. O., and Gerhart, B. (1999), 42, 168
Boyatzis, R. E. (1993), 27, 51, 65, 168
Boyatzis, R. E., and Kolb, D. (1993), 51, 52–53, 54, 168
Bracey, G. W. (1998), 2, 127, 168
Bracey, G. W. (2000), 127, 168
Bracey, G. W. (2002), 4, 127, 168
Bradley, A. (1998), 76, 168
Brandenburg, I. J. (1992), 36, 168
Bryk, A., Sebring, P., Kerbow, D., Rollow, S. and Easton, J. (1998), 34, 168

C

Capie, W., and Cronin, L. (1986), 163, 169
Carlson, R. (1996), 3, 7, 169
Carpenter, W. A. (2000), 2, 127, 169
Carr, D. K., and Johnson, H. J. (1995), 69, 169
Cascio, W. F. (1998), 58, 169
Castetter, W., and Young, I. P. (2000), 58, 169
Chickering, A. W., and Havighurst, R. J. (1981), 50, 169
Childs, T. S., and Shakeshaft, C. (1986), 4, 169

Cicchinelli, L. F., and Zoe, B. (1999), 30, 169
Cleland, D., and King, W. R. (1969), 12, 169
Clotfelter, C. T., and Ladd, H. F. (1996), 82, 169
Conley, D. (1993), 8, 169
Cornett, L. M. (1995), 80, 169
Cornett, L. M., and Gaines L. M. (1994), 43, 80, 169, 170
Covey, S. (1990), 69, 170
Cross, K. P. (1981), 51, 170
Csikszentmihalyi, M. (1990), 16, 18, 120, 170
Cushman, K. (1999), 25, 27, 164, 170

D

Darling-Hammond, L. (1994), 164, 170
Darling-Hammond, L. (1997), 3, 11, 170
Darling-Hammond, L., Wise, A., and Pease, S. (1983), 25, 170
DeBray, E., Parson, G., and Woodworth, D. (2001), 106, 170
DeMitchell, T. A., and Carroll, T. (1999), 34, 170
Dickson, L. (1990), 107, 170
Diessner, R., and Tiegs, J. (2001), 50, 170
Dorman, A., and Fulford, N. (1989), 100, 170
Dorman, A., and Fulford, N. (1990), 36, 170
Drinkard, J. (1999), 37, 171
Drucker, P. (1980, 1998), 69, 171
Drucker, P. (1998), 69, 171
Duttweiler, P. L. and Ramos-Cancel, M. L. (1986), 6, 171
Duttweiler, P. L. and Remos-Cancel, M. L. (1986), 95, 96, 145
Dwyer, C. A. (1994), 25, 171

E

Ebmeier, H., and Good, T. L. (1979), 58, 171
Educational Testing Service (1995), 25, 171

Eisner, E. W. (1999), 25, 171
Eisner, E. W. (2001), 11, 171
Elam, S. M., Gallup, A. M. (1989), 4, 171
Elmore, R. F. (1997), 47, 59, 60, 63–64, 164, 171
Elmore, R. F. (1997, 2002), 121, 171
Elmore, R. F. (2002), 47, 48, 52, 163, 171
Elmore, R. F., and Furhman, S. H. (2001), 59, 105–106, 129, 171
Erikson, E. H. (1982), 50, 171

F

Farnsworth, B., Debenham, J. and Smith, G. (1991), 40, 95, 148, 171
Finn, J. D. (2002), 109, 172
Finn, J. D., and Achilles, C. M. (1999), 109, 171
Firestone, W. (1994), 3, 12, 20, 40, 81, 83, 84, 95, 164, 172
Fisher, R. and Ury, W. (1991), 34, 172
Florida Department of Education (1999a), 164, 172
Florida Department of Education (2000), 25, 172
Fowler, F. C. (2000), 38, 117, 127, 172
Frutrell, M. H. (1989), 1, 10, 165, 172
Fuhrman, S. H. (1993), 11, 172
Fuhrman, S. H. (1999), xiv, 2, 172
Fuhrman, S. H. (2001), 129, 172
Fuhrman, S. H., and Odden, A. (2001), 8, 172
Fullan, M. (1993), 17, 69
Fullan, M. (1993, 1999), 128, 172
Fullan, M. (1999), 9, 34, 36, 84, 119, 172
Futrell, M. H. (1989), 165, 172

G

Gage, N. E., and Berliner, D. (1998), 58, 172
Garris, J. M., and Cohn, E. (1996), 41, 163, 172
Gay, L. R. and Airasian, P. (2000), 27, 172
General Accounting Office (2001),

131, 173
George, P. S. (2001), 166, 173
Gielen, E. (1995), 28, 173
Giunta, A. (1999), 36, 173
Glass, G. V., and Smith, M. L. (1978), 109, 173
Glatthorn, A. (1987), 164, 173
Goertz, M. E. (2001a), 128, 173
Goertz, M. E. (2001b), 127, 173
Goertz, M. E., Duffy, M., and LeFloch, K. C. (2001), 173
Gould, R. (1978), 50, 173
Grissmer, D. et al (2000), 109, 173
Grissmer, D., Flanagan, A., Kawata, J. and Williamson, S. (2000), 4, 37, 42, 131, 173
Guba, E. and Lincoln, Y. (1989), 29, 173
Gupta, N., Schweizer, T. P., and Jenkins, Jr., G. D. (1987), 173
Guskey, T. R. (1999), 49, 173

H

Hall, G. E., Caffarella, E. and Burtlett, E. (1997), 31, 32, 35, 173
Hamilton, M. L. (1995), 27, 173
Hammer, M., and Champy, J. (1993), 69, 173
Hanushek, E. A. (1989), 4, 39, 174
Hargrove, R. (1995), 164, 174
Harty, H. P., Greiner, J. M., and Ashford, B. G. (1994), 79, 81, 84, 92, 96, 106–107, 149, 174
Hassel, B. C. (2002), 3, 79, 85, 92, 96, 174
Hawley, W. D. (1985), 36, 174
Heneman, III, H. G., and Milanowski, A. T. (1999), 102, 174
Herman, J. L. (1997), 22, 29, 174
Herman, R. (1999), 127, 174
Herzberg, F. (1966), 16, 19, 174
Heubert, J. and Hauser, R. (1999), 24, 174
Hibbard, K. M. (1996), 25, 26, 174
Hodge, W., and Jones, J. (2000), 122, 174
Hoover, R. L. (2000), 24, 127, 174

Howey, K., and Vaughn, J. (1983), 48, 174

I

Ingvarson, L., Chadbourne, R., and Culton, W. (1995), 2, 174
Interstate New Teacher Assessment and Support Consortium (INTASC-1995), 25, 175

J

Jackson, P. W., Boostrom, R. E., Hansen, D. T. (1998), 84, 175
Jacobson, L. (2001), 109, 175
Johnson, Jr. H. C. (1985), 4, 175
Johnson, S. M. (1986), 5, 15, 16, 19, 80–81, 94, 106, 161, 162, 175
Joint Committee on Standards for Educational Evaluation (1994), 25, 175
Jones et al (1999), 24, 102, 104–105, 111, 163, 175
Jones, J. J., and Walters, D. L. (1994), 164, 175
Jordan, H. R., Mendro, R. L., and Weerasinghe, D. (1997), 3
Jordan, H. R., Mendro, R. L., and Weerasinglie, D. (1997), 175
Joyce, B. (1995, 1997), 54, 175
Joyce, B., and Belitzky, A. (1997), 47, 48, 54, 57, 175
Joyce, B. and Showers, B. (1995), 28, 58, 60, 61, 121, 164, 175
Jung, S. M. (1984), 84, 90, 175

K

Kelley, C. (1998), 20, 101, 110, 163, 175
Kelley, C. (1999), 100, 102, 176
Kelley, C., and Heneman, H., and Milanowski, A. (2001), 101, 114, 176
Kerchner, C. T., Koppich, J. E., and Weeres, J. G. (1997), 34, 176
King, B. (1991), 25, 176
Knopp, R., and O'Reilly, R. R. (1978), 19, 176
Knowles, M. S., Holton III, E. F.,

Swanson, R. A. (1998), 28, 51, 62, 121, 176
Kohlberg, L. (1969), 50, 176
Kottkamp, R., Provenzo, E. F., and Cohn, M. M. (1986), 16, 176
Krueger, A. B. (1998), 42, 176
Krueger, A. B. (2000), 42, 176

L

LaBoskey, V. K. (2000), 27, 176
Ladd, H. and Hansen, J. (1999), 33, 39, 111, 113, 176
LaFee, S. (1999), 81, 176
Lawler, E. E. III (1971), 16, 176
Lawler, E. E. III (1971, 1998), 69, 176, 177
Lawler, E. E. III (1990), 18, 83, 177
Lawler, E. E. III (1992), 81, 177
Lawler, E. E. III (1998), 20, 65, 72–73, 89, 90, 91, 92, 93–94, 95, 125, 165, 177
Lehaman, T., and Lester, V. (1978), 50, 177
Lemann, N. (1999), 24, 163, 177
Lenord, D., and Tanaka, L. (1996), 4, 82, 177
Levin, B., and Young, J. (1998), 2, 177
Levine, R. A., et al. (1981), 30, 177
Levin, H. M. (1983), 3, 177
Levinson, D. J. A. (1986), 50, 177
Lewis, A. C. (2000), 76, 177
Lewis, A. C. (2002), 56, 59, 177
Lewis, A. C., and Barnett, B. (1999), 9, 177
Lieberman, A. (1995), 11, 16
Lieberman, A. (1999), 164, 177
Lieberman, A., and McLaughlin, M. (1999), 47, 49, 59, 177
Lindblom, C. E. (1959), 8, 177
Little, J. W. (1993), 49, 177
Locke, E. A., and Latham, G. P. (1995), 17, 120, 177
Lockwood, R., and McLean, J. (1993), 4, 178
Loevinger, J. (1976), 50, 178
London, M., and Smither, J. (1999), 49, 178

Lortie, D. (1975), 15, 16, 19, 25, 106, 162, 178
Ludwig, J., and Bassi, L. J. (1999), 4, 178
Lunenburg, F. C. and Ornstein, A. C. (2000), 15, 165, 178

M

McClernon, T. R., and Swanson, R. A. (1995), 178
McGinn, D. (1999), 15, 178
McGinn, D., and Naughton, K. (2001), 165, 178
McNeil, L. (2000a), 127, 178
McNeil, L. M. (2000b), 127, 178
Mak, K. (2000), 2, 178
Malen, B., Ogawa, R. T., and Kranz, J. (1989, May), xiii, 178
Marshall, R., and Tucker, M. (1992), 69, 178
Martin, M. O., and Kelly, D. L. (1996), 2, 178
Maslow, A. (1970), 16, 18, 178
Matthews, Jr. M. (1999), 3, 80, 178
May, W. T. (1993), 27, 178
Mendro, B., Olivarez, R., Maureen, P., Milanowski, T., Kellor, E., and Odden, A. (1999), 40, 82, 83, 84, 179
Merriam, and Brockett, R. C. (1997), 51, 179
Merriam, S. B., and Caffarella, R. S. (1991), 50, 179
Michaels, J. W., and McCulloh, D. H. (1976), 19, 179
Milanowski, T. (1999), 163, 179
Milanowski, T. (2001), 45, 96, 124, 162, 179
Milanowski, T. and Young, P. (1999), 26, 163, 179
Minorini, P., and Sugarman, S. (1999), 39, 179
Mitchell, D. E., Ortiz, F. I., and Mitchell, T. K. (1983), 19, 179
Mizell, H. (1999), 49, 179
Mohrman, S. A., Galbraith, J. R., Lawler III, E. E., and Associates

(1998), 81, 179
Molar, A. et al (1999), 109, 179
Monahan, T. C. (1996), 48, 57, 59, 120, 164, 180
Mungazi, D. A., and Kay, W. L. (1997), 2, 180
Murphy, J. (1990), 165, 180
Murphy, J. (1991), xiii, xiv, 180
Murray, S. L. (1986), 25, 180

N

National Board for Professional Teaching Standards (1996), 26, 180
National Board for Professional Teaching Standards (1999), 27, 180
National Board for Professional Teaching Standards (2002), 86, 180
National Center for Education Statistics (1996), 70, 180
National Center on Education and the Economy (1996), 5, 180
National Staff Development Council (1994), 56, 180
National Staff Development Council (2001), 60, 163, 180
Nelson, W. (2001), 131, 180
Newman, F. N. (1993), 7, 181
Norton, M., and Scott, H. W. (1988), 34, 100, 104, 181

O

Oakley, K. (1998), 25, 26, 181
Odden, A. (1998), 124, 181
Odden, A. (1999a), 42, 92, 181
Odden, A. (1999b), 38, 39, 124, 181
Odden, A. (2000a), 6, 92, 97, 99, 124, 181
Odden, A. (2000b), 54–55, 57, 124, 181
Odden, A. (2001), 40, 84, 130, 181
Odden, A., and Archibald, S., and Tychsen, A. (1999), 42, 181
Odden, A., and Kelley, C. (1997), 6, 72, 80, 81, 83, 100, 107, 162, 181
Odden, A., and Kelley, C. (1997, 2002), 74, 84, 108, 181
Odden, A., and Kelley, C. (2002), 9, 15, 34, 73–74, 96, 97, 104, 106, 181
Odden, A., and Kellor, E. (2000), 79, 181
Odden, A., and Kellor, E., Heneman, H., and Milanowski, A. (1999), 96, 153, 181
Odden, A., and Picus, L. O. (2000), 39, 181
Olson, L. (1999), 83, 163, 164, 181
Orlich, D. C. (2000), 127, 181
Ozcan, M. (1996), 16, 18, 22, 28, 120, 162, 182

P

Packard, R. D., and Dereshiwsky, M. I. (1988a), 99, 182
Packard, R. D., and Dereshiwsky, M. I. (1988b), 107, 108, 182
Parsons, T. N. (1951), 12, 182
Peterson, K. D. (1995), 25, 163, 182
Picus, L. O. (1998), 10, 182
Pogrow, S. (2000), 165, 182
Popham, W. J. (1971, 1988), 25, 182
Popham, W. J. (1995), 26
Portner, H. (1998), 85, 182

Q

Quinn, D. (2000), 2, 182

R

Ravitch, D. (1995), 5, 182
Ravitch, D. (1995, 2000), 3, 11, 182
Reese, C. M., Miller, K. E., Mazzeo, J. and Dossey, J. A. (1997), 24, 182
Reynolds, R. J., and Cruz, J. (1998), 2, 183
Rice, J. K. (1999), 109, 183
Rioux, W. J., and Berla, N. (1993), 163, 183
Rose, L. C. and Gallup, A. M. (2000), 27, 130, 183
Rose, L. C. and Gallup, A. M. (2000, 2001), 128, 183
Ross, S. (2000), 30, 183
Ross, S. M. et al (1997), 30, 183

Rouiller, J. Z., and Goldstein, I. L. (1993), 58, 183, 188

S

Saavedra, R., and Kwan, S. (1993), 25, 183
Sanders, W. L. and Horn, S. P. (1995), 23, 30, 183
Sanders, W. L. and Rivers, J. C. (1996), 3, 23, 183
Seiler, J. A. (1967), 12, 183
Senge et al (1999), 69, 184
Senge, P. (1994), 69, 183
Seyfarth, J. T. (1996), 48, 184
Shanahan, T. (1998), 42, 184
Sheehy, G. (1977), 50, 184
Shiller, R. J. (2001), 165, 184
Shore, T., Shore, L. M., Thorton, III, G. (1992), 25, 184
Showers, B. (1984), 164, 184
Slavin, R. E., and Madden, N. A., (2000), 165, 185
Slavin, R. E. et al (1996), 23–24, 184
Smith, R. E. (1998), 58, 73, 184
Smith, S. S., and Mickelson, R. A. (2000), 113, 127, 184
Smylie, M. A. and Smart, J. C. (1990), 4, 161, 184
Southern Regional Education Board (SREB-1991), 70, 184
Southern Regional Education Board (SREB-1997), 23, 184
Southern Regional Education Board (SREB-1998), 184
Spady, W. G. (1981), 161, 185
Spady, W. G. (1988), 161, 185
Spady, W. G., and Marshall, K. (1991), 161, 185
Sparks, D., and Hirsh, S. (1999), 54, 65, 185
Sparks, D., and Loucks-Horsley, S. (1990), 47, 121, 164, 185
Stake, R. (1998), 24, 185
Stecher, B. M. and Bohrnstedt, G. W. (2002), 109, 185
Stiggins, R. J. (1994), 26, 185
Stringfield, S., Ross, S., and Smith, L. (1996), 6, 9, 99, 123, 165, 185
Stufflebeam, D. L. (1998), 6, 29, 185
Stufflebeam, D. L. (2002), 30, 185
Swanson, C. B. and Holton III, E. F. (1997), 27, 185
Swanson, C. B., and Stevenson, D. L. (2002), 15, 185
Swanson, R. A., and Holton III, E. F. (1997), 49, 185

T

Texas Assessment of Academic Skills, 33
Tomlinson, H. (1996), 3, 161, 185
Traub, J. (2000), 6, 127, 185
Tucker, M. S., and Codding, J. B. (1998), 1, 3, 5, 11, 20, 22, 24, 95, 96, 151, 185
Tyack, D., and Cuban, L. (1995), 2, 186
Tyack, D. B. (1990), 8, 185

U

Uchitelle, L. (2002), 165, 186
UNICEF (2000), 47, 65, 186
U. S. Department of Education (1995), 8, 186
U. S. Department of Education (1998), 15, 186
U. S. Department of Education (1999), 66, 186
U. S. General Accounting Office (2001), 131, 186

V

Viadero, D. (1998), 2, 186
Viadero, D. (2001), 109, 186
Von Bertalanffy, L. (1968), 12, 186
Vroom, V. (1964), 16, 17, 186

W

Wainer, H. (1993), 4, 42, 186
Walberg, H. J. and Greenberg, R. C. (1999), 24, 127, 165, 186
Weathersby, R. (1978), 50, 186
Webb, L. D., and Norton, M. S. (1999),

47, 59–60, 73, 79, 164, 165, 186
Webb, N. M. et al (1998), 85, 186
Webster, W. J., and Mendro, R. L. (1995), 82, 186
Weick, K. E. (1966), 16, 17, 186
Weiss, C. (1992), 127, 187
Wells, C. (2000), 21, 187
Wenglinsky, H. (1998), 4, 42, 187
Whitehead, M. M. (2000), 4, 187
Wholey, J. S., Harty, H. P., and Newcomer, K. E., 30, 187
Wiegman, J., and Binnie, D. (1985), 5, 187
Wiggins, G. (1998; 1999), 26, 187
Willms, J. D. (2000), 109, 187

Wilson, G. (1985), 5, 187
Winerip, M. (2001), 105, 128, 187
Wise, A. E. (1984), 3, 25, 187
Wong, K. K., and Meyer, S. J. (1998), 2, 127, 187
Wood, R. C., and Thompson, D. C. (1996), 38, 39, 46, 124, 187
Wright, S. P., Horn, S. P. and Sanders, W. L. (1997), 30, 188

Z

Zachary, L. J. (2000), 79, 85, 188
Zemelman, S., Daniels, H. and Hyde, A. (1998), 3, 11, 161, 188

SUBJECT INDEX

A

A Nation at Risk (1983), xiii, xiv, 2
Adults as Learners, Cross (1981), 51
Alvarado, Anthony, 63
American Evaluation Association, 24
American Institute for Research, 56
Ames, Iowa Program, 61
Arizona comprehensive career ladder
    program, 107–109
Arizona's Instrument to Measure Standards, 123
Assessing student performance, 23–25, 45
    benefits of, 25
    high stakes testing and, 24–25
    incentive programs and, 114
    performance pay programs and, 25, 122–123, 125, 130, 131
    RAND study of, 131
    standards and tests (ST) evaluation, 23, 28, 163nn13 and 14
    Success for All (SFA) evaluation approach, 23–24
    taught to the test argument, 24
    Tennessee Value-Added Assessment System, 23, 24
Assessing teacher performance
    action research, 27, 45
    assessment centers and, 27
    assessment techniques, 25, 26, 27, 122
    integrating elements in teacher assessment plans, 27–28
    performance pay programs and, 25, 122–123
    performance-based assessment, 25–26
    portfolio assessment, 26–27, 74, 163n11
Augusta Project, Richmond County, Georgia, 61

B

Bennett, William (former Secretary of Education), 38, 39
Bold Plans for School Restructuring: The New American School Designs, Stringfield, Ross and Smith (1996), 9, 185
Bonuses, 83–84, 87, 89, 104, 115
Bush, President George W., 37, 38, 39

C

Charlotte-Mecklenburg School System's (CMS) comprehensive reform initiative, 113
Cincinnati Teacher Quality Plan, 76, 78–79 *figure* 3
CL *vs.* NCL teachers, 107–108
Classroom assessment technique (CAT), 27
Classroom Effectiveness Index (CEI), 82
Collective bargaining, 34
Colorado's Douglas County School District, 31–32, 35
Comprehensive program evaluation
    Dallas Independent School District

(DISD), 32–33
dimensions of assessment for, 32
"fourth generation evaluation", 29, 31
hierarchy of evaluation strategies, 30
JCSEE mode, 28–29
models for, 28–30
New American Schools Corp. process, 30, 31 *fig-* 2
"parallel criteria" for, 29
Comprehensive School Reform Demonstration Program (CSRDP), xiv, xv, 2, 99–100
education and policy research agencies studies in, 1
Florida A+ System of School Improvement and Accountability and, 12–13
observation of studies, xiv, 1
teacher compensation and, 12
theory of action in, 8
United States Department of Education and, 12
Comprehensive School Reform Teacher Questionnaire, 30
Comprehensive Test of Basic Skills, 41
Consortium for Policy Research in Education (CPRE), 110, 114

D

Dallas Independent School District (DISD), 32–33, 111–112
Dallas performance reward system, 40, 124
Denver Classroom Teacher Association, 36, 119
Differentiated pay programs, 85

E

Education Programs that Work, U.S. DOE, 1983, 8, 186
Educational reform
acceptable teacher incentive programs, 73, 75 *table* 5
Arizona comprehensive career ladder program example, 107–109
career ladder system and, 106–107, 161nn1 and 2
characteristics of, 2
collaborative cultures for, 119
comprehensive accountability in, 15, 118–119, 128, 129, 166n31
comprehensive program evaluation, 123–124
comprehensive reform programs and, 126–127
Comprehensive School Reform Demonstration Program (CSRDP) and, 15, 99–100
comprehensive *vs.* disjointed change in, 12
determination of initiatives for, 3
direct or indirect compensation programs in, 72
disadvantages in incentive programs, 87
discontinuous change in, 8–9
Florida's A+ System of School Improvement and Accountability and, 12–13
global economy and, 2
group-based performance programs, 81
high standards/high involvement model of, 9–10
high-stakes testing impact and, 126, 127–128
incentive programs and, 42, 117–118, 133–143 *appendix* A, 145–159 *appendix* B
incremental change in, 8, 9
merit pay systems and, 106–107
moral purpose and, 17, 128
pay structures shift (traditional) and, 73, 86–87
performance pay programs and, 45–46, 69, 117–118, 126, 130
private sector and, 69
privatization and, 128
professional development and, 57, 66, 67, 120–121
reform initiatives failure, 99
research, lack of, 89, 97, 99–100

self-interest groups and, 127, 131
standardized testing, 128–129, 157–159 *appendix* C
standards of adequacy in, 118–119
standards-based reform, 5–6, 10, 22, 92, 99, 161*nn*3 and 4
standards-driven programs and, 127–128
systemic models in, 6
teacher compensation and, 3
teacher motivation and, 15–22, 119–120
teacher shortage and, 126
Texas accountability system and, 127
theoretical frameworks for, 7–8
values of, 117
whole-school reform, 9, 117, 128, 129, 131
Educational Testing Service's PRAXIS Series, 25, 122, 123
Eisenhower Professional Development Project, 48, 49, 57, 65–67, 121
Expenditures *vs.* student achievement, 4

F

"First wave" reform initiatives, xii–xiv
Florida's A+ System of School Improvement and Accountability, 12–15
Florida Comprehensive Assessment Test (FCAT), 14, 121, 123
Goal 3 Standards, 12–13, 14
Master Teacher Program, 4–5
monetary rewards, bonuses and, 20–21
Sunshine Standards, 13 *figure* 1
Funding performance pay programs, 37–46
adequacy-accountability-quality philosophy of, 39, 45–46
adequate, sustained funding, 40, 124
district role in, 40
equitable distribution of resources, 41

equity approach to, 38
federal money for, 37–38
federal role in, 40
full-state funding based on student performance, 41, 42
incentive programs and, 40–41, 42
performance pay programs and, 39
rewards programs, 42, 43 *table* 3, 44–45 *table* 4
South Carolina foundation system of funding, 41
standards-based reform and, 40
state role in (four elements), 39–40
"up-front budget allocation" for, 40–41

G

Getting to Yes: Negotiating Agreement Without Giving In, Fisher and Ury (1991), 34
Goal 3 Standards, 12–13, 14
Granite School District of Salt Lake City, Utah, 40
Group-based/School Award Systems, 81–84
advantages of, 83–84
bonuses *vs.* base pay, 83–84, 87
Dallas, Texas program, 82–84
measurable standards for, 81–82
Waco, Texas program, 81–82

H

High-stakes accountability programs, 99, 105–106

I

Incentive program design and planning
adequacy guidelines standards, 95–97
appropriate processes for, 91, 92
basic assumptions in, 90–91
choosing objectives, 94, 95
core values in compensation systems, 91, 92
criteria for functional incentive pay systems, 96–97
critical factors in, 117–118,

133–143 *appendix* A, 145–159 *appendix* B
fairness, perception of, 106
gainsharing and, 91
goals and objectives of incentive programs, 92–95, 165n26
high-stakes accountability programs and, 105–106, 115
Lawler, E. E., III on, 89–91
motivation and performance, 100–102
participation *vs.* hierarchical control, 90
practices and structures for, 91, 92
Research Findings on Effective Program Designs and Methodologies, Packard & Dereshiwsky (1988a), 99
research, lack of, 89, 97, 99
restructuring teacher pay systems, 92
reward programs factors in, 92–93
reward systems and, 92, 101
school-based performance award programs (SBPA), 101, 102
Schools and Staffing Survey (SASS-1988), National Center for Education Statistics report and, 102–104, 103 *table* 7
synopsis of six objectives for, 93–94*figure* 4
teacher attitudes and, 102–105
teacher incentives, distinguishing among, 94–95
teacher quality and, 92
Incentive program teachers (IPT), 104–105
Individual classroom performance incentive program, 86, 87
INTASC assessment techniques, 25
Interstate Teacher Assessment and Support Consortium, 26
Iowa Test of Basic Skills (ITBS), 107

J

JCSEE, 28–29
Joint Committee on Standards for Educational Evaluation, 123

K

Kentucky Accountability Program rewards and sanctions, 101, 109(2), 110, 112 *table* 8

L

Lawler, E. E., III, 91, 176–177

M

Mentor teacher plans, 79, 85–86
Michigan Education Assessment Program, 123
Mombassa School Improvement, Kenya, 65
Moral purpose, 17
Motivational theories
content or process theories in, 15, 17–19 *table* 1, 161n5, 162n6
motivational concepts in, 15–16
"Multivariable syndrome", 60, 131

N

National Association of State Directors of Teacher Education and Certification (NASDTEC), 26
National Board for Professional Teaching Standards (NBPT), 85–86, 123
National Center for Education Statistics (NCEE), 70–71
National Commission on Teaching and America's Future (NCTAF), 6
National School Reform Faculty Project, 27
National Staff Development Council (NSDC), 54, 55–56, 163n10
NBC (National Board Candidates), 85–86
NBPTS standards, 25, 26, 76, 122
New American Schools Corporation, 30, 123, 126, 127
New Teacher Assessment and Support Consortium, 122
No Child Behind Act (2001), 38

P

Paying Teachers for What They Know and Do, Odden and Kelley (1997, 2002), 6, 74, 108
Performance assessment, 22–28
  outcomes *vs.* process measures, 22
  student achievement and, 22, 23–25, 109
  teacher assessment and, 25–26
  teachers' performance and, 22
Performance Pay Standards of Adequacy Checklist (PPSAC), Hodge, Warren, 96
Performance pay systems. *see also* Funding Performance Pay Programs
  assumptions in designing performance pay systems, 90–91
  career ladder programs, 4, 79–81, 85, 99, 100, 106–107, 108–109
  Cincinnati's compensation and awards program, 74
  classify pay configurations terms, 73
  collaborative cultures for, 36–37, 119–120
  collective bargaining, 35
  Colorado's Douglas County School District performance pay plan, 31–32, 35–36
  competency pay, 73–74
  comprehensive program evaluation and, 28–29, 123–124
  criteria and standards for, 11, 28, 29
  Denver Classroom Teacher Association and, 36
  differentiated pay programs, 85
  dimensions of assessment for, 32
  direct or indirect compensation programs, 72
  effective collaboration in, 37, 119
  evaluation and performance assessment, 22, 124–125
  "fourth generation evaluation" and, 31
  group-based/school awards systems, 81–84
  implementation of, 45–46
  incentive programs and, 40–41, 42, 45
  individual classroom performance program, 86, 87
  "inside-out" principle of collaboration in, 34, 45
  JCSEE strands for, 28–29
  mentor teacher plans, 79, 85–86, 87
  merit pay systems, 4–5, 85, 104, 106–107
  National Center for Education Statistics (NCEE) study (1996), 70–71
  New York City Schools example of, 36
  North Carolina's accountability performance pay program, 111
  null hypotheses for, 35
  "parallel criteria" for, 29
  participation and collaboration in, 34–35, 36, 119
  perception of fairness and, 106
  performance assessment and, 22, 122–123, 124–125
  performance pay plan (PPP) and, 32, 35
  performance portfolios, 74
  professional development and, 50, 55, 63, 67, 120–121
  public support of, 130
  radical pay schemes, 69–72
  RAND study of, 131
  recognition incentive programs, 84–85
  reform efforts and, 30
  research base, inadequate, 114
  research findings, 125–126, 130
  research, lack of, 89, 97, 99
  reward system and, 91–92
  skills and competency-based pay programs, 79
  skills-based or knowledge-based pay programs, 73–74, 77 *table* 6, 80–81
  Southern Regional Education Board (SREB) study of, 69–70

student achievement and, 25, 109, 122–123, 125, 130, 131
systemic school reform efforts and, 118–119
teacher attitudes toward, 104–105
teacher motivation and, 19–20 *table* 2, 114–115, 119–120
traditional pay structures shift in, 73, 86
Phase theory of adult development, 50
Policy Studies for Educational Leaders, Fowler, F. C. (2000), 117
Portfolio Assessment System (PAS), 26, 27
Position Statement on High Stakes Testing in PreK-12 Education, American Evaluation Association, 24
PRAXIS III assessment technique, 25
Professional development
andragogy *vs.* pedagogy, 51, 62, 66
Boyatzis and Kolb model for, 52–53
California's Subject Matter Networks and, 59
coordinated system for, 49–50
critical factors in, 50
development and learning theories in, 50–51, 66
district-wide approach to, 63–65
education accountability and, 66
effective staff development study, 48–49
Eisenhower Professional Development Project, 48, 49, 57, 65–67
employee satisfaction and, 49
exemplars of comprehensive approaches to, 60–66
funding of, 54–55, 57, 66
incentive programs and, 47, 48, 50
Joyce and Showers' Student Achievement Through Staff Development Model (1995), 60, 61–62
Knowles' Human Resources Development Performance and Improvement Model (1998), 60, 62
learning principles and, 51–52, 62, 66
learning questions, focus points for, 52
levels of success in, 65
Maryland's Regional Staff Development Centers and, 59
mixed models for, 50
models and approaches for, 51, 58–60
modes of growth, adaptation in adult learning, 53
National Council on Staff Development guidelines, 65
National Staff Development Council (NSDC) recommendation for, 54
National Staff Development Council (NSDC) standards and guidelines for, 55–57, 60
New York City Community School District 2 Model (1997), 60, 63–66, 121
performance pay systems and, 50, 55, 63, 67
phase and stage theories in, 50
planning processes in, 59–60
private sector and, 49
programs for, 47–48, 49
qualities of successful programs for, 62
reform approaches to, 59
short-term strategies for, 59
staff development program design, 51–54, 58–60
State of Florida and, 55
student achievement linkage in, 55, 60, 61
technical assistance for, 59
time allocation for, 54–55, 66, 162n9
traditional pay structures shift and, 66
transfer of learning from, 58, 66
Webb and Norton's five steps for planning processes, 59–60
whole-school reform movement and, 57

R

Recognition incentive programs, 84–85, 87
Reflecting on Ten Years of Incentive Program, Cornett and Grimes (1994), 80
Research Findings on Effective Program Designs and Methodologies, Packard & Dereshiwsky (1988a), 99
Restructuring teacher pay systems, 92–95
Robbinsdale Area Schools, Minneapolis, Minn., 74, 76
Rose v. Council for Better Education, Inc. (1989), 109

S

Schenley Project, Pittsburgh, Penn., 61
School Climate Survey, 30
School Effectiveness Indexes, 82
School Effectiveness Index (SEI), 82
School Improvement Programs, Block, Evans, & Gurksey, 1995, 168
School Improvement Programs, Block, Everson, & Guskey, 1995, 8–9
School Observation Measure, 30
School-based performance award programs (SBPA), 101
Schools and Staffing Survey (SASS-1988), National Center for Education Statistics, 102–104
Skills, knowledge-based incentive programs, 73–81
    career ladder programs and, 79–80, 85, 99, 100, 106–107, 108–109
    Cincinnati Teacher Quality Plan, 76, 77 *table*6, 78–79 *figure* 3
    competency programs, 79
    disadvantages of, 80–81
    mentor teacher plans, 79, 85–86
    Robbinsdale Area Schools example, 74, 76
    single salary schedules and, 74
South Carolina's full-state funding program, 124
Stage theory of adult development, 50
Standards for Our Schools, Tucker and Codding (1998), 96
Standards-based reform, 5–6, 10
    evaluation and performance assessment, 22
Stufflebeam's CIPP Model (1974), 123
Success for All (SFA), 23–24

T

Teacher compensation. *see also* Performance pay systems
    ancillary rewards, 16, 21, 49
    bonuses, 83–84, 87, 89, 103, 104
    career ladder programs, 4, 79–81, 85, 99, 100, 104, 106–107, 106–107, 108–109, 108–109
    essential precursors to, 11, 165n23
    evaluation process in, 4–5
    extrinsic rewards, 16, 21, 45, 120
    individual salaries, 3
    intrinsic rewards, 16, 21, 120
    merit pay systems, 4–5, 85, 104, 106–107
    minority and disadvantaged students and, 4
    moral purpose and, 17, 85
    motivational theories and, 15–16, 17–19 *table* 1
    performance-based assessment and, 26
    professional efficacy and, 16–17, 21, 120
    rewards and, 16, 21, 45, 49, 120, 162nn6 to 8
    single salary schedule, 3, 4
    standards-based, 5, 6–7, 10
    teacher skills and, 3–4
Teacher motivation, 15–16
    ancillary, extrinsic, intrinsic, 16, 21, 45, 120
    fear of sanctions and, 101
    high-stakes accountability programs and, 105–106
    holistic view of, 21–22
    incentive programs and, 100–101, 114
    key motivator, 16–17

moral purpose and, 17
performance pay programs and,
    101, 114–115
professional efficacy and, 16–17,
    21
research findings on, 100–101
reward systems and, 16, 40, 92–93.
    101
Schools and Staffing Survey
    (SASS-1988), National Center
    for Education Statistics report,
    102–104
teachers' attitudes and, 102–106,
    115
Tennessee Value-Added Assessment
    System, 23, 24

Texas Assessment of Academic Skills
    (TAAS), 33, 123
The Adult Learner, Knowles and Associates (1984, 1998), 51
The Profession and Practice of Adult Learning, Merriam and Brokett (1997), 51

U

UNICEF (2000), 65
United Mind Workers, Kerchner, Kippich, and Weeres (1997), 34

```
LB2842.22 .H63 2003
Hodge, Warren A.
The role of performance pay
systems in comprehensive
school reform :
considerations for policy
making and planning
```